Roger H. C. Smith

English for
ELECTRICAL
ENGINEERING

in Higher Education Studies
Teacher's Book

Series editor: Terry Phillips

Published by
Garnet Publishing Ltd.
8 Southern Court
South Street
Reading RG1 4QS, UK

www.garneteducation.com

First published 2014.
Reprinted 2016.

ISBN 978-1-90757-533-4

British Cataloguing-in-Publication Data
A catalogue record for this book is available from
the British Library.

Production
Series editor: Terry Phillips
Project management: Claire Forsyth, Matthew George
Editorial team: Stephen Brierley, Karen Kinnair-Pugh,
                        Matthew George, Sue Coll
Specialist review: Liana Marmol, Oswaldo Cadenas
Design: Mike Hinks, Bob House

Audio recorded at Silver Street Studios.

Printed and bound in Lebanon by International Press:
interpress@int-press.com

Contents

Book map

Unit	Topics
1 What is electrical engineering? Listening · Speaking	• what is included in the subject of Electrical Engineering • different branches of Electrical Engineering: computing and electric power • different aspects of Electrical Engineering, e.g., definitions of some basic electrical terms, measuring devices
2 The history of electrical and electronic engineering Reading · Writing	• the history of Electrical Engineering from the 19th century to modern days • key figures in the discipline: their main achievements and inventions • the more recent history of Electronic Engineering: solid-state electronics
3 Electric and magnetic circuits Listening · Speaking	• Ohm's law • the applications of Ohm's law to simple electric circuits • the limitations of Ohm's law for circuit elements that do not have a constant resistance • how Ohm's law can be applied to magnetic circuits
4 The computer Reading · Writing	• the development of the computer • the invention of the integrated circuit, or microchip: its advantages and its impact on society • the use of computers in education • a guide to a more efficient use of the internet and computers in research
5 The television – from CRT to LCD and 3D Listening · Speaking	• small electrical items: the technology behind different types of television set and screen • some examples of television technology and devices • 3D televisions: two types of lens used in 3D technology: passive and active
6 Control systems Reading · Writing	• control system design • a common feedback loop controller: *PID* • examples of control systems: setting the temperature of a domestic oven, cruise control for cars
7 Electric power generation, transmission and distribution Listening · Speaking	• how electric power is generated in various kinds of power station, such as wind turbines • how it is transmitted across long distances • how it is delivered to customers • issues involved in the power transmission process: energy loss, voltage choices, transformers
8 Telecommunications Reading · Writing	• the history of telecommunication: the main inventions and developments • the processes involved in telecommunication: key stages, elements and related devices • examples of the main applications of telecommunication: radio broadcasting, the mobile phone • the influence that telecommunication has had on the world
9 Signal processing Listening · Speaking	• analogue and digital signal processing • different types of signal and how and why they are processed • filters and processors for both analogue and digital signals • applications of signal processing: active noise control and speech recognition technologies
10 Electric cars Reading · Writing	• the reasons why electric cars have become popular, their advantages and disadvantages • the problems that electric cars pose for electrical engineers: the need to balance issues of efficiency, weight, environmental concerns etc.
11 Microelectromechanical systems Listening · Speaking	• MEMS and NEMS (micro- and nanoelectromechanical systems): how they are manufactured • applications: examples of devices using MEMS and NEMS • potential future developments
12 Lighting engineering Reading · Writing	• the main lighting devices: incandescent light bulbs, fluorescent lamps and LEDs • how these devices work, their applications, and their advantages and disadvantages • technical report writing in the field of simple circuits with LEDs

Vocabulary focus	Skills focus		Unit
• words from general English with a special meaning in electrical engineering • prefixes and suffixes	Listening	• preparing for a lecture • predicting lecture content from the introduction • understanding lecture organization • choosing an appropriate form of notes • making lecture notes	**1**
	Speaking	• speaking from notes	
• English–English dictionaries: headwords · definitions · parts of speech · phonemes · stress markers · countable/uncountable · transitive/intransitive	Reading Writing	• using research questions to focus on relevant information in a text • using topic sentences to get an overview of the text • writing topic sentences • summarizing a text	**2**
• stress patterns in multi-syllable words • prefixes	Listening	• preparing for a lecture • predicting lecture content • making lecture notes • using different information sources	**3**
	Speaking	• reporting research findings • formulating questions	
• computer jargon • abbreviations and acronyms • discourse and stance markers • verb and noun suffixes	Reading Writing	• identifying topic development within a paragraph • using the Internet effectively • evaluating Internet search results • reporting research findings	**4**
• word sets: synonyms, antonyms, etc. • the language of trends • common lecture language	Listening Speaking	• understanding 'signpost language' in lectures • using symbols and abbreviations in note-taking • making effective contributions to a seminar	**5**
• synonyms, replacement subjects, etc., for sentence-level paraphrasing	Reading Writing	• locating key information in complex sentences • reporting findings from other sources: paraphrasing • writing complex sentences	**6**
• compound nouns • fixed phrases from electrical engineering • fixed phrases from academic English • common lecture language	Listening Speaking	• understanding speaker emphasis • asking for clarification • responding to queries and requests for clarification	**7**
• synonyms • nouns from verbs • definitions • common 'direction' verbs in essay titles (discuss, analyze, evaluate, etc.)	Reading Writing	• understanding dependent clauses with passives • paraphrasing • expanding notes into complex sentences • recognizing different essay types/structures: descriptive · analytical · comparison/evaluation · argument • writing essay plans and writing essays	**8**
• fixed phrases from electrical engineering • fixed phrases from academic English	Listening Speaking	• using the Cornell note-taking system • recognizing digressions in lectures • making effective contributions to a seminar • referring to other people's ideas in a seminar	**9**
• 'neutral' and 'marked' words • fixed phrases from electrical engineering • fixed phrases from academic English	Reading Writing	• recognizing the writer's stance and level of confidence or tentativeness • inferring implicit ideas • writing situation–problem–solution–evaluation essays • using direct quotations • compiling a bibliography/reference list	**10**
• words/phrases used to link ideas (*moreover*, *as a result*, etc.) • stress patterns in noun phrases and compounds • fixed phrases from academic English • words/phrases related to research	Listening Speaking	• recognizing the speaker's stance • writing up notes in full • building an argument in a seminar • agreeing/disagreeing	**11**
• verbs used to introduce ideas from other sources (*X contends/suggests/asserts that* …) • linking words/phrases conveying contrast (*whereas*), result (*consequently*), reasons (*due to*), etc. • words for quantities (*a significant minority*)	Reading Writing	• understanding how ideas in a text are linked • deciding whether to use direct quotation or paraphrase • incorporating quotations • writing research reports • writing effective introductions/conclusions	**12**

Introduction

The ESAP series

The aim of the titles in the ESAP series is to prepare students for academic study in a particular discipline. In this respect, the series is somewhat different from many ESP (English for Specific Purposes) series, which are aimed at people already working in the field, or about to enter the field. This focus on *study* in the discipline rather than *work* in the field has enabled the authors to focus much more specifically on the skills which a student of engineering studies needs.

It is assumed that prior to using titles in this series students will already have completed a general EAP (English for Academic Purposes) course such as *Skills in English* (Garnet Publishing), up to the end of at least Level 3, and will have achieved an IELTS level of at least 5.

English for Electrical Engineering

English for Electrical Engineering is designed for students who plan to take an engineering course entirely or partly in English. The principal aim of *English for Electrical Engineering* is to teach students to cope with input texts, i.e., listening and reading, in the discipline. However, students will also be expected to produce output texts in speech and writing throughout the course.

The syllabus concentrates on key vocabulary for the discipline and on words and phrases commonly used in academic and technical English. It covers key facts and concepts from the discipline, thereby giving students a flying start for when they meet the same points again in their faculty work. It also focuses on the skills that will enable students to get the most out of lectures and written texts. Finally, it presents the skills required to take part in seminars and tutorials and to produce essay assignments. For a summary of the course content, see the book map on pages 4–5.

Components of the course

The course comprises:
- the student Course Book
- this Teacher's Book, which provides detailed guidance on each lesson, full answer keys, audio transcripts and extra photocopiable resources
- audio CDs with lecture and seminar excerpts

Organization of the course

English for Electrical Engineering has 12 units, each of which is based on a different aspect of electrical engineering. Odd-numbered units are based on listening (lecture/seminar extracts). Even-numbered units are based on reading.

Each unit is divided into four lessons:

Lesson 1: vocabulary for the discipline; vocabulary skills such as word-building, use of affixes, use of synonyms for paraphrasing

Lesson 2: reading or listening text and skills development

Lesson 3: reading or listening skills extension. In addition, in later reading units, students are introduced to a writing assignment which is further developed in Lesson 4; in later listening units, students are introduced to a spoken language point (e.g., making an oral presentation at a seminar) which is further developed in Lesson 4

Lesson 4: a parallel listening or reading text to that presented in Lesson 2, in which students have to use their new skills (Lesson 3) to decode; in addition, written or spoken work is further practised

The last two pages of each unit, *Vocabulary bank* and *Skills bank*, are a useful summary of the unit content.

Each unit provides between four and six hours of classroom activity with the possibility of a further two to four hours on the suggested extra activities. The course will be suitable, therefore, as the core component of a faculty-specific pre-sessional or foundation course of between 50 and 80 hours.

Vocabulary development

English for Electrical Engineering attaches great importance to vocabulary. This is why one lesson out of four is devoted to vocabulary and why, in addition, the first exercise at least in many of the other three lessons is a vocabulary exercise. The vocabulary presented can be grouped into two main areas:

- key vocabulary for electrical engineering
- key vocabulary for academic English

In addition to presenting specific items of vocabulary, the course concentrates on the vocabulary skills and strategies that will help students to make sense of lectures and texts. Examples include:

- understanding prefixes and suffixes and how these affect the meaning of the base word
- guessing words in context
- using an English–English dictionary effectively
- understanding how certain words/phrases link ideas
- understanding how certain words/phrases show the writer/speaker's point of view

Skills development

Listening and reading in the real world involve extracting communicative value in real time – i.e., as the spoken text is being produced or as you are reading written text. Good listeners and readers do not need to go back to listen or read again most of the time. Indeed, when listening to formal speech such as a lecture, there is no possibility of going back. In many ELT materials second, third, even fourth listenings are common. The approach taken in the ESAP series is very different. We set out to teach and practise 'text-attack' skills – i.e., listening and reading strategies that will enable students to extract communicative value at a single listening or reading.

Students also need to become familiar with the way academic 'outputs' such as reports, essays and oral presentations are structured in English. Conventions may be different in their own language – for example, paragraphing conventions, or introduction–main body–conclusion structure. All students, whatever their background, will benefit from an awareness of the skills and strategies that will help them produce written work of a high standard.

Examples of specific skills practised in the course include:

Listening
- predicting lecture content and organization from the introduction
- following signposts to lecture organization
- choosing an appropriate form of lecture notes
- recognizing the lecturer's stance and level of confidence/tentativeness

Reading
- using research questions to focus on relevant information
- using topic sentences to get an overview of the text
- recognizing the writer's stance and level of confidence/tentativeness
- using the Internet effectively

Speaking
- making effective contributions to a seminar
- asking for clarification – formulating questions
- speaking from notes
- summarizing

Writing
- writing notes
- paraphrasing
- reporting findings from other sources – avoiding plagiarism
- recognizing different essay types and structures
- writing essay plans and essays
- compiling a bibliography/reference list

Specific activities

Certain types of activity are repeated on several occasions throughout the course. This is because these activities are particularly valuable in language learning.

Tasks to activate schemata

It has been known for many years, since the research of Bartlett in the 1930s, that we can only understand incoming information, written or spoken, if we can fit it into a schemata. It is essential that we build these schemata in students before exposing them to new information, so all lessons with listening or reading texts begin with one or more relevant activities.

Prediction activities

Before students are allowed to listen to a section of a lecture or read a text, they are encouraged to make predictions about the contents, in general or even specific terms, based on the context, the introduction to the text or, in the case of reading, the topic sentences in the text. This is based on the theory that active listening and reading involve the receiver in being ahead of the producer.

Working with illustrations, diagrams, figures

Many tasks require students to explain or interpret visual material. This is clearly a key task in a field which makes great use of such material to support written text. Students can be taken back to these visuals later on in the course to ensure that they have not forgotten how to describe and interpret them.

Vocabulary tasks

Many tasks ask students to group key engineering words, to categorize them in some way or to find synonyms or antonyms. These tasks help students to build relationships between words which, research has shown, is a key element in remembering words. In these exercises, the target words are separated into blue boxes so you can quickly return to one of these activities for revision work later.

Gap-fill

Filling in missing words or phrases in a sentence or a text, or labelling a diagram, indicates comprehension both of the missing items and of the context in which they correctly fit. You can vary the activity by, for example, going through the gap-fill text with the whole class first orally, pens down, then setting the same task for individual completion. Gap-fill activities can be photocopied and set as revision at the end of the unit or later, with or without the missing items.

Breaking long sentences into key components

One feature of academic English is the average length of sentences. Traditionally, EFL classes teach students to cope with the complexity of the verb phrase, equating level with more and more arcane verb structures, such as the present perfect modal passive. However, research into academic language, including the corpus research which underlies the *Longman Grammar of Spoken and Written English,* suggests that complexity in academic language does not lie with the verb phrase but rather with the noun phrase and clause joining and embedding. For this reason, students are shown in many exercises later in the course how to break down long sentences into kernel elements, and find the subject, verb and object of each element. This receptive skill is then turned into a productive skill, by encouraging students to think in terms of kernel elements first before building them into complex sentences.

Activities with stance marking

Another key element of academic text is the attitude (or stance) of the writer or speaker to the information which is being imparted. This could be dogmatic, tentative, incredulous, sceptical and so on. Students must learn the key skill of recognizing words and phrases marked for stance.

Crosswords and other word puzzles

One of the keys to vocabulary learning is repetition. However, the repetition must be active. It is no good if students are simply going through the motions. The course uses crosswords and other kinds of puzzles to bring words back into the students' consciousness through an engaging activity. However, it is understood by the writers that such playful activities are not always seen as serious and academic. The crosswords and other activities are therefore made available as photocopiable resources at the back of the Teacher's Book and can be used at the teacher's discretion, after explaining to the students why they are valuable.

Methodology points

Setting up tasks

The teaching notes for many of the exercises begin with the word *Set ...* . This single word covers a number of vital functions for the teacher, as follows:

- Refer students to the rubric (instructions).
- Check that they understand what to do – get one or two students to explain the task in their own words.
- Tell students how they are to do the task, if this is not clear in the Course Book instructions – as individual work, pairwork or in groups.
- Go through the example, if there is one. If not, make it clear what the target output is – full sentences, short answers, notes, etc.
- Go through one or two of the items, working with a good student to elicit the required output.

Use of visuals

There is a considerable amount of visual material in the book. This should be exploited in a number of ways:

- before an exercise, to orientate students, to get them thinking about the situation or the task, and to provide an opportunity for a small amount of pre-teaching of vocabulary (be careful not to pre-empt any exercises, though)
- during the exercise, to remind students of important language
- after the activity, to help with related work or to revise the target language

Comparing answers in pairs

This is frequently suggested when students have completed a task individually. It provides all students with a chance to give and explain their answers, which is not possible if the teacher immediately goes through the answers with the whole class.

Self-checking

Learning only takes place after a person has noticed that there is something to learn. This noticing of an individual learning point does not happen at the same time for all students. In many cases, it does not even happen in a useful sense when a teacher has focused on it. So learning occurs to the individual timetable of each student in a group. For this reason, it is important to give students time to notice mistakes in their own work and try to correct them individually. Take every opportunity to get students to self-check to try to force the noticing stage.

Confirmation and correction

Many activities benefit from a learning tension, i.e., a period of time when students are not sure whether something is right or wrong. The advantages of this tension are:

- a chance for all students to become involved in an activity before the correct answers are given

- a higher level of concentration from the students (tension is quite enjoyable!)
- a greater focus on the item as students wait for the correct answer
- a greater involvement in the process – students become committed to their answers and want to know if they are right and, if not, why not

In cases where learning tension of this type is desirable, the teacher's notes say, *Do not confirm or correct (at this point)*.

Feedback

At the end of each task, there should be a feedback stage. During this stage, the correct answers (or a model answer in the case of freer exercises) are given, alternative answers (if any) are accepted, and wrong answers are discussed. Unless students' own answers are required (in the case of very free exercises), answers or model answers are provided in the teacher's notes.

Highlighting grammar

This course is not organized on a grammatical syllabus and does not focus on grammar specifically. It is assumed that students will have covered English grammar to at least upper intermediate level in their general English course. However, at times it will be necessary to focus on the grammar, and indeed occasionally the grammar is a main focus (for example, changing active to passive or vice versa when paraphrasing).

To highlight the grammar:

- focus students' attention on the grammar point, e.g., *Look at the word order in the first sentence.*
- write an example of the grammar point on the board
- ask a student to read out the sentence/phrase
- demonstrate the grammar point in an appropriate way (e.g., numbering to indicate word order; paradigms for verbs; time lines for tenses)
- refer to the board throughout the activity if students are making mistakes

Pronunciation

By itself, the mispronunciation of a single phoneme or a wrong word stress is unlikely to cause a breakdown in communication. However, most L2 users make multiple errors in a single utterance, including errors of word order, tense choice and vocabulary choice. We must therefore try to remove as many sources of error as possible. When you are working with a group of words, make sure that students can pronounce each word with reasonable accuracy in phonemic terms, and with the correct stress for multiple syllable words. Many researchers have found that getting the stress of a word wrong is a bigger cause of miscommunication than getting individual phonemes wrong.

Pair and group activities

Pairwork and group activities are, of course, an opportunity for students to produce spoken language. As mentioned above, this is not the main focus of this course. But the second benefit of these interactional patterns is that they provide an opportunity for the teacher to check three points:

- Are students performing the correct task, in the correct way?
- Do students understand the language of the task they are performing?
- Which elements need to be covered again for the benefit of the class, and which points need to be dealt with on an individual basis with particular students?

Vocabulary and Skills banks

Each unit has clear targets in terms of vocabulary extension and skills development. These are detailed in the checks at the end of the unit (*Vocabulary bank* and *Skills bank*). However, you may wish to refer students to one or both of these pages at the start of work on the unit, so they have a clear idea of the targets. You may also wish to refer to them from time to time during lessons.

1 WHAT IS ELECTRICAL ENGINEERING?

This introductory unit explores what is included in the subject of electrical engineering. Students listen to an extract from a lecture which describes different branches of electrical engineering, such as computing and electric power. Many of these branches will be explored in more detail in subsequent units. The students also listen to a series of mini-lectures which introduce different aspects of electrical engineering, from definitions of some basic electrical terms to measuring devices.

Skills focus

🎧 Listening

- preparing for a lecture
- predicting lecture content from the introduction
- understanding lecture organization
- choosing an appropriate form of notes
- making lecture notes

Speaking

- speaking from notes

Vocabulary focus

- words from general English with a special meaning in electrical engineering
- prefixes and suffixes

Key vocabulary

alternator	ground	professional body
ampere	in series	proton
battery	inductor coil	radiation
certification	infrared	resistance
charge (n)	kilowatt	spark
circuit board	law	thermal
current	leakage	transistor
electromagnet	luminous intensity	transmission
electron	magnetic	ultrasonic
device	microwave	voltage
dish	node	wave (n)
fibre-optics	noise	wire (n)
field	ohmmeter	
gigabyte	overload	

1.1 Vocabulary

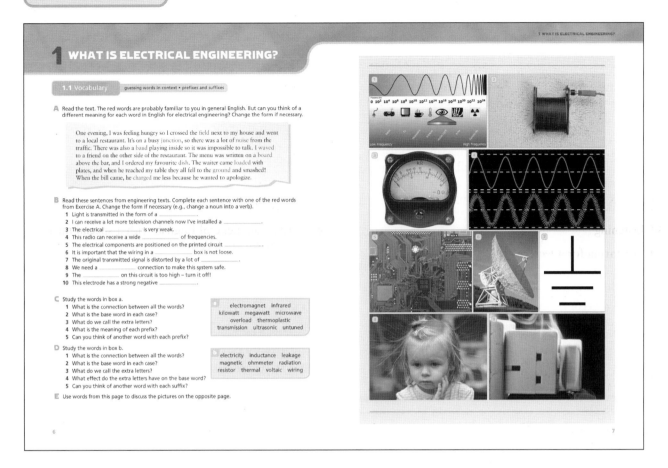

1 WHAT IS ELECTRICAL ENGINEERING?

1.1 Vocabulary guessing words in context • prefixes and suffixes

A Read the text. The red words are probably familiar to you in general English. But can you think of a different meaning for each word in English for electrical engineering? Change the form if necessary.

> One evening, I was feeling hungry so I crossed the field next to my house and went to a local restaurant. It's on a busy junction, so there was a lot of noise from the traffic. There was also a band playing inside so it was impossible to talk. I waved to a friend on the other side of the restaurant. The menu was written on a board above the bar, and I ordered my favourite dish. The waiter came loaded with plates, and when he reached my table they all fell to the ground and smashed! When the bill came, he charged me less because he wanted to apologize.

B Read these sentences from engineering texts. Complete each sentence with one of the red words from Exercise A. Change the form if necessary (e.g., change a noun into a verb).
1 Light is transmitted in the form of a _____
2 I can receive a lot more television channels now I've installed a _____.
3 The electrical _____ is very weak.
4 This radio can receive a wide _____ of frequencies.
5 The electrical components are positioned on the printed circuit _____
6 It is important that the wiring in a _____ box is not loose.
7 The original transmitted signal is distorted by a lot of _____
8 We need a _____ connection to make this system safe.
9 The _____ on this circuit is too high – turn it off!
10 This electrode has a strong negative _____

C Study the words in box a.
1 What is the connection between all the words?
2 What is the base word in each case?
3 What do we call the extra letters?
4 What is the meaning of each prefix?
5 Can you think of another word with each prefix?

> **a** electromagnet infrared kilowatt megawatt microwave overload thermoplastic transmission ultrasonic untuned

D Study the words in box b.
1 What is the connection between all the words?
2 What is the base word in each case?
3 What do we call the extra letters?
4 What effect do the extra letters have on the base word?
5 Can you think of another word with each suffix?

> **b** electricity inductance leakage magnetic ohmmeter radiation resistor thermal voltaic wiring

E Use words from this page to discuss the pictures on the opposite page.

6

7

General note

Read the *Vocabulary bank* at the end of the Course Book unit. Decide when, if at all, to refer students to it. The best time is probably at the very end of the lesson or the beginning of the next lesson, as a summary/revision.

Lesson aims

- identify words for the discipline in context, including words which contain affixes
- gain fluency in the target vocabulary

Introduction

Write the following sentences on the board:

1 *My teenage son is going through a difficult phase at the moment – he doesn't talk to anyone!*

2 *The two oscillators are out of phase with each other.*

Ask students the meaning of *phase* in the two sentences:

- In sentence 1 it has a *general* English meaning – i.e., a temporary stage in the development of something – a person's growing up in this case.

- In sentence 2 the meaning is particular to electrical engineering. However, if we start with the general

English meaning, to be 'out of phase' is where two things are reaching the same stage at different times, i.e., they are unsynchronized. Therefore, the meaning in sentence 2 refers to where two oscillators have the same frequency, but there is a time lag between the two.

Ask students to think of some phrases with *phase* in them. If you like, you can ask them to check in their dictionaries. Ask them to distinguish between those with a general English meaning and those related to electrical engineering. For example:

in phase

three-phase current

single phase

the first phase

a difficult phase

Note: Don't spend too long on this.

Exercise A

Set for individual work and pairwork checking. Point out that this is a text which introduces some important basic vocabulary related to electrical engineering – although it may not seem like that, at first glance. Do the first one as an example, e.g., *In general English, a field is an area of grass on a farm. In English for electrical*

11

engineering, it means the space surrounding electrically charged particles or in which a magnetic force is present.

Point out that there is often a relationship with the general English meaning, and if you know the general English meaning it can help to guess the meaning used in electrical engineering (as in the case of *dish* or *noise*). Remind students to change the form if necessary, e.g., from verb to noun. Check students understand grammar or other changes.

Feed back, putting the electrical engineering English meanings in a table on the board. Tell students to use these structures where possible:

- *a(n) X is (a(n)) … to define a noun*
- *to X is to Y to define a verb*

Make sure students can say the words correctly. For example:

- diphthong in *load* /əʊ/, *ground* /aʊ/, *noise* /ɔɪ/
- long vowels in *board* /ɔː/, *field* /iː/, *branch* /ɑː/ (also *charge* /ɑː/)
- schwa /ə/ in last syllable of *power*
- role of final *e* in *noise*, *wave*, *charge*

Answers

See table below.

Students may not be familiar with all meanings in general English, e.g., *junction* = where two or more roads cross; *loaded* = the past participle of *load* used as an adjective; *charge* = request payment for goods or services.

Exercise B

Set for individual work and pairwork checking. Do the first sentence as an example.

Feed back with the whole class. Ask students for any other words they know which have a special meaning in electrical engineering.

Answers

Model answers:

1 Light is transmitted in the form of a <u>wave</u>.
2 I can receive a lot more television channels now I've installed a <u>dish</u>.
3 The electrical <u>field</u> is very weak.
4 This radio can receive a wide <u>band</u> of frequencies.
5 The electrical components are positioned on the printed circuit <u>board</u>.
6 It is important that the wiring in a <u>junction</u> box is not loose.
7 The original transmitted signal is distorted by a lot of <u>noise</u>.
8 We need a <u>ground</u> connection to make this system safe.
9 The <u>load</u> on this circuit is too high – turn it off!
10 This electrode has a strong negative <u>charge</u>.

Examples of other possible words from general English in electrical engineering:

tolerance (n) – the total amount by which a quantity is allowed to vary, i.e., the algebraic difference between the maximum and minimum limits

frequency (n) – the repetition rate of a periodic signal expressed in units of hertz (Hz)

packet (n) – a unit of data which is sent over a network

Word	Meaning	Comments
field	the space surrounding electrically charged particles or in which a magnetic force is present	goes with *magnetic, electric, gravitational*
junction	the connection between two or more conductors, or the contact between two dissimilar metals or materials, as in a thermocouple	similar to general English meaning
noise	in reference to sound, an unwanted disturbance caused by waves that originate from man-made or natural sources	uncountable noun here
band	a limited continuous range of frequencies, especially in the radio spectrum	goes with *of frequencies*
wave	oscillation of an electric charge, which has the characteristic time and spatial relations associated with progressive wave motion	change from verb to countable noun
board	a flat, insulating surface upon which printed wiring and miniaturized components are connected in a predetermined design and attached to a common base	used with *printed circuit*
dish	a microwave antenna shaped like a dish	goes with *satellite*
load	power consumed by a device or circuit in performing its function	change from verb to countable noun
ground	the point in a circuit used as a common reference point for measuring purposes, usually connected to earth	related to general English meaning
charge	represents electrical energy – a material having an excess or shortage of electrons is said to have a negative or positive charge, respectively	change from verb to uncountable noun

bus (n) – a data path connecting the different subsystems or modules within a computer system

brush (n) – a conductor, usually carbon or a carbon–copper mixture, that makes sliding electrical contact to the rotor of an electrical machine

Exercise C

Set the first question for pairwork. See which pair can work out the answer first.

Set the remainder for pairwork. Feed back, building up the table in the Answers section on the board.

Answers

Model answers:

1 They all have a base word + extra letters at the beginning/prefixes.
2 See table below.
3 Prefix.
4 See table.
5 See table.

> ### Language note
>
> English is a lexemic language. In other words, the whole meaning of a word is usually contained within the word itself, rather than coming from a root meaning plus prefixes or suffixes (affixes). In most texts, written or spoken, there will only be a tiny number of words with affixes. However, these often add to a base meaning in a predictable way and it is important that students learn to detach affixes from a new word and see if they can find a recognizable base word.

Some words beginning with letters from prefixes are NOT in fact base + prefix, e.g., *refuse*. In other cases, the base word does not exist anymore in English and therefore will not help students, e.g., *transfer, transit,*

although even in these cases the root meaning of the prefix may be a guide to the meaning of the whole word.

Exercise D

Repeat the procedure from Exercise C.

Answers

Model answers:

1 They all have a base word + extra letters at the end/suffixes.
2 See table on next page.
3 Suffix.
4 See table.
5 See table.

> ### Language note
>
> Note that with prefixes we rarely change the form of the base word. However, with suffixes, there are often changes to the base word, so students must:
>
> - take off the suffix
> - try to reconstruct the base word

Exercise E

Set for pairwork. Try to elicit more than just the words from this lesson. Students should describe the pictures as fully as they can at this stage.

Students may use the following words in their discussion of each picture:

1 **frequency band** for **infrared** radiation
2 **electromagnet** showing an **electric field**
3 **ohmmeter** for measuring resistance
4 **waveform** with and without **noise**
5 **printed circuit board** showing components

Prefix	Base word	Meaning of prefix	Another word
electro	magnet	concerning electricity	electromotive, electrostatic
infra	red	below	infrasonic
kilo	watt	a factor of one thousand = 10^3	kilometre
mega*	watt	a factor of one million = 10^6	megaohms
micro	wave	very small	microcircuit, microphone
over	load	do more than enough	overcharge, overdriven
thermo	plastic	concerning heat	thermocouple
trans	mission	from one place/state to another	transform, transmitter
ultra	sonic	beyond a specified range	ultrahigh
un	tuned	not, opposite	unbalanced

*mega = 10 to the power of 6, or one million; other common, related prefixes are kilo = one thousand (10^3), giga = one billion (10^9) and tera = one trillion (10^{12})

Base word	Suffix	Effect/meaning of suffix	Another word
electric	~ity	adjective → noun	sensitivity
leak	~age	verb → noun	wastage
magnet	~ic	noun → adjective	electronic
induct	~ance	verb → noun indicating the act or fact of the activity described by the verb	disturbance
ohm	~meter	noun → noun indicating an instrument for measuring	voltmeter, ammeter
radia(te)	~tion	verb → noun	production
resist	~or	verb → noun	detector, regulator
therm	~al	noun → adjective	electrical, accidental
volt	~aic	noun → adjective	algebraic
wir(e)	~ing	countable noun → uncountable noun referring to an action	zeroing, switching

6 antenna satellite **dish**

7 **ground** symbol

8 hair standing up because of an **electric charge**

9 dangerous electrical **wiring**

Closure

If you have not done so already, refer students to the *Vocabulary bank* at the end of Unit 1. Tell students to explain how this lesson can help them deal with new words in context. If you wish, make three groups. Group A looks at the first section, *Using related words*. Group B looks at the second section, *Removing prefixes*. Group C looks at the third section, *Removing suffixes*. Then make sets of three with an ABC in each to explain to each other.

1.2 Listening

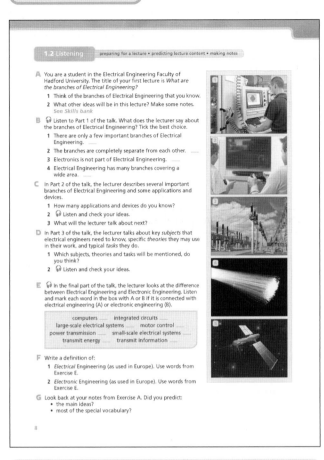

1.2 Listening   preparing for a lecture • predicting lecture content • making notes

A You are a student in the Electrical Engineering Faculty of Hadford University. The title of your first lecture is *What are the branches of Electrical Engineering?*
  1 Think of the branches of Electrical Engineering that you know.
  2 What other ideas will be in this lecture? Make some notes.
  See *Skills bank*

B Listen to Part 1 of the talk. What does the lecturer say about the branches of Electrical Engineering? Tick the best choice.
  1 There are only a few important branches of Electrical Engineering.
  2 The branches are completely separate from each other.
  3 Electronics is not part of Electrical Engineering.
  4 Electrical Engineering has many branches covering a wide area.

C In Part 2 of the talk, the lecturer describes several important branches of Electrical Engineering and some applications and devices.
  1 How many applications and devices do you know?
  2 Listen and check your ideas.
  3 What will the lecturer talk about next?

D In Part 3 of the talk, the lecturer talks about key *subjects* that electrical engineers need to know, specific *theories* they may use in their work, and typical *tasks* they do.
  1 Which subjects, theories and tasks will be mentioned, do you think?
  2 Listen and check your ideas.

E In the final part of the talk, the lecturer looks at the difference between Electrical Engineering and Electronic Engineering. Listen and mark each word in the box with A or B if it is connected with electrical engineering (A) or electronic engineering (B).

  computers ___ integrated circuits ___
  large-scale electrical systems ___ motor control ___
  power transmission ___ small-scale electrical systems ___
  transmit energy ___ transmit information ___

F Write a definition of:
  1 *Electrical* Engineering (as used in Europe). Use words from Exercise E.
  2 *Electronic* Engineering (as used in Europe). Use words from Exercise E.

G Look back at your notes from Exercise A. Did you predict:
  • the main ideas?
  • most of the special vocabulary?

8

General note

The recording should only be played once, since this reflects what happens in a real lecture. Students should be encouraged to listen for the important points, since this is what a native speaker would take from the text. However, students can be referred to the transcript at the end of the lesson to check their detailed understanding and word recognition, or to try to discover reasons for failing to comprehend.

Read the *Skills bank* at the end of the Course Book unit. Decide when, if at all, to refer students to it. The best time is probably at the very end of the lesson or the beginning of the next lesson, as a summary/revision.

Lesson aims

- prepare for a lecture
- predict lecture content
- make notes

Introduction

1 Show students flashcards of some or all of the words from Lesson 1.1. Tell students to say the words correctly and quickly as you flash them. Give out each word to one of the students. Say the words again. The student with the word must hold it up. Repeat the process saying the words in context.

2 Refer students to the photos. Briefly elicit ideas of what they depict. (They will look at the different areas of electrical engineering in more detail in Exercise C.)

Exercise A

1 Set for pair or group work. Feed back, but do not confirm or correct at this time.

2 Set for pairwork. Elicit some ideas but do not confirm or correct.

Methodology note

You may want to refer students to the *Skills bank/Making the most of lectures* at this point. Set the following for individual work and pairwork checking. Tell students to cover the points and try to remember what was under each of the *P*s – Plan, Prepare, Predict, Produce. Then tell students to work through the points to make sure they are prepared for the lecture they are about to hear.

🎧 Exercise B

Give students time to read the choices. Point out that they are only going to hear the introduction once, as in an authentic lecture situation. Play Part 1. Feed back. If students' answers differ, discuss which is the best answer and why.

Answers

4 Electrical engineering has many branches covering a wide area.

Transcript 🎧 1.1

Part 1

Good morning, everyone. In this lecture, we are going to look at exactly what is included in the field of Electrical Engineering. This is an important topic because it will show you a wide variety of career paths that are possible for students of this subject. This lecture might help you choose your future job!

OK. There are many different branches within Electrical Engineering. Practising electrical engineers work in a variety of areas, doing very different things. Today we are going to look at some of the most important branches. Some electrical engineers work in only one of these branches, but many deal with a combination of them. As we will see, many branches are closely linked to each other. This is particularly true in the case of electronics. As well as the different branches, I will also mention a few of the applications and devices related to Electrical Engineering.

🎧 Exercise C

1 Set for pairwork discussion before listening. Tell students to make notes.

2/3 Play Part 2 for students to check their ideas and listen for question 4. Feed back, building up a diagram on the board. Explain that this is a *classification* diagram. Finally, check the answer to question 4.

Answers

Model answers:

1/2 See below.

4 The lecturer is now going to answer the question: 'What does a practising engineer do?/What are the typical work activities of a practising electrical engineer and what knowledge is required?'

Part 2

So what are the different branches of Electrical Engineering? What activities are involved in these branches? Well, let's start with the first branch of Electrical Engineering – the one concerned with computing. This branch deals with the design of both hardware and software for computers. When designing computer hardware, an engineer can be involved in the design and interconnection of very small electronic devices for use in an integrated circuit. This is known as *microelectronics*. Of course, the range of applications of the computer is huge. Computers vary from those used to control an industrial plant, down to desktop computers and computer-like devices such as DVD players and video game consoles. This is the perhaps the largest of the branches of Electrical Engineering.

Another very important branch is the one that concerns electric light and power – the generation, transmission and distribution of electricity. Related applications include transformers, turbines, electric generators and electric motors. This field often involves the use of high voltages in an electrical network called a *power grid*. The grid covers a wide area – often a whole country – connecting generators with users, who buy the electrical energy for their homes and businesses.

A third major branch is communications. This involves telephony, but also satellite communications and the transmission of laser signals through optical-fibre networks. This branch is closely connected to computer engineering since

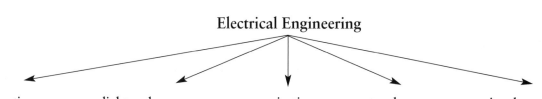

Electrical Engineering

computing (largest branch)	light and power	communications	control	signal processing
hardware design	generation, transmission, distribution of electricity	telephony	electronic controllers	analysis/manipulation of digital/analogue signals
software design		satellite communications	dynamic systems	
controllers for integrated circuits (microelectronics)	high voltages	laser signals	aircraft flight systems	amplify/filter analogue audio
	power grid	optical-fibre networks	factory automation	
control an industrial plant	transformers	computer communication using wires, microwaves, satellite circuits		compress/correct digital signals
desktop computers	turbines			radios
DVD players	generators			mobile phones
consoles	motors			missile guidance
				radars

computers can communicate with each other by sending digital data via wires, microwaves and satellite circuits.

Control engineering is another branch of Electrical Engineering. It involves the design of electronic controllers that make a wide range of dynamic systems behave in a particular way. Applications include the flight systems of aircraft and automation systems in factories.

The last area I want to talk about today is signal processing. This involves the analysis and manipulation of signals – both analogue and digital. An engineer can amplify or filter analogue signals, for example for audio equipment. He or she can also compress and correct errors of digitally sampled signals. This field of Electrical Engineering has a very wide range of applications, from radios and mobile phones, to missile guidance and radars.

So, as you can see, Electrical Engineering covers a wide range of subjects. Several of the areas are closely connected to each other, particularly by their use of computers and microelectronics. Now perhaps we should ask the question a little differently: 'What does a practising engineer do?' In other words, we are asking 'What exactly are the typical work activities of a practising electrical engineer and what knowledge is required?'

🎧 Exercise D

Write the words *subjects*, *theories* and *tasks* on the board. Ask for some examples of each. Set the questions for pairwork. Play Part 3. Feed back.

Answers

Model answers:

Word	Example
subjects	Mathematics, Physics, Computing
theories	depends on branch: ● circuit theory is important for most electrical engineers ● integrated circuit design requires quantum mechanics and solid state physics
tasks	preparing project schedules, meeting clients, managing other engineers

Transcript 🎧 1.3

Part 3

As we have seen, electrical engineering is involved in the development of a wide range of technologies. So practising electrical engineers design, develop, test and supervise all sorts of electrical systems and devices. Physics and mathematics are key subjects

for electrical engineers, and most engineering work now uses computers.

Circuit theory is a requirement for most engineers, but other theories may be used by some engineers and not others. Take, for example, engineers who design integrated circuits. They will need to have knowledge of quantum mechanics and solid state physics. However, these theories may not be relevant to engineers working in areas such as power transmission or telecommunication systems.

Apart from technical work, practising electrical engineers also spend time on other tasks. They prepare project schedules and meet clients. At higher levels they manage other engineers in a team. So, as you can see, the job of an electrical engineer can be very varied and stimulating and can also involve working in a variety of environments.

Methodology note

Up to this point, you have not mentioned how students should record information. Have a look around to see what students are doing. If some are using good methods, make a note and mention that later in the unit.

🎧 Exercise E

Point out that we often give examples of things to help clarify definitions. Give students plenty of time to look at the words in the box, then play Part 4. Feed back.

Answers

computers	B
integrated circuits	B
large-scale electrical systems	A
motor control	A
power transmission	A
small-scale electrical systems	B
transmit energy	A
transmit information	B

Transcript 🎧 1.4

Part 4

One thing I want to mention is the relationship between electrical engineering and electronic – or electronics – engineering. Are they different subjects? Or are they related, and if so, how? The answer is that, to some extent, it depends on where you are in the world. In the United States, Electrical Engineering is the main subject that is studied at university and it contains all the other branches, including electronics.

In Europe, however, it's a little different. A distinction is made between electrical and electronic engineering. Electrical engineering deals with large-scale electrical systems. Here, electrical engineers are generally involved with using electricity to transmit *energy*. Examples of applications of electrical engineering would be power transmission and motor control. Electronic engineering, on the other hand, deals with small-scale systems, and electronic engineers use electricity to transmit *information*. Examples would be computers and integrated circuits.

So let's summarize. In America, *Electrical Engineering* covers all electrical disciplines and so includes electronics. In Europe, *Electronic Engineering* is often considered a subject in its own right, and there may be separate university departments for Electrical and Electronic Engineering.

2 Ask students what definition of electrical and electronic engineering they are familiar with and what they use in their country. Do they think they should be considered separate subjects with different university departments?

3 Refer students to the *Skills bank* if you have not done so already and work through the section *Making the most of lectures*.

Exercise F

Set for individual work and pairwork checking. Feed back, building up the two definitions on the board.

Answers

Possible answer:

Electrical engineering deals with large-scale electrical systems, using electricity to transmit energy, and includes applications such as power transmission and motor control.

Electronic engineering deals with small-scale systems, using electricity to transmit information, and includes applications such as computers and integrated circuits.

Exercise G

Refer students back to their notes from Exercise A.

Closure

1 Look at the pictures of the various electrical engineering activities. Ask for suggestions for subjects, theories and tasks for each one.

Possible answers:

- a computer in an industrial plant – computing, circuit theory, systems theory, solid state physics, control theory, calculating, communicating
- a video game console – computing, programming, circuit theory, information theory
- a power grid – physics, transmission, generation, distributing of electricity, design
- an optical fibre – physics, wave theory, transmitting, receiving information
- a telecommunications satellite in space – physics, mathematics, circuit theory, control theory, signal theory, transmitting, receiving information

1.3 Extending skills

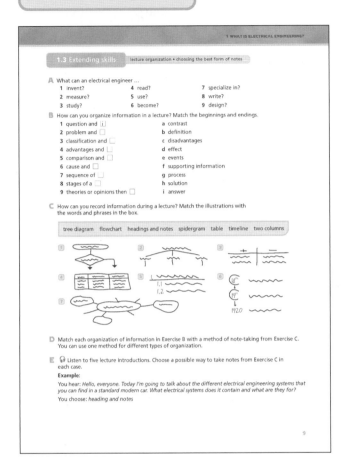

Lesson aims

- identify different types of lecture organization
- use the introduction to a lecture to decide the best form of notes to use

Introduction

Tell students to build up the four Ps of preparing for and attending a lecture: Plan, Prepare, Predict, Produce. You could put students into four groups, each group working on one of the stages, then feeding back to the rest of the class.

Exercise A

These words will occur in the listening texts. Set for pairwork. Feed back orally. The more students can say about these words, the better. Accept anything correct but let students explain their choice if they choose a combination not given below.

Answers

Possible answers:

1	invent	applications, devices, new theories
2	measure	quantities, parameters (e.g., resistance, temperature, etc.)
3	study	a subject (e.g., Mathematics), for a degree/MSc/PhD, a report
4	read	journals, reports
5	use	equipment, instruments, symbols, theories
6	become	a recognized professional, a certified engineer, experienced
7	specialize in	one branch of Electrical Engineering, a particular field
8	write	equations, reports, articles for journals, notes
9	design	electrical circuits, electrical systems, appliances

Exercise B

Point out that you can understand a lecture better if you can predict the order of information. Point out also that there are many pairs and patterns in presenting information, e.g., question and answer, or a sequence of events in chronological order.

Set for pairwork. Feed back orally. Check pronunciation. Point out that lecturers may not actually use these words, but if you recognize that what a lecturer is saying is the first of a pair, or the beginning of a sequence, you are ready for the second or next stage later in the lecture.

Answers

1 question and	i answer
2 problem and	h solution
3 classification and	b definition
4 advantages and	c disadvantages
5 comparison and	a contrast
6 cause and	d effect
7 sequence of	e events
8 stages of a	g process
9 theories or opinions then	f supporting information

Exercise C

Identify the first form of notes – a flow chart. Set for individual work and pairwork checking. Feed back, using datashow or other visual medium if possible.

Answers

1 flow chart
2 tree diagram
3 two columns

4 table

5 headings and notes

6 timeline

7 spidergram

> **Methodology note**
>
> You might like to make larger versions of the illustrations of different note types and pin them up in the classroom for future reference.

Exercise D

Work through the first one as an example. Set for pairwork.

Feed back orally and encourage discussion. Demonstrate how each method of note-taking in Exercise C can be matched with an organizational structure. Point out that:

- a tree diagram is useful for hierarchically arranged information, such as when the information moves from general to specific/examples
- a spidergram is more fluid and flexible, and can be used to show connections between things, such as interactions or causes and effects

Answers

Possible answers:

1 question and answer = headings and notes

2 problem and solution = headings and notes or two-column table

3 classification and definition = tree diagram or spidergram

4 advantages and disadvantages = two-column table

5 comparison and contrast = table

6 cause and effect = spidergram

7 sequence of events = timeline or flow chart

8 stages of a process = flow chart (or circle if it is a cycle)

9 theories or opinions then supporting information = headings and notes or two-column table

🎧 Exercise E

Explain that students are going to hear the introductions to several different lectures. They do not have to take notes, only decide what kind of information organization they are going to hear. Work through the example.

Play each introduction. Pause after each one and allow students to discuss then feed back. Students may suggest different answers in some cases. Establish that sometimes lecturers move from one information organization to another, e.g., classification then cause and effect.

Answers

Model answers:

1 heading and notes (question and answer)

2 spidergram (classification and definition)

3 tree diagram (classification and definition)

4 table (classification and definition)

5 flow chart (stages of a process)

Transcript 🎧 1.5

Introduction 1

Hello, everyone. Today I'm going to talk about the different sorts of electrical engineering systems that you can find in a standard modern car. What electrical systems does it contain and what are they for? I think the answer really shows us what a wide range of areas are included in the subject of Electrical Engineering. To demonstrate this, I will briefly describe some of these systems in turn.

Introduction 2

Shall I start? OK. As students of Electrical Engineering, you need to know all about the systems of units that are used. So, in this lecture, we are going to look at these different units and their symbols. These appear in the formulas and laws that electrical engineers need and use every day in their jobs.

Introduction 3

Good morning, everyone. This week I'm going to talk about the earliest accounts of electricity and its very first developments. In particular, we'll look at important terms such as *charge* and *current*. We'll also learn about *Kirchhoff's current law*, and how it helps in the design of large electrical circuits.

Introduction 4

Good afternoon. I think we can start now. In my lecture this week, I want to look at some of the measuring devices that are such an important part of an electrical engineer's work. I'll be looking at three of these devices, their characteristics and how they are used.

Introduction 5

Right. Let's have a look at the process that most electrical engineers go through in order to become recognized practising professionals. As you will find out, there are two main stages in this process. Most of you here today are at the beginning of the first stage, so there's quite a long way to go yet!

Closure

1 Test students on the pairs from Exercise B. Correct pronunciation again if necessary.

2 Refer students to the *Skills bank – Making perfect lecture notes*.

1.4 Extending skills

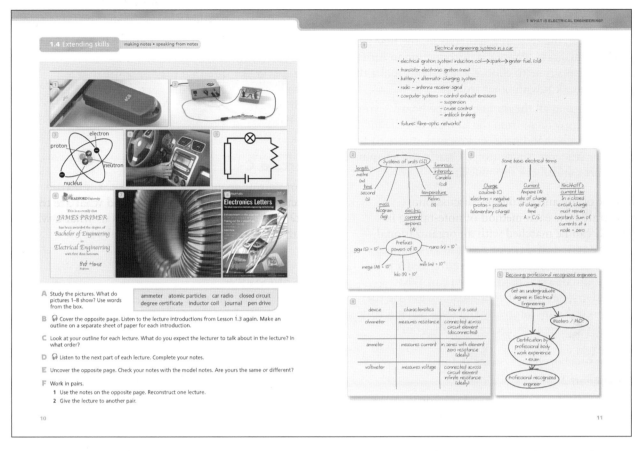

Lesson aims

- make outline notes from lecture introductions
- make notes from a variety of lecture types
- speak from notes

Further practice in:

- predicting lecture content

Introduction

Elicit as much information from the lecture in Lesson 1.2 as possible. If necessary, prompt students by reading parts of the transcript and pausing for students to complete in their own words.

Exercise A

Set for individual work and pairwork checking. Feed back orally but still do not confirm or correct. Point out that students are going to hear about all these things in today's lesson. You will return to these illustrations at the end.

For reference, the illustrations show:

- a 4Gb **pen drive**
- an **ammeter** in series as an element in an electric circuit

- an atom with its **atomic particles** – a nucleus containing positively charged protons, surrounded by negatively charged electrons
- a **closed circuit** with a light bulb and a resistor – the junction where two or more conductors are connected is a 'node'
- a **car radio** – the antenna receives electromagnetic waves via the antenna and decodes these signals to reproduce the original sounds
- a **degree certificate** in Electrical Engineering
- an **inductor coil** for generating a voltage
- an electronics **journal**

Methodology note

It is best that students close the book at this stage, so they are not tempted to look at the model notes. You can give the instructions for the next few stages orally as required.

🎧 Exercise B

Make sure students understand that they are going to hear the introductions from Lesson 1.3 again. Ask them briefly if they can remember any of the content from the introductions. Spend a few moments on this if students are able to contribute. Elicit suggestions for types of notes (Lesson 1.3, Exercise E).

Explain that this time they must create an outline using an appropriate type of notes. (You can refer them again to the *Skills bank – Making perfect lecture notes*.) Make sure students understand that they don't need to write a lot at this stage – outlines may consist of just a few words, e.g., the start of a spidergram, the first part of a table or diagram. Play each introduction in turn and give students time to choose a note-type, make the outline and check it with other students.

Feed back, getting all the outlines on the board – you may wish to copy them from the first part of the model notes on the right-hand page, or you may prefer to follow your students' suggestions. Clarify the meaning of new words and check pronunciation.

Transcript 1.5

Introduction 1

Hello, everyone. Today I'm going to talk about the different sorts of electrical engineering systems that you can find in a standard modern car. What electrical systems does it contain and what are they for? I think the answer really shows us what a wide range of areas are included in the subject of Electrical Engineering. To show this, I will briefly describe some of these systems in turn.

Introduction 2

Shall I start? OK. As students of Electrical Engineering, you need to know all about the systems of units that are used. So, in this lecture, we are going to look at these different units and their symbols. These appear in the formulas and laws that electrical engineers need and use every day in their jobs.

Introduction 3

Good morning, everyone. This week I'm going to talk about the earliest accounts of electricity and its very first developments. In particular, we'll look at important terms such as *charge* and *current*. We'll also learn about *Kirchhoff's current law*, and how it helps in the design of large electrical circuits.

Introduction 4

Good afternoon. I think we can start now. In my lecture this week, I want to look at some of the measuring devices that are such an important part of an electrical engineer's work. I'll be looking at three of these devices, their characteristics and how they are used.

Introduction 5

Right. Let's have a look at the process that most electrical engineers go through in order to become recognized practising professionals. As you will find out, there are two main stages in this process. Most of you here today are at the beginning of the first stage, so there's quite a long way to go yet!

Methodology note

Spiral bound or stitched/stapled notebooks are not the best way to keep lecture notes. It is impossible to reorganize or add extra information at a later date, or make a clean copy of notes after a lecture. Encourage students, therefore, to use a loose leaf file, but make sure that they organize it in a sensible way, with file dividers, and keep it tidy. Tell students to use a separate piece of paper for each outline in this lecture.

Exercise C

Set for pair or group work. Feed back, but do not confirm or correct. Students should be able to predict reasonably well the kind of information which will fit into their outline.

Exercise D

Before you play the next part of each lecture, refer students to their outline notes again. Tell them to orally reconstruct the introduction from their notes. They don't have to be able to say the exact words, but they should be able to give the gist.

Remind students that they are only going to hear the next part of each lecture once. Play each extract in turn, pausing if necessary to allow students to make notes but not replaying any section. Tell students to choose an appropriate type of notes for this part of the lecture – it could be a continuation of the type they chose for the introduction, or it could be a different type.

Explain to students that different countries use different abbreviations for university qualifications. For example, a postgraduate Engineering qualification in the UK would be referred to as an MSc in Engineering, whereas in the USA this would be referred to as an MS in Engineering. Qualifications and professional certification will be discussed in Lecture 5.

Transcript

1.6

Lecture 1

It's not just modern cars that have electrical systems – even older cars had them. They used an electric circuit to start the engine. This was achieved by using a starting handle to trigger the ignition phase. In this circuit, an inductor coil generates a high voltage and sends a spark across the gap in the spark plug. This spark then ignites the air and fuel mixture. The coil is supplied with a DC voltage by a battery. However, in modern cars, this traditional electrical ignition system has been replaced by electronic ignition with transistors. This device lasts much longer and is more reliable.

The car battery is a self-contained electric power system. But, like all batteries, it gradually loses its power. In order to make it last as long as possible, the car has a charging system, involving an alternator. First we have the inductor coil, then there is the battery which supplies power to other electrical components such as the lights and radio. The radio is yet another electrical system. It receives electromagnetic waves via the antenna and decodes these signals to reproduce the original sounds, sent from a long way away.

More recently, computer systems have been used in cars. Computer systems are used, for example, to control exhaust emissions. Let's look at this control system in a little more detail. A microprocessor receives signals from sensors and these contain information about things such as the composition of gases in the exhaust. From the processed information, the computer in the car can decide how to make the engine work as cleanly as possible. The use of computer systems in cars is becoming more and more common in all sorts of ways. Examples of recent uses of on-board computers are electronically controlled suspension, electronic cruise control and anti-lock braking. In the future, fibre-optic networks may replace traditional wire systems.

🎧 **1.7**

Lecture 2

The main system electrical engineers use is the International System of Units – also known as SI units. These are used by all engineering professional bodies. SI units are based on six fundamental quantities, which are length, mass, time, electric current, temperature and luminous intensity. I'll repeat those slowly – length, mass, time, electric current, temperature and luminous intensity.

The unit of length is the metre, and the symbol is a small *m*. The unit of mass is the kilogram, with the symbol *kg*. The unit of time is the second, as I'm sure you know, and the symbol is a small *s*. Electric current is measured in amperes, and the symbol is a capital *A*. In everyday life, we usually measure temperature in degrees Celsius, but as electrical engineers we need to use the Kelvin, and the symbol for that is a capital *K*. The last SI unit is the one for luminous intensity and its unit is the candela. Its symbol is small *cd*. All other units can be derived from these six fundamental units. For example, a coulomb is the amount of electric charge transported in one second by one ampere of current.

The other thing we need to look at is the prefixes we can use to denote different powers of ten of SI units. We will also discuss the other units that can be derived from these. These prefixes are very

useful because we often need to describe quantities that occur in large multiples or small fractions of a unit. In engineering, units are usually expressed in powers of ten that are used in multiples of three.

Let me give you an example. If we are talking about weight, we can talk about a kilogram. *Kilo* is a prefix to describe ten to the power of three, so a kilogram is one thousand grams. We write it with a small *k* before the symbol for grams – which is *g* – so that makes *kg*. *Mega* means ten to the power of six, so a megawatt is one million watts. Its symbol is a capital *M*. *Giga* is ten to the power of nine, with a capital *G* as the symbol. That's a very large number!

We can also use prefixes to describe very *small* numbers of units. This is particularly important for engineers working with microelectronics. For example, the prefix *milli* – with the symbol small *m* – is ten to the power of minus three, whereas *nano* is ten to the power of minus nine. Its symbol is a small *n*.

🎧 **1.8**

Lecture 3

First, let's look at the term 'charge'. It's been known for over 2,000 years that it is possible to create a static charge on certain objects, for example on a piece of amber – that's a piece of fossilized tree resin. A charged object is capable of attracting very light objects, for example small feathers. This is an example of static electricity – an electric charge on the surface of an object. But what exactly is this charge?

Alessandro Volta invented the battery using copper and zinc metals. He showed that electricity flows through the wires attached to the battery. This is an example of current, or moving charge, electricity. Initially it wasn't clear what the connection was between static and current, but Volta showed that they were both part of the same fundamental mechanism. And this mechanism involves the atomic structure of matter, in other words a nucleus – made up of neutrons and protons – surrounded by electrons. Charge is measured in a unit called the *coulomb* – with a capital *C* as its symbol. The two main particles that carry a charge are the *electron*, with a negative charge, and the *proton*, with a positive charge. Electrons and protons are known as *elementary charges*.

The next quantity we need to look at is *current*. Electric current is defined as the rate of change of charge passing through an area – usually the cross-sectional area of a metal wire – per unit of time. It is therefore measured in terms of *coulombs per second*, and one coulomb per second is known as an *ampere*, symbolized by a capital *A* as mentioned in the last lecture. In metallic conductors, current is carried by negative charges – these are the *free electrons*. The free electrons are only weakly attracted to the atomic structure in metallic elements. As a result, they can move easily in the presence of electric fields.

In order for current to flow, there must be a *closed circuit*. An example of a simple closed circuit is a battery connected to a light bulb. The German scientist Kirchhoff observed that the current flowing from the light bulb to the battery is equal to the current flowing from the battery to the light bulb. This means that no charge is lost around the closed circuit. Kirchhoff's current law states that because charge must remain constant, the sum of currents at a node must equal zero. A node is a junction of two or more device terminals or conductors. Thanks to Kirchhoff's law, it is possible to express currents in a circuit in terms of each other. For example, it is possible to express the current leaving a node in terms of all other currents at the node. This makes it possible to write equations and this can help in designing and understanding large electrical circuits.

🎧 **1.9**

Lecture 4

The three devices I'm going to talk about today measure three basic electrical parameters: current, voltage and resistance.

The first practical measuring device is the ohmmeter. When the ohmmeter is connected across a circuit element, it can measure the resistance of the element. However, you need to remember one important rule here: we can only measure the resistance of an element when it is disconnected from any other circuit.

The ammeter is the second device I want to mention. When the ammeter is connected in series with a circuit element, such as a resistor, it can measure the current flowing through the element. There are two important things to remember if you want an accurate reading. First, as I just mentioned, the ammeter must be placed in series with the element, and not across it as in the case with the ohmmeter. Secondly, the ammeter should not affect the flow of current in any way. If it does this, it will cause a voltage drop and the measurement will no longer be the true current flowing in the circuit. Therefore, we can say that an ideal ammeter has zero internal resistance.

The last device I want to look at today is the voltmeter. This can measure the voltage across a circuit element. Voltage, as you probably remember, is the difference in potential between two points in a circuit, so the voltmeter needs to be connected across the element. There are a couple of points you need to remember about the voltmeter. First, as I just mentioned, the voltmeter needs to be placed in parallel with the element, and not in series with it. Secondly, the voltmeter should not take any current away from the element whose voltage it is measuring. Otherwise, it won't be able to measure the true potential difference. So, the voltmeter should have an infinite internal resistance. This, of course, is the complete opposite of what we said about the ideal ammeter.

So for both the ammeter and the voltmeter, we need to consider the practical limitations of the devices we use. There will always be some series resistance to the circuit because of the presence of the ammeter. Similarly, a voltmeter will always draw some current away from the measured circuit. This is simply part of the difference between a perfect world, and the world as we know it!

🎧 **1.10**

Lecture 5

The first step in becoming a recognized electrical engineer is to study for an academic degree in Electrical Engineering. As you know, it can take four or five years to get a bachelor's degree. This involves studying a range of subjects, including physics, mathematics, computer science and other specific topics. At the beginning of a university programme, students take courses in all the branches of Electrical Engineering. They can then choose to specialize in one or more branches in the final years.

Having completed an undergraduate degree programme, some electrical engineers decide to take a postgraduate degree such as an MSc in Engineering or a PhD in Engineering. The MSc can consist of either research or coursework, while a PhD involves a significant research component. Getting an MSc or PhD is, however, optional for most engineers. The important thing in the process of becoming a practising engineer is obtaining a bachelor's degree.

After graduation, the next step is to obtain certification by a professional body. For this, a set of requirements must be satisfied. These usually include work experience, and there is often a written exam too. After certification, engineers are given the title of Professional Engineer or Chartered Engineer, depending on the part of the world where they live and work. Obtaining certification is an important step because in many countries only certified engineers can do certain important jobs. In some countries, if you are not certified, you cannot work as an engineer at all.

There are several important professional bodies for electrical engineers. One of these is the Institute of Electrical and Electronics Engineers, abbreviated as IEEE or 'I triple E'. Another is the Institution of Engineering and Technology, or IET. These bodies have members worldwide and publish literature for the profession, such as journals. They also help practising electrical engineers keep up to date with new skills and new information, which change more and more rapidly each year. These are therefore very important reasons for being a member.

Exercise E

Allow students to uncover the opposite page or open their books. Give them plenty of time to compare their answers with the model notes. Feed back on the final question.

Exercise F

1 Ask students to work in pairs. Assign a set of notes to each pair. They must try to reconstruct the lecture orally – including the introduction – from the notes.

2 Put the pairs together in groups of four, with different topics. Each pair should give their lecture to the other pair.

Closure

1 Work on any problems you noticed during the pairwork (Exercise F).

2 Refer back to the pictures at the top of the Course Book page. Students should now be able to name them with confidence.

Extra activities

1 Work through the *Vocabulary bank* and *Skills bank* if you have not already done so, or as a revision of previous study.

2 Use the *Activity bank* (Teacher's Book additional resources section, Resource 1A).

A Set the crossword for individual work (including homework) or pairwork.

Answers

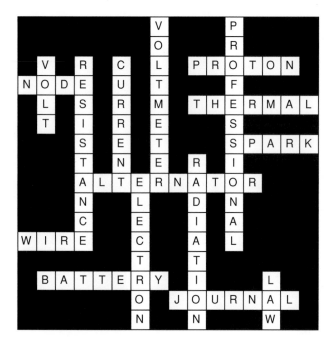

B Play noughts and crosses in pairs. There are two boards. The first contains words with affixes, the second contains concepts related to electrical engineering.

Teach students how to play noughts and crosses if they don't know – they take it in turns to choose a word/phrase and try to use it in context or explain what it means. If they succeed, they can put their symbol – a nought **0** or a cross **X** – in that box. If a person gets three of their own symbols in a line, they win.

First board: Tell students to remove the affixes to find the basic word in each case. Make sure they can tell you the meaning of the basic word (e.g., *magnetic* for *electromagnetic)* but don't elicit the meaning of the affixed word at this stage. Put students in pairs to play the game. Monitor and adjudicate.

Second board: Put students in different pairs to play the second game. Clearly, this time they have to actually remember the facts from the lectures. Don't let them look back at notes.

3 Each of the mini-lectures from Lesson 1.4 can lead on to a great deal more work. Tell students to research one of the following, according to which group they ended in. Explain that they must come back and report to the rest of the class in the next lesson/next week.

Lecture	Research
1	The electrical engineering systems in a typical home.
2	Other units used in electrical engineering (e.g., *volt*), derived from the six fundamental quantities.
3	Other fundamental laws of circuit analysis.
4	Other measuring devices (e.g., wattmeter).
5	Recognized journals for electrical engineers and certification for electrical engineers in your country.

4 Brainstorm note-taking techniques. For example:

- use spacing between points
- use abbreviations
- use symbols
- underline headings
- use capital letters
- use indenting
- make ordered points
- use different colours
- use key words only

2 THE HISTORY OF ELECTRICAL AND ELECTRONIC ENGINEERING

Unit 2 looks at the history of electrical engineering from the 19th century to modern days, charting the key figures in the discipline and their main achievements and inventions. The more recent history of electronic engineering, with its focus on solid-state electronics, is also examined.

Note that students will need dictionaries for some exercises in this unit.

Skills focus

Reading

- using research questions to focus on relevant information in a text
- using topic sentences to get an overview of the text

Writing

- writing topic sentences
- summarizing a text

Vocabulary focus

- English–English dictionaries:
  headwords
  definitions
  parts of speech
  phonemes
  stress markers
  countable/uncountable
  transitive/intransitive

Key vocabulary

advancement	electron	microprocessor
amplifier	electronics	network
application	element	safety
broadcast	filament	semiconductor
commercially	foundation	signal (n)
components	generator	switch (n and v)
conductor	grid	technique
current	incandescent	telegraph
demand	induction (n and adj)	transistor
development	insulated	triode
device	integrated circuit	vacuum
discover	invent	voltage
distribution	light bulb	wireless

2.1 Vocabulary

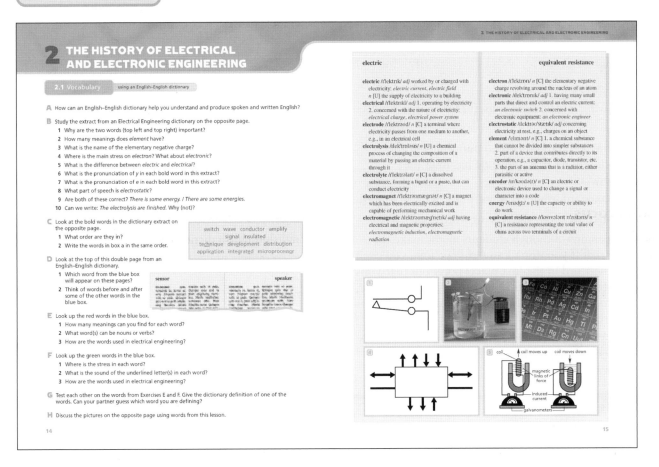

General note

Take in a set of English–English dictionaries.

Read the *Vocabulary bank* at the end of the Course Book unit. Decide when, if at all, to refer students to it. The best time is probably at the very end of the lesson or the beginning of the next lesson, as a summary/revision.

Lesson aims

- learn how to make full use of an English–English dictionary
- gain fluency in the target vocabulary

Introduction

1 Revise the vocabulary from the last unit. Check:
   - meaning
   - pronunciation
   - spelling

2 Ask students whether they use a translation (bilingual) dictionary or an English–English (monolingual) dictionary. Elicit the advantages and disadvantages of a translation dictionary.

Answers

Possible answers:

Advantages	Disadvantages
good when you know the word in your own language and need a translation into English	not good when there is more than one possible translation of a word – which is the correct one?
when you look up an English word, the translation into your language is easy to understand	English–English dictionaries often have more examples and precise definitions of each word

Methodology note

Recent research has shown that, despite the insistence of generations of language teachers on the use of English–English dictionaries in class, nearly 90 per cent of students use a translation dictionary when studying on their own.

Exercise A

Ask the question as a general discussion. Confirm but do not explain anything. Point out that the next exercise will make the value of this kind of dictionary clear.

Answers

Model answers:

The following information is useful for spoken English:

- stress
- pronunciation of individual phonemes – particularly when a phoneme has multiple pronunciations

The following information is useful for written English:

- information about the type of word – C/U; T/I
- the spelling – although students might make the point that if you don't know the spelling, you can't find the word in the first place; point out that you can often guess the possible spelling – for example, *electrolyte* could be *electrolite*, but if you don't find it there, you can try it with a *y* in the middle …
- some synonyms for lexical cohesion – this is a very important point, although you may not want to elaborate on this now

Exercise B

Set for individual work and pairwork checking. Feed back, ideally using an OHT or other visual display of the dictionary extract to highlight points. You might suggest that students annotate the dictionary extract in their books, highlighting symbols, etc., and writing notes on the meaning and value.

Answers

Model answers:

1. They tell you the first and last words on the pages to help you locate the word you want.
2. Three.
3. An electron.
4. *Electron* – on the second syllable; *electronic* – on the third syllable.
5. There is some overlap in the usage of the two adjectives when they are used to describe devices that are worked by electricity. However, *electrical* is the more general term, being used for anything concerned with the nature of electricity.
6. The *y* may be pronounced as /iː/, such as *energy*, or /ə/ (schwa sound), as in *electrolysis*. Ask what other pronunciation *y* can have, and elicit examples such as *electrolyte*, *dynamo*, *electrify* (/aɪ/) and system (/ɪ/).

7. Four possible pronunciations: /ɪ/ usually at the beginning of a word (e.g., *electric*, *encoder*, *equivalent*); /e/ in the middle of a word (e.g., second *e* in *electric*, *electrical*, *electrode*) and sometimes at the beginning of a word (e.g., *element*, *energy*). It may also be pronounced with the /ə/ sound (schwa sound) in words such as *current*, *power* and *system*, and the second *e* in *energy*. Occasionally the *e* is not pronounced, especially when it is at the end of the word (e.g., *electrode*, *electrolyte*, *charge*).
8. Adjective – *ic* marks an adjective.
9. The first is correct because *energy* is an uncountable noun, so it is always singular. It is incorrect to say: *I put all my energies into making it work.*
10. No. Although *electrolysis* ends in an *s*, it is an uncountable noun, so it is singular.

Exercise C

Note: If students are from a Roman alphabet background, you may want to omit this exercise.

1. Students should quickly be able to identify alphabetical order.
2. Set for individual work and pairwork checking. Feed back, getting the words on the board in the correct order. Don't worry about stress and individual phonemes at this point – students will check this later with their dictionaries.

Language note

It may seem self-evident that words in a dictionary are in alphabetical order. But students from certain languages may not automatically recognize this. In the famous Hans Wehr dictionary of written Arabic, for example, you must first convert a given word to its root and look that up, then find the derived form. So *aflaaj* (the plural of *falaj* = irrigation channel) will not be found under A but under F since the root is *f-l-j*.

Exercise D

1. Set for pairwork. Feed back orally, explaining the principle if necessary.
2. Set for pairwork. Ask each pair to choose five words to work on. Ask them to find words connected with electric engineering if they can. Feed back orally.

Answers

1. *Signal* will appear on the double page spread.
2. Answers depend on which words students choose.

Exercise E

Give out the dictionaries, if you have not already done so.

Remind students that dictionaries number multiple meanings of the same part of speech and multiple parts of speech. Remind them also of the countable/uncountable and transitive/intransitive markers. (Note that different dictionaries may use different methods for indicating these things. The *Oxford Advanced Learner's Dictionary*, for example, uses [V] for intransitive verbs and [Vn] for transitive verbs.)

Write the headings of the table in the Answers section on the board, and work through the first word as an example.

Set for pairwork. Feed back, building up the table in the Answers section on the board. (Students' answers will vary – accept any appropriate meanings and definitions.)

Answers

Model answers:

	Part of speech	Type	Main meaning in electrical engineering	Main meaning(s) in general English
switch	n	C	a device used to open or close a circuit	a device to turn an electrical machine on and off
	v	T	to connect, disconnect or change the connections in an electric circuit	to turn an electrical machine on and off
wave	n	C	a variation of an electromagnetic field in the propagation of radiation through space	an undulation that moves across the surface of the sea caused by wind
	v	I	not commonly used	to move your hand from side to side in the air to say hello or goodbye
conductor	n	C	1. a material with a large number of free electrons; 2. a material that easily permits electric current to flow	1. the person who stands in front of an orchestra and directs it; 2. the person who works on a bus or train and sells or checks tickets
amplify	v	T	to increase the strength of electrical signals	to increase the level of sound using a device
signal	n	C	a general term used to describe any AC or DC in a circuit	a gesture, sound or action that sends a message
	v	I	not commonly used	to make a gesture, sound or action in order to send a message
insulated	adj		separated from other conducting surfaces by something that offers a high resistance to the passage of current	similar use: 1. covered by plastic to prevent electric shocks; 2. protected from cold or noise by covering with a thick layer of material

Exercise F

Remind students how stress and the pronunciation of individual phonemes are shown in a dictionary. Refer them to the key to symbols if necessary. Write the headings of the table in the Answers section on the board, and work through the first word as an example.

Set for pairwork. Feed back, building up the table from Answers section on the board.

Answers

Model answers:

Stress	Sound	Part of speech	Type	Main meaning in electrical engineering
tech'nique	/k/	n	C	a particular way of doing an activity, involving practical skills
de'velopment	/e/	n	C /U	the spread of something over space or time
distri'bution	/ʃ/	v	T	the spread of something over space or time countable: a wide distribution uncountable: some distribution
appli'cation	/eɪ/	n	C	the use of a particular theory or rule in a specific, practical situation
'integrated	/ɪ/	adj		to describe a circuit in which many elements are fabricated and connected by a single process into a single chip
micro'processor	/ə/(/r/)	n	C	the central processing chip in a piece of electronic equipment

Exercise G

Demonstrate how to do the exercise by giving a few definitions and getting students to tell you the word (without reading from the board or their books, if possible). Stick to electrical engineering usage rather than general English and encourage students to do the same. Point out that dictionaries often use a small set of words that help to define, e.g., *place, set, method, kind, type, principle, person*. Give definitions using these words and ask students to identify what you are defining, e.g., *It's a method of closing a circuit; It's a type of material that allows current to flow*; etc.

Exercise H

Work through the pictures. Check that students understand what they show and the relationship to electrical engineering.

For reference, the pictures show:

1 an electronic **switch**
2 an **electrolysis** experiment, with two **electrodes**; some students may be able to describe what happens in the experiment
3 the periodic table of the **elements**
4 a **microprocessor**
5 an illustration of **electromagnetic induction**, showing an electric **circuit**, a coil, and a **magnet**; some students may be able to explain how magnetic induction works

Closure

Remind students that you can identify the part of speech of an unknown word by looking at the words before or after the word, i.e.,

- nouns often come before and after verbs, so if you know that X is a verb, the next content word before or after is probably a noun
- nouns often come immediately after articles
- verbs often come after names and pronouns
- adjectives come before nouns or after the verb *be*

Come back to this point when you are feeding back on the reading texts in this unit.

2.2 Reading

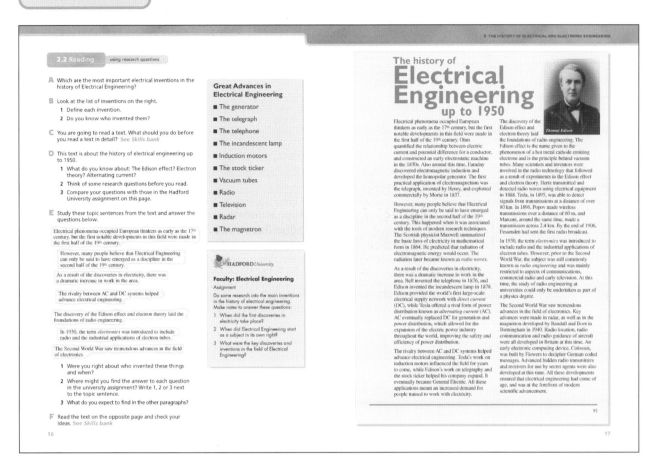

General note

Take in an English–English dictionary.

Read the *Skills bank* section on doing reading research at the end of the Course Book unit. Decide when, if at all, to refer students to it. The best time is probably at the very end of the lesson or the beginning of the next lesson, as a summary/revision. Alternatively, you could refer students to the *Skills bank* after Exercise C.

Lesson aims

- prepare for reading research
- use research questions to structure reading research

Introduction

1 Hold up an English–English dictionary and say a word from Lesson 2.1. Ask students where approximately they will find it in the dictionary – i.e., beginning, middle, two-thirds of the way through, etc. Follow their advice and read the word at the top left. Ask students if the target word will be before or after. Continue until you get to the right page. Repeat with several more words from Lesson 2.1.

2 Give definitions of some of the words from Lesson 2.1 for students to identify.

Exercise A

Set the question for pairwork. Feed back ideas to the whole class.

Exercise B

Refer students to the list of inventions. Set questions for pairwork. General discussion to pool answers. Don't say if they are right or wrong at this stage, since they will find out most of the answers from the text.

Invention	Definition	Who invented them?
the generator	a machine that converts physical energy into electrical energy	Faraday
the telegraph	a communications system that transmits and receives simple unmodulated electric impulses	Henry / Morse
the telephone	an instrument that converts voice and other sound signals into a form that can be transmitted to remote locations and that receives and reconverts waves into sound signals	Bell
the incandescent lamp	an electric lamp in which a filament is heated to incandescence by an electric current	Edison
induction motors	an alternating-current motor in which a primary winding on one member (usually the stator) is connected to the power source, and a secondary winding on the other member (usually the rotor) carries only current induced by the magnetic field of the primary	Tesla
the stock ticker	one of the first applications of transmitting text over a wire to a printing device	Calahan / Edison
vacuum tubes	an electron tube from which all or most of the gas has been removed, permitting electrons to move with low interaction	Edison / Tesla / others
radio	the wireless transmission through space of electromagnetic waves in the approximate frequency range from 10 kilohertz to 300,000 megahertz	Marconi / Popov
television	the transmission of dynamic or sometimes static images, generally with accompanying sound, via electric or electromagnetic signals, and the apparatus that receives these signals	John Logie Baird
radar	a method of detecting distant objects and determining their position, velocity, or other characteristics by analysis of very high frequency radio waves reflected from their surfaces	Robert Alexander Watson-Watt
the magnetron	a microwave tube in which electrons generated from a heated cathode are affected by magnetic and electric fields in such a way as to produce microwave radiation	Habann

Exercise C

Students may or may not be able to articulate preparation for reading. Elicit ideas. One thing they must identify – reading for a purpose. Point out that they should always be clear about the purpose of their reading. A series of questions to answer, or **research questions**, is one of the best purposes.

Refer students to the *Skills bank* at this stage if you wish.

Exercise D

1 Set for pairwork. Elicit ideas and feed back.
2 Set for pairwork. Elicit some ideas.
3 Refer students to the Hadford University research questions at the bottom of the page. Check comprehension. If students have come up with better research questions, write them on the board for consideration during the actual reading.

Answers

Possible answers:
1 The Edison effect – the flow of a current between two metal wires in a vacuum, one of which is heated.

Electron theory – the idea that electricity is the movement of electrons through a conductor. In the Edison effect, the current flows because it is carried by free electrons.

Alternating current – in alternating current, the movement of electric charge periodically reverses direction. In direct current, the flow of electric charge is only in one direction.

Exercise E

Remind students about topic sentences if they haven't mentioned them already in Exercise C. Give them time to read the topic sentences in this exercise. Point out that the topic sentences are in order, so they give a rough overview of the whole text. Some topic sentences clearly announce what the paragraph will be about. Others may only give a hint of how it will develop.

1 Set for group discussion.
2 Remind students of the research questions. Look at the first research question as an example, then set for pairwork. Point out that they may match a research question to more than one topic sentence, and that some topic sentences may not relate to the research questions (i.e., they don't have to write a number for each topic sentence).
3 Explain that here students look at the topic sentences they *didn't* number in question 2, and try to work out the likely content of each paragraph.

Do the first two as examples, then set for pairwork. Feed back, eliciting and checking that they are reasonable possibilities, based on the topic sentence. You can accept multiple ideas for the same paragraph provided they are all possible.

Answers

Possible answers:

1 Refer students back to their predictions in Exercise B.

2 The following is probably the best prediction:

Electrical phenomena occupied European thinkers as early as the 17th century, but the first notable developments in this field were made in the first half of the 19th century.	1/3
However, many people believe that Electrical Engineering can only be said to have emerged as a discipline in the second half of the 19th century.	1/3
As a result of the discoveries in electricity, there was a dramatic increase in work in the area.	1/3
The rivalry between AC and DC systems helped advance electrical engineering.	
The discovery of the Edison effect and electron theory laid the foundations of radio engineering.	
In 1930, the term *electronics* was introduced to include radio and the industrial applications of electron tubes.	
The Second World War saw tremendous advances in the field of electronics.	1

3 Answers depend on the students. Discuss.

Exercise F

Point out, if students have not already said this, that the topic sentences are normally the first sentences of each paragraph. Tell students to compare the contents of each paragraph with their predictions. Encourage them to take notes as they read.

If necessary, the reading can be set for homework.

Closure

1 Unless you have set the reading for homework, do some extra work on oral summarizing as a comprehension check after reading (see *Skills bank – Using topic sentences to summarize*). Students work in pairs. One student says a topic sentence and the other student summarizes the paragraph from memory in his/her own words, or if necessary reads the paragraph again and then summarizes it without looking.

2 You may also want to redo the text as a jigsaw – the text is reproduced in the additional resources section at the back of this Teacher's Book (Resource 2B) to facilitate this.

3 As a further activity after reading, remind students of the note-taking skills practised in Unit 1. Discuss appropriate note-taking forms for this text. They can then write notes on the text. Tell them to keep their notes, as they will be useful for the summary exercise in Lesson 2.3.

2.3 Extending skills

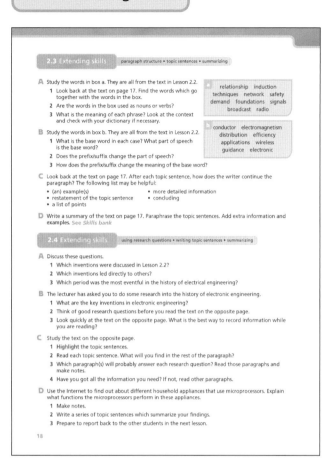

2.3 Extending skills   paragraph structure • topic sentences • summarizing

A Study the words in box a. They are all from the text in Lesson 2.2.

  1 Look back at the text on page 17. Find the words which go together with the words in the box.

  2 Are the words in the box used as nouns or verbs?

  3 What is the meaning of each phrase? Look at the context and check with your dictionary if necessary.

relationship induction
techniques network safety
demand foundations signals
broadcast radio

B Study the words in box b. They are all from the text in Lesson 2.2.

  1 What is the base word in each case? What part of speech is the base word?

  2 Does the prefix/suffix change the part of speech?

  3 How does the prefix/suffix change the meaning of the base word?

conductor electromagnetism
distribution efficiency
applications wireless
guidance electronic

C Look back at the text on page 17. After each topic sentence, how does the writer continue the paragraph? The following list may be helpful:

• (an) example(s)
• restatement of the topic sentence
• a list of points
• more detailed information
• concluding

D Write a summary of the text on page 17. Paraphrase the topic sentences. Add extra information and examples. See Skills bank

2.4 Extending skills   using research questions • writing topic sentences • summarizing

A Discuss these questions.

  1 Which inventions were discussed in Lesson 2.2?

  2 Which inventions led directly to others?

  3 Which period was the most eventful in the history of electrical engineering?

B The lecturer has asked you to do some research into the history of electronic engineering.

  1 What are the key inventions in electronic engineering?

  2 Think of good research questions before you read the text on the opposite page.

  3 Look quickly at the text on the opposite page. What is the best way to record information while you are reading?

C Study the text on the opposite page.

  1 Highlight the topic sentences.

  2 Read each topic sentence. What will you find in the rest of the paragraph?

  3 Which paragraph(s) will probably answer each research question? Read those paragraphs and make notes.

  4 Have you got all the information you need? If not, read other paragraphs.

D Use the Internet to find out about different household appliances that use microprocessors. Explain what functions the microprocessors perform in these appliances.

  1 Make notes.

  2 Write a series of topic sentences which summarize your findings.

  3 Prepare to report back to the other students in the next lesson.

18

General note

Take in a set of English–English dictionaries.

Lesson aims

- identify paragraph structure
- produce good topic sentences
- summarize a text

Further practice in:

- vocabulary from Lesson 2.2

Introduction

Test students on the factual information in the text, e.g., *What were some of the key inventions of the 19th century? Who were the scientists mentioned?* If a student says, accurately: *I didn't read about that. It wasn't relevant to my research*, accept it and praise the student.

Exercise A

Set for pairwork. Feed back orally, asking students for the location of the phrase.

Methodology note

Don't help students to find words in a text. It's a key reading skill to be able to pattern match, i.e., get a word in your mind's eye and then find it on the page.

Answers

Possible answers:

Phrase	Noun or verb phrase?	Meaning
quantified the relationship	verb phrase	understood mathematically how two factors depended on each other
electromagnetic induction	noun phrase	the production of a voltage in a coil due to a change in the number of magnetic lines of force passing through the coil
modern research techniques	noun phrase	ways of doing research that use recently developed tools
electrical supply network	noun phrase	a system that provides electrical power to buildings
improving the safety (of something)	verb phrase	making (something) less dangerous
increased demand (for something)	noun phrase	an increase in the amount or number (of something) that people want
laid the foundations	verb phrase	did something that provided initial support, which others can build on later
detect signals	verb phrase	receive a message or sign
sent the first radio broadcast (to someone)	verb phrase	gave a message via radio waves to someone who couldn't be see or spoken to directly
commercial radio	noun phrase	a service provided by a radio station that is run as a business to make a profit (as opposed to public radio)

Exercise B

Set for individual work and pairwork checking. Students can check these points in a dictionary. Feed back, taking apart the words and showing how the affixes can change the meaning.

Answers

Model answers:

Word	Base word	Affix and meaning
conductor	conduct (v)	~or = verb → noun – the thing performing the action
electromagnetism	electromagnet (n)	~ism = the effect produced by the base noun
distribution	distribute (v)	~ion = verb → noun
efficiency	efficient (adj)	~y = adjective → noun
applications	apply (v)	~ation = verb → noun
wireless	wire (n)	~less = without
guidance	guide (v)	~ance = verb → noun
electronic	electron (n)	~ic = noun → adjective

Exercise C

Do the first paragraph first, then set the rest for individual work followed by pairwork checking.

Feed back with the whole class. Ask students to locate the discourse markers used which help to identify the way in which the paragraph is continued. Build the table in the Answers section below on the board (or on an OHT or PowerPoint slide).

An alternative procedure would be to look at each topic sentence in turn and feed back before moving on to the next topic sentence.

Discourse note

In academic writing, topic sentences often consist of a general point. The sentences that follow then support the general statement in various ways, such as:

- giving a definition and/or a description
- giving examples
- giving lists of points (e.g., arguments or reasons)
- restating the topic sentence in a different way to help clarify it
- giving more information and detail on the topic sentence to clarify it

Often – but not always – the type of sentence is shown by a 'discourse marker' – e.g., *for example*, *first of all*, etc. This helps to signal to the reader how the writer sees the link between the sentences and is therefore a good clue as to purpose of the sentences following the topic sentence.

Answers

Possible answers:

Topic sentence	Possible paragraph content	Discourse markers
Electrical phenomena occupied European thinkers as early as the 17th century, but the first notable developments in this field were made in the first half of the 19th century.	examples of developments	Also around this time … The first …
However, many people believe that Electrical Engineering can only be said to have emerged as a discipline in the second half of the 19th century.	more information and detail on the topic sentence to clarify it	This happened when …
As a result of the discoveries in electricity, there was a dramatic increase in work in the area.	examples of the increase in work	… while … … eventually …
The rivalry between AC and DC systems helped advance electrical engineering.	last sentence: restatement of the topic sentence in a different way to help clarify it	All these applications …
The discovery of the Edison effect and electron theory laid the foundations of radio engineering.	a chronological list of examples of the increase in resulting radio technology	… in 1888 … in 1895 In 1896 … … around the same time … By the end of 1906, …
In 1930, the term *electronics* was introduced to include radio and the industrial applications of electron tubes.	a list of contrasting points (reasons why *electronics* was not a common term)	However, … At this time, … only …
The Second World War saw tremendous advances in the field of electronics.	a list of examples of the advances	Key advances were … … was built by … … also developed …
	concluding last sentence forms conclusion to piece	All these developments …

Exercise D

Students can work individually (for homework) or in pairs (in class). Ask them to write a summary in about 150 words. They should use their own words as far as possible, but they should also try to incorporate the vocabulary they have practised so far. Refer students to the *Skills bank – Using topic sentences to summarize*.

Methodology note

There are two reasons for students to use their own words in written work (except when quoting and acknowledging sources):

1. The work involved in rewording information and ideas helps us to mentally process them and to retain them in memory.

2. Copying whole sentences from the work of other writers is plagiarism (unless the quotation is acknowledged). Universities disapprove of plagiarism and may mark down students who plagiarize. In the commercial world, an accusation of plagiarism can cause legal problems, and in the academic world, it can severely damage a teacher's reputation and career.

Closure

Tell students to define some of the electrical engineering terms from the text on page 17. Alternatively, give definitions of some of the words and tell students to identify the words.

2.4 Extending skills

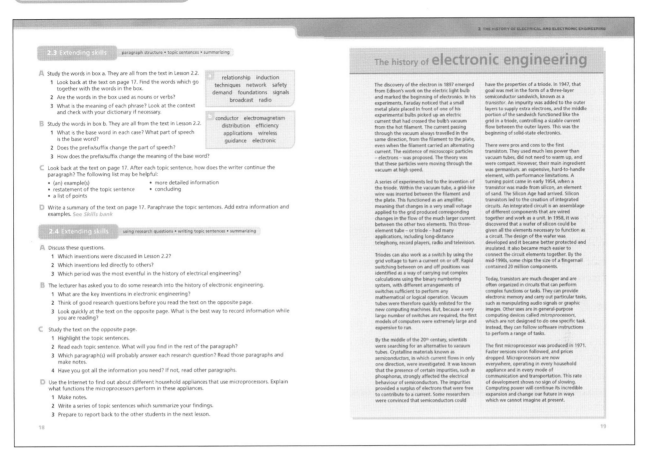

Lesson aims

- use research questions to structure reading research
- write topic sentences for a short research report/summary

Introduction

Give a word from the text in Lesson 2.2 which is part of a phrase. Ask students to try to complete the phrase. It's probably better if you give the first word in the phrase, but you might also try giving the second word at times or at the end of the exercise.

Possible two-word phrases:

electric	*current*
potential	*difference*
electromagnetic	*induction*
electrical	*engineering*
research	*techniques*
mathematical	*form*
electromagnetic	*energy*
radio	*waves*
incandescent	*lamp*
supply	*network*
power	*distribution*
induction	*motor*
vacuum	*tube*

Exercise A

Do this with students' books closed.

1 Give prompts if students can't remember some of the inventions, e.g., give the name of the inventor (see Answers table in Lesson 2.2 Exercise B).

2 See what students can remember here and prompt them if necessary. Encourage a class discussion. Refer back to the article for details.

Answers

Model answers (see next page):

What inventions were discussed?	Which inventions led directly to others?	Which period was the most eventful?
• the generator • the telegraph • the telephone • the incandescent lamp • induction motors • the stock ticker • vacuum tubes • wireless transmissions • radio • television • radar • the magnetron	vacuum tubes → incandescent lamp/radio/television/magnetron radio → radar/magnetron	The second half of the 19th century, when radio technology was developed

3 Encourage students to give their own opinions. Probably the Second World War produced the most new developments in electronics. However, the 1830s were a key period in the advancement of the theory of electricity, and the 1880s saw a range of practical applications of newly discovered inventions.

Exercise B

1 This question relates to the reading text on page 19 and acts as a pre-question. Set for pairwork. Feed back orally.

2 Remind students of the importance of research questions – reading for a purpose. Set for pairwork. Feed back, writing up suitable questions on the board.

3 Elicit the different kinds of notes you can use – see Unit 1 *Skills bank*. Remind students to think about the best kind of notes before and while they are reading.

Methodology note

It is good for students to get into the habit of thinking about the form of their notes before they read a text in detail. If they don't do this, they will tend to be drawn into narrative notes rather than notes which are specifically designed to help them answer their research questions.

Answers

Possible answers:

1 Accept all reasonable answers.

2 Questions such as: *When did electronic engineering start? What discoveries led to the invention of the integrated circuit? What are the main applications of electronic engineering?* etc.

3 See Unit 1 *Skills bank*.

Exercise C

1/2 Remind students of the importance of topic sentences. Set for individual work and pairwork checking. Encourage students not to read ahead. Perhaps you should ask students to cover the text and only reveal each topic sentence in turn, then discuss possible contents of the paragraph. Remind them that this is technique for previewing a text and at this point they do not need to read every part of the text. This will come later. If you have an OHP or other visual display, you can tell students to close their books and just display the topic sentences (additional resources section, Resource 2C), or you can give them out on a handout.

3 Set the choice of paragraphs for pairwork. Students then read individually, make notes and compare them. Monitor and assist.

4 Give students time to read other paragraphs if they need to.

Answers

Possible answers:

2

Topic sentence	Possible paragraph content
The discovery of the electron in 1897 emerged from Edison's work on the electric light bulb and marked the beginning of electronics.	how this discovery occurred and what happened afterwards
A series of experiments led to the invention of the triode.	a description of these experiments; definition of a *triode*.
Triodes can also work as a switch by using the grid voltage to turn a current on or off.	explanation of this works; the results of this discovery
By the middle of the 20th century, scientists were searching for an alternative to vacuum tubes.	how they did this and what they found
There were pros and cons to the first transistors.	a list of the advantages and disadvantages
Today, transistors are much cheaper and are often organized in circuits that can perform complex functions or tasks.	some practical applications of this
The first microprocessor was produced in 1971.	explanation of what it is and what it is used for

3 The appropriate paragraphs to read depend on the research questions from Exercise B.

Discourse note

It is as well to be aware (though you may not feel it is appropriate to discuss with students at this point) that in real academic texts, the topic sentence may not be as obvious as in the texts in this unit. Sometimes there is not an explicit topic sentence, so that the overall topic of the paragraph must be inferred. Or the actual topic sentence for the paragraph can be *near* rather than *at* the beginning of the paragraph. Sometimes, also, the first sentence of a paragraph acts as a topic statement for a succession of paragraphs.

Exercise D

Set the task for homework and feed back next lesson. Encourage students to make notes on the points as given, i.e.,

1 Different household appliances that use microprocessors.

2 What functions the microprocessor performs in each.

Make sure students realize that they only have to write the topic sentences. They can add the details orally.

Closure

1 Focus on some of the vocabulary from the text, including:

alternating current
electron
triode
filament
vacuum tube
amplifier
voltage
audio signals
switch (n)
turn on/off (v)
binary numbering system
logical operation
semiconductor
impurities
transistor
solid-state electronics
warm up (v)
integrated circuits
microprocessors
chips
components
insulated
audio signals
device
software instructions
household appliance

2 You may also want to redo the text as a jigsaw, as before – the text is reproduced in the additional resources section (Resource 2D) to facilitate this.

1 Work through the *Vocabulary bank* and *Skills bank* if you have not already done so, or as a revision of previous study.

2 Use the *Activity bank* (Teacher's Book additional resources section, Resource 2A).

A Set the wordsearch for individual work (including homework) or pairwork.

Answers

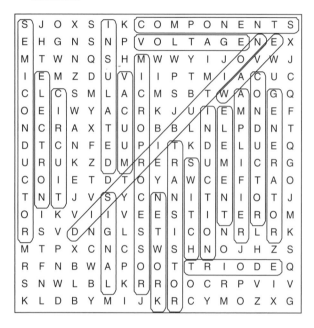

B Do the quiz as a whole class, or in teams, or set for homework – students can re-read the texts to get the answers if necessary.

Answers

1 a A transistor.

  b A switch.

  c An integrated circuit.

2 a Radio waves were transmitted and detected using electrical equipment (by Hertz).

  b The transistor was invented (by Shockley, Bardeen and Brattain).

3 Direct current/alternating current.

4 a Telephone, incandescent lamp, large-scale supply network, stock ticker.

  b Radar, magnetron, early computing devices, hidden radio transmitters.

3 Ask students to work in small groups to research the experiments and inventions of a famous electrical scientist or engineer. They should:

- choose an example of a famous electrical scientist or engineer
- research the inventions and experiments of this scientist/engineer

If students are going to do research on the Internet, a good place to start (at the time of writing) is: http://www.enchantedlearning.com/inventors/

Alternatively, you can do this research before the lesson and print off some pages for students to work from. Remind students that they can't possibly read everything they find, so they must use the topic sentences to decide if a paragraph is worth reading.

4 You can get students to practise their reading aloud – a skill which is not vital but is sometimes useful – by following this approach.

Photocopy and cut up one of the jigsaw texts in the additional resources section (Resources 2B and 2D). Give topic sentences to Student A and the corresponding paragraphs to Student B.

Student A reads out a topic sentence.

Student B finds the corresponding paragraph and reads it out.

An alternative is to give Student A the topic sentences and Student B a set of sentences chosen from each paragraph (one sentence per paragraph). Student A reads out the topic sentences one by one. Student B decides which of his/her sentences is likely to appear in the same paragraph as the topic sentence. Both students have to agree that the paragraph sentence matches the topic sentence.

5 Have a competition to practise finding words in a monolingual dictionary. Requirements:

- an English–English dictionary for each student (or pair of students if necessary)
- Unit 2 key vocabulary list

Put students in teams with their dictionaries closed. Select a word from the vocabulary list and instruct students to open their dictionaries and find the word. The first student to find the word is awarded a point for their team. Additional points can be awarded if the student can give the correct pronunciation and meaning.

3 ELECTRIC AND MAGNETIC CIRCUITS

Unit 3 looks at Ohm's law: what it is, its limitations, and its applications to electromagnetism. The first lecture defines Ohm's law and looks at how it is used in simple electric circuits. The second lecture examines the limitations of the law for circuit elements that do not have a constant resistance. The second lecture also shows how Ohm's law can be applied to magnetic circuits.

Skills focus

🎧 **Listening**

- preparing for a lecture
- predicting lecture content
- making lecture notes
- using different information sources

Speaking

- reporting research findings
- formulating questions

Vocabulary focus

- stress patterns in multi-syllable words
- prefixes

Key vocabulary

application	glow	polarity
battery	heat up	potential
calculations	incandescent	proportional
coil (n)	increase (n and v)	relationship
circuit	linear	reluctance
compass	magnet	resistance
conductor	measurement	resistor
constant	mmf	resolution
current	multimeter	rise (n)
degeneration	multiplication	supply (n)
demagnetize	non-linear	temperature
electromagnetic	ohmic	terminals
empirical	Ohm's law	turns (n)
equation	perpendicular	
filament	photovoltaic	

3.1 Vocabulary

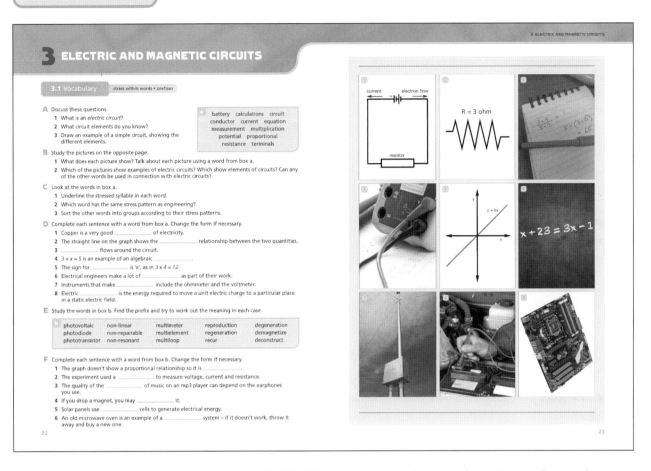

3 ELECTRIC AND MAGNETIC CIRCUITS

3.1 Vocabulary   stress within words • prefixes

A Discuss these questions.
1 What is an *electric circuit*?
2 What circuit elements do you know?
3 Draw an example of a simple circuit, showing the different elements.

> battery calculations circuit
> conductor current equation
> measurement multiplication
> potential proportional
> resistance terminals

B Study the pictures on the opposite page.
1 What does each picture show? Talk about each picture using a word from box a.
2 Which of the pictures show examples of electric circuits? Which show elements of circuits? Can any of the other words be used in connection with electric circuits?

C Look at the words in box a.
1 Underline the stressed syllable in each word.
2 Which word has the same stress pattern as *engineering*?
3 Sort the other words into groups according to their stress patterns.

D Complete each sentence with a word from box a. Change the form if necessary.
1 Copper is a very good _____ of electricity.
2 The straight line on the graph shows the _____ relationship between the two quantities.
3 _____ flows around the circuit.
4 $3 + x = 5$ is an example of an algebraic _____.
5 The sign for _____ is 'x', as in $3 \times 4 = 12$.
6 Electrical engineers make a lot of _____ as part of their work.
7 Instruments that make _____ include the ohmmeter and the voltmeter.
8 Electric _____ is the energy required to move a unit electric charge to a particular place in a static electric field.

E Study the words in box b. Find the prefix and try to work out the meaning in each case.

photovoltaic	non-linear	multimeter	reproduction	degeneration
photodiode	non-repairable	multielement	regeneration	demagnetize
phototransistor	non-resonant	multiloop	recur	deconstruct

F Complete each sentence with a word from box b. Change the form if necessary.
1 The graph doesn't show a proportional relationship so it is _____.
2 The experiment used a _____ to measure voltage, current and resistance.
3 The quality of the _____ of music on an mp3 player can depend on the earphones you use.
4 If you drop a magnet, you may _____ it.
5 Solar panels use _____ cells to generate electrical energy.
6 An old microwave oven is an example of a _____ system – if it doesn't work, throw it away and buy a new one.

22

23

General note

Read the *Vocabulary bank* at the end of the Course Book unit. Decide when, if at all, to refer your students to it. The best time is probably at the very end of the lesson or the beginning of the next lesson, as a summary/revision.

Dictionaries will be useful in this lesson.

Lesson aims

- gain a greater understanding of the importance of stress within words and some of the common patterns
- extend knowledge of words which contain prefixes
- gain fluency in the target vocabulary

Introduction

1 Revise the vocabulary from the first two units. Check:
- meaning
- pronunciation
- spelling

2 Revise the terms from Unit 1: *charge*; *electron*; *current*; *circuit*; *battery*; *bulb*; *Kirchhoff's current law*. Ask students for the definitions of these terms. Ask students what they remember about the German scientist Ohm – he is briefly mentioned in the first reading text in Unit 2: The history of electrical engineering up to 1950.

Exercise A

Put the following words up on the board: *device*; *current*; *resistors*; *inductors*; *capacitors*; *passive*; *generate*. Have students cover page 23. Tell students that the answers to these questions should involve some of these words. Put students in pairs to discuss the questions. Feed back orally, assisting with terminology if necessary.

Answers

Possible answers:

1 An electric circuit is an electrical *device* that provides a path for electrical *current* to flow.

2 Circuit elements include *resistors*, *inductors* and *capacitors*. These are *passive* elements because they do not *generate* electricity.

3 See the diagram on the opposite page of the Course Book for an example.

Exercise B

1 Refer students to the pictures on the opposite page. Ask what students can see in the first picture. Elicit *It's a simple electric circuit.* Ask which word from box a could be used to say something *more* about the picture. Accept any suggestions which use the words *current*, *terminals* or *battery*, e.g., *The arrow indicates the flow of current around the circuit. The symbol with two lines shows the battery. The positive battery terminal is the short line, and the negative terminal is the long one.*

Set the remaining pictures for pairwork. Students should make two statements: first what they can see and then a further comment about each picture using at least one word from box a. If necessary, they should check the meanings of the words in their dictionaries. All the words are relevant. Feed back with the whole class. Accept any reasonable suggestions. Check/correct pronunciation, especially the stress patterns.

2 Set for pairwork. Students should consider how the words they have used in question 1 can be used in connection with electric circuits. Feed back orally, but do not confirm or correct at this stage.

Answers

Possible answers:

1

1 It's a simple electric 'circuit, showing a 'battery with a positive 'terminal and a negative 'terminal. The arrows show the direction of 'current flowing around the circuit.

Subject note

As shown in the Course Book diagram, the actual electron flow is in the opposite direction to the conventional direction of current.

2 This shows the two possible symbols for a re'sistor in a circuit.

3 These are calcu'lations; some of them involve multipli'cation.

4 This is an ammeter which gives a 'measurement of current.

5 The two quantities in this graph are pro'portional, i.e., the relationship is a straight line.

6 This is an algebraic e'quation.

7 The device shown here is a lightning con'ductor.

8 This is a car battery, showing terminals and cells.

9 A computer motherboard, showing its circuits.

2 Picture 1 shows an electric circuit. Pictures 1 and 2 show elements of circuits, e.g., resistors, conductors and batteries. Some of the other words can be used in connection with electric circuits, e.g., *We can make calculations that involve multiplication about circuits using equations; We can take a measurement of the potential across an element in a circuit.*

Methodology note

From now on, whenever you present a group of words in a box, as here, ask students for the part of speech of each word. This is good practice and also good preparation for changing the form of the word if a different part of speech is required in the associated exercise(s).

Exercise C

Write *engineering* on the board. Ask students to say how many syllables there are in the word (there are four). Draw vertical lines to divide the syllables. Then ask students to say where the main stress is and draw a line under the syllable:

en | gi | <u>neer</u> | ing

Point out the importance of stressed syllables in words – see *Language note* below.

1 Set for pairwork. Tell students to divide the words into syllables first, then to underline the strongest stress. Feed back.

2 Ask students to find the word which has the same stress pattern as *engineering*. Write it on the board like this:

en | gi | <u>neer</u> | ing

cal | cu | <u>la</u> | tions

3 Set for pairwork. Students should match words with the same number of syllables and with main stresses in the same place.

Language note

In English, speakers emphasize the stressed syllable in a multi-syllable word. Sometimes listeners may not even hear the unstressed syllables. Vowels, in any case, often change to schwa or a reduced form in unstressed syllables. Therefore, it is essential that students can recognize key words from the stressed syllable alone, when they hear them in context. Stress sometimes moves to fit common patterns when you add a suffix, *e.g.,* 'calculate, calcu'lation.

Other suffixes, such as *~ment* or *~al*, don't affect the stress of the root word, e.g., 'measure, 'measurement; e'lectric, e'lectrical.

Sometimes it is difficult to be sure exactly how a word should be divided into syllables. Use vowel sounds as a guide to the number of syllables. If in doubt, consult a dictionary.

Answers

1 <u>ba</u>ttery
   cal<u>cu</u>lations
   <u>cir</u>cuit
   con<u>duc</u>tor
   <u>cur</u>rent
   e<u>qua</u>tion
   <u>mea</u>surement
   multipli<u>ca</u>tion
   po<u>ten</u>tial
   pro<u>por</u>tional
   re<u>sis</u>tance
   <u>ter</u>minals

3 <u>ba</u>ttery, <u>cir</u>cuit, <u>cur</u>rent, <u>mea</u>surement, <u>ter</u>minals
   con<u>duc</u>tor, e<u>qua</u>tion, po<u>ten</u>tial, pro<u>por</u>tional, re<u>sis</u>tance
   multipli<u>ca</u>tion

Exercise D

Set for individual work and pairwork checking. Not all the words are needed. Feed back orally.

Answers

1 Copper is a very good <u>conductor</u> of electricity.
2 The straight line on the graph shows the <u>proportional</u> relationship between the two quantities.
3 <u>Current</u> flows around the circuit.
4 *3 + x = 5* is an example of an algebraic <u>equation</u>.
5 The sign for <u>multiplication</u> is '×', as in *3 × 4 = 12*.
6 Electrical engineers perform a lot of <u>calculations</u> as part of their work.
7 Instruments that take <u>measurements</u> include the ohmmeter and the voltmeter.
8 Electric <u>potential</u> is the energy required to move a unit electric charge to a particular place in a static electric field.

Language note

See Lesson 3.4 Exercise F for information about how mathematical operations are said verbally. We do not usually use the noun.

Exercise E

Set for pairwork. Students should look at all three words in each column to find and then deduce the meaning of the prefix. Encourage them to use a phrase as a definition rather than a single-word translation. They need to develop a sense of the broader meaning of the prefix. Feed back, getting the meanings on the board.

Answers

Model answers:

   photo = connected to light
   non = not
   multi = many
   re = to do again, repetition
   de = to remove from, to decrease, to change in the opposite direction

Methodology note

With some of these words it is difficult to work out the base word, e.g., *cur* in the word *recur*. However, you can point out that you can sometimes understand roughly what a word means if you understand the prefix, e.g., *recur* must be something to do with changing something or doing something *again*, so context will help you to guess the rough meaning.

Exercise F

This is further practice in using words with prefixes. Remind students that they must make sure the form of the word fits into the sentence. If students are struggling, point out that all but one of the missing words are from the top row of the box.

Feed back, checking pronunciation and stress patterns.

Answers

Model answers:

1 The graph doesn't show a proportional relationship so it is <u>non-linear</u>.
2 The experiment used a <u>multimeter</u> to measure voltage, current and resistance.
3 The quality of the <u>reproduction</u> of music on an mp3 player can depend on the earphones you use.
4 If you drop a magnet, you may <u>demagnetize</u> it.
5 Solar panels use <u>photovoltaic</u> cells to generate electrical energy.
6 An old microwave oven is an example of a <u>non-repairable</u> system – if it doesn't work, throw it away and buy a new one.

Closure

1 Ask students what other electrical engineering terms they know with these prefixes. Discuss ideas with the whole class.

2 If you have not already done so, refer students to the *Vocabulary bank* at the end of Unit 3. Work through some or all of the stress patterns.

Language note

The patterns shown in the *Vocabulary bank* in Unit 3 are productive, i.e., they enable you to make more words or apply the rules accurately to other words. The words with unusual patterns tend to be the more common ones, so if students come across a new multi-syllable word at this level, it is likely to conform to the patterns shown. Native speakers recognize the patterns and will naturally apply them to unusual words, e.g., proper nouns. How, for example, would you pronounce these nonsense words?

felacom

bornessity

shimafy

emtonology

scolobility

nemponary

cagoral

andimakinise

ortepanimation

3.2 Listening

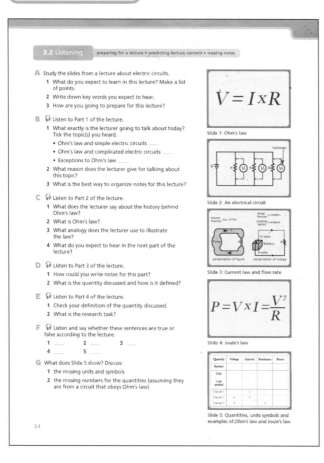

Lesson aims

Further practice in:

- planning and preparing for a lecture
- predicting lecture content
- choosing the best form of notes
- making notes

Introduction

Review key vocabulary by:

- using flashcards
- playing the alphabet game in the extra activities section at the end of this unit

Exercise A

Refer students to Slides 1 and 2. Write the title *Simple circuits* on the board.

1/2 Set for individual work and pairwork checking. Feed back, eliciting some ideas.

3 Brainstorm to elicit key words. Allow the class to decide whether a word should be included.

4 Elicit some points – the four Ps (Plan, Prepare, Predict, Produce). If necessary, refer students to Unit 1 *Skills bank* to review the preparation for a lecture. One way to help the students to make provisional notes is to:

- brainstorm what they would include
- organize their topics into a logical sequence

Answers

Answers depend on the students.

🎧 Exercise B

1 Tell students they are only going to hear the introduction to the lecture. Ask what information they expect to get from the introduction (i.e., the outline of the lecture).

Give students time to read the choices of topics. Check that they understand the meaning and relevance. Remind them they will only hear the introduction once, as in a lecture. Play Part 1. Allow them to compare answers.

Feed back. Ask them to justify their choice by saying what they heard related to it. Confirm the correct answer.

2 Elicit ideas. Confirm or correct.

3 Elicit ideas.

Answers

Model answers:

1 Ohm's law and simple electric circuits. The lecturer says that the other topics will be covered in future lectures.

2 So the students are ready to deal with more complicated circuits later on in the course.

3 Since the lecture is about a law which shows the relationship between different quantities, heading and bullet points is probably the best format to use.

Ohm's law

- …
- …

Transcript 🎧 1.11

Part 1

Good morning, everyone. Shall we start? OK. Today we will look at some of the basic concepts of electricity and circuit theory. I realize that some of you may already be familiar with these concepts, but I think it's important to revise them before we consider more complicated topics. In this lecture, I want to concentrate on simple circuits and how current, voltage and resistance are related. Ohm's law gives the relationship between these quantities, but as we will see later, this is not a law in the strictest sense. It's actually derived from empirical data, which means it relates to experiment and observation rather than theory. The law holds true in most situations, but there are exceptions and it is important to be aware of these, so I'll be discussing them in my next lecture. Today, though, we'll see how Ohm's law can be used to perform calculations for a simple circuit. Later on in the course, we'll be examining more complicated circuits, but the principle is basically the same. That's why I think it's important to make sure that we all feel completely confident with the basic terminology and equations now – before it's too late!

🎧 Exercise C

Before playing Part 2, refer students to Slide 1. Ask students what they expect to hear. Give them time to read questions 1–3. Tell them to write only brief notes. The main task is to absorb the meaning.

Play Part 2. Give them time to answer questions 1–3. Allow them to compare their answers. Feed back.

When they thoroughly understand Ohm's law, ask them what they expect in the next part of the lecture (question 4). Elicit ideas but do not confirm or correct.

Answers

Model answers:

1 Ohm did his experiments in the 19th century. His theory was a very important step for the study of electricity, and although it seems almost intuitive to us nowadays, it was greeted initially with criticism.

2 Ohm's law states that in a circuit the voltage is equal to the current multiplied by the resistance, or V = IR.

3 The lecturer used the analogy of water flowing through a pipe to illustrate current flowing through a circuit.

4 Answers depend on the students.

Transcript 🎧 1.12

Part 2

Georg Ohm was born in Bavaria (now Germany) in 1789. He was a teacher of science and mathematics and did some important research on resistance, publishing his first results in 1827 in a book called *The Galvanic Circuit Investigated Mathematically* – except it was written in German, not English! Historically speaking, Ohm's law is one of the most important, if not *the* most important, early quantitative descriptions of the physics of electricity. However, when Ohm first published his work, critics were very hostile and voiced their disagreement very angrily.

So, what is Ohm's law? Well, Ohm's law describes the relationship between current, voltage and resistance. Ohm discovered that the amount of electric current through two points of a metal conductor in an electrical circuit is directly proportional to the potential difference or voltage across those two points. I'll say that again, because it's a very important point. Ohm discovered that the current through most materials is directly proportional to the potential difference applied across the material. Moreover, the current is inversely proportional to the resistance between the two points, meaning as one goes up the other goes down. This law can be expressed by the simple algebraic equation V equals I times R, as we can see in the first slide. In this equation, V is the potential difference measured across the resistance in units of volts; I is the current through the resistance in units of amperes; and R is the resistance of the conductor in units of ohms. I'll repeat that – V is measured in volts, I in amperes and R in ohms. Ohm's law states that the quantity R in this relationship is constant, independent of the current.

It might be useful to describe Ohm's law in terms of the analogy of water. Think of water flowing through pipes and this might make the concept a bit easier to understand. Let's consider a horizontal pipe, where the rate of water flowing through the pipe corresponds to current. If we do something that restricts the flow of the water, for example if we make the diameter of the pipe smaller, then this behaves just as a resistor does in an electric circuit. In this analogy, the difference in water pressure between two points of the pipe, for example before and after the restriction, corresponds to electrical voltage in a circuit. Ohm's law would say that the rate of water flow through the restricted part of the pipe is proportional to the difference in water pressure across the restriction. You can see this in Slide 3.

Now let's see how Ohm's law can help us analyze simple circuits. In a very simple circuit, the source of voltage is the battery. Ohm's law states that if we know the values of any two of the three quantities – voltage, current and resistance – we can use the law to calculate the value of the third quantity. For example, here we have a voltage of 3 volts and a resistance of 6 ohms. This means that the amount of current passing through the circuit is equal to V divided by R, which works out to be 0.5 amperes.

🎧 Exercise D

Play the first two sentences of Part 3. Ask the first question. Set the second question for individual work and pairwork checking. Play the rest of the recording. Tell students to take notes. Allow students to compare their definitions. Don't, at this stage, confirm the answers.

Answers

Model answers:

1 A table is good for definitions.
2 See Exercise E.

Transcript 🎧 1.13

Part 3

OK. So far, we've talked about Ohm's law, which involves current, resistance and voltage, but there is another measurement in circuits we need to look at now and that is *power*. First, we need to define power, then we can analyze it in an electric circuit.

Power is a measurement of how much *work* can be performed in a certain amount of time. The electric power associated with a complete electric circuit or a circuit component represents the rate at which energy is converted from the electrical energy of the moving charges into some other form, for example heat, mechanical energy or energy stored in electric fields or magnetic fields.

The equation that expresses the relationship between power, voltage and current is *P* equals *I* times *V*. So, for a resistor in a DC circuit, the power is given by the applied voltage multiplied by the electric current. You can see this in Slide 4. This is known as *Joule's law*. Joule was an English physicist who lived in the 19th century, and this was just one of his discoveries. In Joule's law, power, written as the capital letter *P*, is exactly equal to current – capital *I* – times voltage – capital *V*. The unit of measurement of power is the *watt* and its symbol is a capital *W*.

🎧 Exercise E

Part 4 summarizes the definition of power. Tell students that this is the last part of the lecture. What do they expect to hear? Confirm that it is a summary. Play Part 4.

1 Students should check their definitions as they listen. After the summary has finished, they should correct their definitions and complete their notes. Guide them to the correct answer: that is, the correct meaning, not necessarily the words given here.

2 Elicit ideas. (If you wish, you could ask your students to do some research on this topic themselves. However, it is not essential at this stage.

Students are asked to do a separate research task at the end of Lesson 3.3 and feed back on that in Lesson 3.4.)

Answers

Model answers:

1

Quantity	Definition	Unit	Symbol
power	P = IV	watts	W

2 The research task is to look at the limitations of Ohm's law and the application of the law to electromagnetism – also known as electromagnetics.

Transcript 🎧 1.14

Part 4

So let's summarize what power means in terms of electrical circuits. Joule's equation says that power equals current times voltage. It's clear, then, that we aren't talking about a proportional relationship here. And we can see that neither voltage nor current alone constitutes power. Power is a combination of both voltage and current – it is the voltage multiplied by the current, or in other words the product of the two quantities.

In practical terms, a circuit with a high voltage and a low current may involve the same amount of power as a circuit with a low voltage and a high current. Let's think about an open circuit – this is where the circuit is incomplete. In an open circuit, where a voltage is present between the terminals of a battery but there is no current flow, the power is equal to zero. And this is true even if the voltage is very high.

OK, I think that's enough for now. Do you remember me saying at the beginning of the lecture that Ohm's law isn't a real law? Well, next time, we'll have a look at some of the limitations of the law. We'll also see how the law can be applied to electromagnetism. So don't forget to do some research on this topic before then. Thank you and see you next time.

🎧 Exercise F

These are sentences about the ideas in the lecture.

Set for pairwork. Say or play the sentences. Give time for students to discuss and then respond. Students must justify their answers.

Transcript 🎧 1.15

1 Ohm's law is always true.
2 In the hydraulic analogy, current is the rate of flow of water through the pipe.
3 A resistor helps current flow more easily through a circuit.
4 Power is the amount of work done in a given time.
5 A circuit with a high voltage has more power than a circuit with a low voltage.

Answers

1 false	Ohm's law holds true only in certain conditions, e.g., constant temperature.
2 true	
3 false	A resistor restricts current flow through a circuit.
4 true	
5 false	A circuit with a high voltage but very high resistance may have less power than a circuit with low voltage but very low resistance.

Exercise G

This exercise practises making questions and describing information in a table.

Ask students to think of three questions they could ask about the table in Slide 5 using Wh~ question words such as *What ...? How many ...?* etc. Elicit some examples and write these on the board. For example:

What is the unit of resistance?

What is the symbol for unit of current?

What is the power in circuit 1?

How many ohms is the resistor in circuit 2?

How much current is flowing in circuit 3?

Put students in pairs to ask each other their questions. Check.

Answers

Possible answers:

Quantity	Voltage	Current	Resistance	Power
Symbol	V	I	R	P
Unit	volt	ampere	ohm	watt
Unit symbol	V	A	Ω	W
Circuit 1	3	3	1	9
Circuit 2	6	3	2	18
Circuit 3	4	2	2	8

Closure

Ask students to:

● give definitions of resistance – current – voltage – power
● define Ohm's law and Joule's law

Note: Students will need their lecture notes from Lesson 3.2 in the next lesson.

3.3 Extending skills

General note

Read the *Skills bank* at the end of the Course Book unit. Decide when, if at all, to refer students to it. The best time is probably at the beginning of this lesson or the end of the next lesson, as a summary/revision.

Lesson aim

This lesson is the first in a series about writing an assignment or giving a presentation based on research. The principal aim of this lesson is to introduce students to sources of information.

Introduction

1 Tell students to ask you questions about the information in the lecture in Lesson 3.2 as if you were the lecturer. Refer them to the *Skills bank* for typical language if you wish.

2 Put students in pairs. Student A must ask Student B about the information in the lecture in Lesson 3.2 to help him/her complete the notes from the lecture. Then they reverse roles. Go round, helping students to identify gaps in their notes and to think of good

questions to get the missing information. Refer them to the *Skills bank* if you wish for language they can use in the pairwork.

Pairs then compare notes and decide what other information would be useful and where they could get it from. For example, more technical definitions of the key words might be useful, from a specialist dictionary or an encyclopedia. In the feedback, write a list of research sources on the board, at least including dictionaries, encyclopedias, specialist reference books and the Internet.

Point out that dictionaries are good for definitions, although you may need to go to a specialist dictionary for a technical word. Otherwise, try an encyclopedia, because technical words are often defined in entries when they are first used. You could also try Google's 'define' feature, i.e., type *define: power; electrical engineering*. But remember you will get definitions from other disciplines, not just your own, so you need to scan to check the relevant one. (*Power* is a term that is used in a wide variety of contexts and subjects.)

When doing an Internet search it is also useful to try both American and British English spellings. British spelling: *analogue*; US: *analog*.

🎧 Exercise A

Point out the importance of stressed syllables in words – see *Language note* below.

In this exercise, students will hear each word with the stressed syllable emphasized, and the rest of the syllables underspoken.

Play the recording, pausing after the first few to check that students understand the task. Feed back, perhaps playing the recording again for each word before checking. Ideally, mark up an OHT of the words.

Language note

In English, speakers emphasize the stressed syllable in a multi-syllable word. Sometimes listeners may not even hear the unstressed syllables. Vowels, in any case, often change to schwa or a reduced form in unstressed syllables. Therefore it is essential that students can recognize key words from the stressed syllable alone when they hear them in context.

Answers

application	3
circuit	6
compass	1
constant	16
electromagnetic	9
empirical	15
filament	17
incandescent	2
increase	11
linear	4
magnet	18
polarity	14
relationship	5
resistor	12
supply	8
temperature	13
terminal	10
zero	7

Transcript 🎧 1.16

1 'compass
2 incan'descent
3 appli'cation
4 'linear
5 re'lationship
6 'circuit
7 'zero
8 su'pply
9 electromag'netic
10 'terminal
11 'increase
12 re'sistor
13 'temperature
14 po'larity
15 em'pirical
16 'constant
17 'filament
18 'magnet

Exercise B

Erase the words or turn off the visual display. Ask students to guess or remember where the stressed syllable is on each word. Tell them to mark their idea with a light vertical stroke in pencil. Elicit and drill. Refer students to the *Vocabulary bank* at this stage if you wish.

Answers

See transcript for Exercise A.

Exercise C

Set for pair or group work. Go round and assist/correct.

Exercise D

1 Refer students to the device and vocabulary lists on the right. Elicit question forms for this discussion such as:

What is the relationship between resistance and an incandescent lamp?

How is ... related to ... ?

How does a ... work?

Why do you think ... is connected to ...?

Put students in small groups or pairs to discuss the questions.

Feed back, building up the flow charts in the Answers section on the board. The more details students can give, the better.

2 Discuss with the whole class. Accept any reasonable suggestions.

Answers

Model answers:

Device 1: Incandescent lamp

Filament of metal wire is connected up to an electric circuit with a voltage source

↓

The circuit is closed and current flows

↓

The filament offers resistance to the current

↓

The filament heats up

↓

It glows white hot and emits light

Device 2: Electromagnet

Metal wire is formed into a coil with a number of turns

↓

An electric current passes through the wire

↓

A magnetic field is produced, perpendicular to the direction of the current flow

↓

The magnetic fields in the coil produce a stronger field with clear north–south polarity

2 Simple electrical devices include: energy meter, current transformer, single-phase motor, battery charger, switch, lighting, guitar amplifier.

Exercise E

Remind students again about the four Ps. Refer students to the lecture topics and the questions. Make sure they understand that all three questions relate to before, rather than during, the lecture. Work through as a whole class if you wish.

Answers

Model answers:

1 Look up key words in a dictionary/encyclopedia/on the Internet. Check pronunciation so you will recognize the words in the lecture.

2 Lecture 1: a table containing different metals and examples of different types of wire, with their resistance and related characteristics.

Lecture 2: a table presenting examples of different types of lamp, with lists of components and characteristics.

Lecture 3: a spidergram showing different unwanted effects; related problems; examples; solutions to these problems.

Lecture 4: heading and list of factors that affect the magnetic field; how they can be maximized; equations; examples.

3 Tables; spidergram (so that it is easier to brainstorm with fellow students and cover all the possible areas that the lecturer might focus on); heading and list.

Exercise F

Set for pairwork, giving each member of the pair a different research task. If students have access in class to reference material, allow them to at least start the activity in class. Otherwise, set for homework. Before the feed back to partner stage in Lesson 3.4, refer students to the *Skills bank – Reporting information to other people*.

Closure

Dictate sentences with words from Exercise A in context for students to identify the words again.

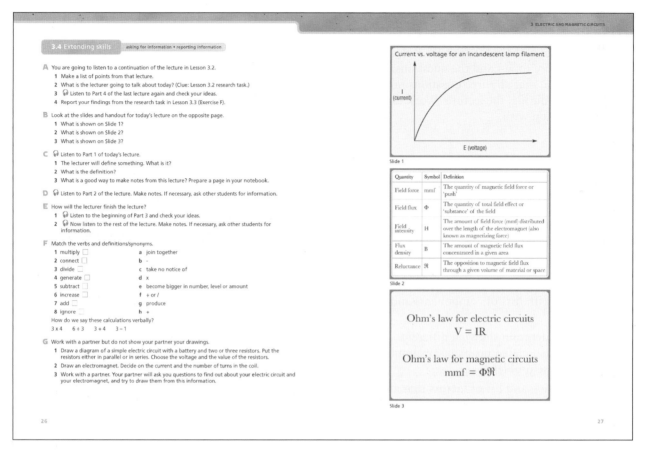

Lesson aims

- ask other people for information

Further practice in:

- choosing the best form of notes
- making notes
- reporting information

Introduction

1 Elicit as much information from the lecture in Lesson 3.2 as possible. If necessary, prompt students by reading parts of the transcript and pausing for students to complete in their own words.

2 Remind students of the language involved in asking for information from other people – see *Skills bank*. Drill some of the sentences if you wish.

🎧 Exercise A

1/2 Set for pairwork. Encourage students to ask each other for information.

3 Play Part 4 of the lecture from Lesson 3.2 to enable students to check their answers. Feed back.

4 Elicit information from the students' research (Lesson 3.3). Do not confirm or correct at this stage except pronunciation mistakes on key words.

Answers

Model answers:

1 Main points of lecture in 3.2:

- Georg Ohm – his research into resistance
- Ohm's law expresses the relationship between current, resistance and voltage in an electric circuit: V = IR
- A hydraulic analogy of Ohm's law
- An example of a calculation using Ohm's law
- Joule's law: P = IV
- What Joule's law means in practical terms

2/3 The limitations of Ohm's law and its application to electromagnetics.

Transcript 🎧 1.14

Part 4

So let's summarize what power means in terms of electrical circuits. Joule's equation says that power equals current times voltage. It's clear, then, that we aren't talking about a proportional relationship here. And we can see that neither voltage nor current alone constitutes power. Power is a combination of both voltage and current – it is the voltage multiplied by the current, or in other words the product of the two quantities.

In practical terms, a circuit with a high voltage and a low current may involve the same amount of power as a circuit with a low voltage and a high current. Let's think about an open circuit – this is where the circuit is incomplete. In an open circuit, where a voltage is present between the terminals of a battery but there is no current flow, the power is equal to zero. And this is true even if the voltage is very high.

OK, I think that's enough for now. Do you remember me saying at the beginning of the lecture that Ohm's law isn't a real law? Well, next time, we'll have a look at some of the limitations of the law. We'll also see how the law can be applied to electromagnetism. So don't forget to do some research on this topic before then. Thank you and see you next time.

Exercise B

Refer students to the lecture slides. Set for pairwork discussion. Feed back.

Answers

Model answers:

1 A graph showing a non-linear relationship of current and voltage for a lamp. The lamp does not obey Ohm's law here.

Subject note: voltage can be given the symbol V, E or *emf*, although in this book V is used for consistency.

2 A table presenting the symbols and definitions of some key quantities of electromagnetism.

3 A comparison of Ohm's law for electric circuits (voltage, current and resistance) and Ohm's law for electromagnetics (mmf, flux and reluctance).

🎧 Exercise C

Set for individual work, then pair or group discussion. Play Part 1 of the lecture.

Methodology note

Don't tell students words they can't remember. It would be quite normal in a lecture that they can't write all of them down. If they don't remember them all this time, they should at least put the key words they remember in order. They can then listen for the other key words as the text develops.

Answers

Model answers:

1 Ohmic resistors.

2 An ohmic resistor has a constant resistance over a range of operating conditions.

3 The notes for the next part of the lecture that are not ohmic could be set out in a table. The application of Ohm's law to electromagnetism could be organized as a heading and bullet points. (See answers to Exercises D and E in this lesson.)

Transcript 🎧 1.17

Part 1

In the last lecture, we talked about Ohm's law and its application to simple electrical circuits. Today, we are going to continue looking at Ohm's law, but I want to do this in a little more depth. In the first half, I'll explain the limitations of the law. Then, in the second half of the lecture, I'll look at the very important influence Ohm's law has had in various fields, particularly in electromagnetics.

So, in the first part of this lecture, we will look at an example of a resistor that does not behave as Ohm's law suggests. A resistor can be defined as a circuit element that makes the passage of electric charge around the circuit more difficult. If you remember, in my last lecture, I used the analogy of water flowing through a pipe to illustrate Ohm's law. According to this analogy, a resistor corresponds to a restriction of the flow of water – for example, a narrowing of the pipe. If Ohm's law is to work, a resistor must have a specific resistance R – and this value should be constant. A resistor that restricts the passage of electric charge according to Ohm's law is known as an *ohmic resistor*. An ohmic resistor therefore has a single value of resistance over a range of operating conditions. I now want to show you that ohmic resistors are not part of the real world! This can create all sorts of problems, and I want to give you an example and look at the consequences of these problems.

🎧 Exercise D

Play Part 2 of the lecture. Students should recognize the rhetorical structure – see Answers section below– and complete a table. When students have done their best individually, put them in pairs or small groups to complete their notes by asking for information from the other student(s).

In the feedback, allow the correct meaning, not just these words.

Answers

Model answers:

Problem	Example	Consequences
materials used in circuits have resistance that changes with temperature	an incandescent lamp – the resistance of the filament increases with temperature.	• usually the consequences are negligible and can be ignored • with incandescent lamps, an increase in voltage does not necessarily mean an increase in current

Transcript 🎧 1.18

Part 2

As I said in my last lecture, Ohm's law is not a real law – it is an empirical observation. This means that it seems to be true in most situations. I now want to look at situations when it is no longer true. The main problem is that the resistance of the materials used in an electrical circuit tends to change with temperature. For example, in an incandescent lamp, a thin filament of metal wire is connected in an electric circuit and this wire offers resistance to the current flow. As a result of this resistance, the wire heats up to the point that it glows white-hot and emits light. The resistance of this wire increases dramatically as it warms up from room temperature to working temperature. This has an unusual consequence. It means that we could increase the supply voltage to the lamp circuit, and the increase in current would cause the filament to get even hotter. But this would increase its resistance and in reality prevent any further increases in current. This is clearly a very different relationship between current, voltage and resistance than the one described in Ohm's law. The resistance of the incandescent lamp's filament does not remain constant or stable for different currents.

This is not an isolated problem. Resistance changing with variations in temperature is common to nearly all metals. And, of course, wires are made of metal. Often these changes in resistance are very small and can be ignored when making calculations. However, in some cases, such as metal lamp filaments, the change is very large. If you look at the first slide, this shows the graph of the current in a lamp circuit for different values of battery voltage. As you can see, the graph is no longer a straight line. As the voltage increases from zero, the graph rises sharply. Then it begins to flatten out, as the circuit needs more and more voltage to achieve the same increase in current. Clearly, if we try to apply Ohm's law to find the resistance of this lamp circuit, we arrive at many different values depending on the temperature. The resistance is

non-linear and it increases with current and voltage. The effects of high temperature on the metal wire in the lamp filament cause this non-linearity.

Therefore we can say that Ohm's law is true for a conductor at a constant temperature. But, as we have seen, the resistance, or *resistivity*, of materials is usually affected by temperature.

🎧 Exercise E

Ask the initial question and elicit ideas, but do not confirm or correct at this stage.

1 Play the first two sentences of Part 3. Feed back. Ask the students what they think the best approach to note-taking is for this part of the lecture.

2 Play the rest of Part 3. Give students time to do their own work, then set for pair or group completion.

Answers

Model answers:

1 Ohm's law applied to electromagnetics.

2 Ohm's law for electromagnetics
   • describes the relationship between field force, field flux and reluctance
   • is similar to Ohm's law for electric circuits
   • can be represented by the equation: mmf $= \Phi\Re$

Transcript 🎧 1.19

Part 3

OK, so much for the limitations of Ohm's law. Now let's look at the application of Ohm's law to electromagnetics.

As I'm sure you remember, the orientation of the magnetic field produced by an electric current is always perpendicular to the direction of the current flow. This magnetic field is usually very weak in most situations – it can make a compass needle move, but not much else. To produce a stronger magnet with the same amount of current, we need to make the wire into a coil. The magnetic fields around the wire join together and create a much larger field with a clear north and south polarity.

The amount of magnetic field force generated by this coil is proportional to the current through the wire, multiplied by the number of turns of wire in the coil. Magnetic field force is known as *magnetomotive force* and it has the symbol *mmf* – written in lower case letters. It's very similar to the idea of electromotive force E, or *emf*, in an electric circuit. Magnetomotive force is just one important quantity associated with magnetism – there are several more quantities that you need to know about. We don't have time to look at all of these in detail, but on Slide 2 you will see a useful list. The ones we need today are field flux and reluctance. *Field flux* is the quantity of total field effect or 'substance' of the field. This is similar to electric current. *Reluctance* is the opposition to magnetic field flux through a given volume of space or material. Reluctance is therefore similar to electrical resistance.

So, to summarize, let's look at Slide 3. Just as Ohm's law describes the relationship between voltage, current and resistance in electric circuits, a very similar equation describes the relationship between field force, field flux and reluctance in magnetic circuits. This is a good illustration of how important Ohm's law has proved to be and I think Ohm himself would be very surprised!

Exercise F

Set for pairwork. Monitor and assist. Feed back, writing the words on the board as the students correctly identify them. Check pronunciation and stress patterns.

Answers

Model answers:

1 multiply	d	× NB: this could also be matched with 'become bigger in number, level or amount' since 'multiply' is a type of 'increase'.
2 connect	a	join together
3 divide	f	÷ or /
4 generate	g	produce
5 subtract	b	−
6 increase	e	become bigger in number, level or amount
7 add	h	+
8 ignore	c	take no notice of

Language note

The verbs *multiply*, *divide*, *add* and *subtract* for the four mathematical symbols are not always used when we say these operations verbally, as shown here:

3×4	3 times 4 / 3 multiplied by 4
$6 \div 3$	6 divided by 3 / 6 over 3
$3 + 4$	3 and 4 / 3 plus 4 / 3 add 4
$3 - 1$	3 minus 1 / 3 subtract 1 / 3 take away 1 / 3 take 1

Exercise G

1 Set for individual work. Students should draw a simple electric circuit with a battery and two or three resistors with specific values. If students do not know what a parallel circuit is, an example of one can be found in Slide 2 in Lesson 3.2. Feed back. Accept any reasonable suggestions. Write a few on the board.

2 Set for individual work. Students should draw a simple electromagnet with a coiled wire with a specific number of turns.

3 Put students in different pairs to do the information gap activity. They need to ask for the necessary information to draw their partner's circuit and electromagnet. They can then ask questions about the current, using Ohm's law. Remind students of the ways of asking politely for information (refer to *Skills bank* if necessary).

Answers

Answers depend on the students.

Methodology note

End all listening lessons by referring students to the transcript at the back of the Course Book, so they can read the text while the aural memory is still clear. You could set this as standard homework after a listening lesson. You can also get students to highlight key sections and underline key sentences.

Closure

Ask students to list similarities and differences between electric and electromagnetic circuits.

Similarities

● both involve electric circuits with current flowing through wire

● there are a lot of mathematical analogies between the two types of circuits, e.g., magnetic field = electrical field / reluctance = electrical resistance.

● Magnetic circuit laws are similar to electrical circuit laws

Differences

● the way the wire is positioned is important in electromagnetic circuits, but not in electric circuits

● Electric currents represent the flow of particles (electrons) and carry power, which is dissipated as heat in resistances. Magnetic fields don't represent the 'flow' of anything, and no power is dissipated in reluctances.

● The current in typical electric circuits is confined to the circuit, with very little 'leakage'. In typical magnetic circuits, not all of the magnetic field is confined to the magnetic circuit, and there is leakage of flux in the space outside.

Extra activities

1 Work through the *Vocabulary bank* and *Skills bank* if you have not already done so, or as a revision of previous study.

2 Use the *Activity bank* (Teacher's Book additional resources section, Resource 3A).

   A Set the crossword for individual work (including homework) or pairwork.

   Answers

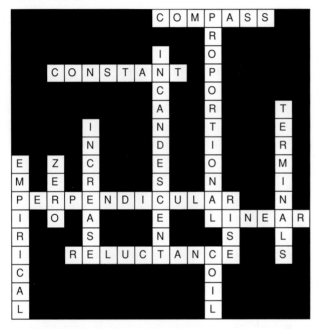

   B This game practises pronunciation and meaning recognition. It can only be played in groups in class.

Students must think of one word for each of the categories on the bingo card. Allow them to use any of the vocabulary from this unit. They should write their words on card 1, or copy the bingo grid into their notebooks.

Each student says one of their own words at random once only, concentrating on the pronunciation. The others must identify the category and cross it out on card 2.

The winner is the first student to identify the correct category for all the words. If the teacher keeps a record of which words have been said, he/she can say when a successful card could have been completed.

3 Students can play this alphabet game by themselves or as a group/class. The aim is to think of a word related to electrical engineering for each letter of the alphabet. For example:

   Student A: **a**lternator
   Student B: alternator, **b**attery
   Student C: alternator, battery, **c**harge
   Each student adds something for the next letter of the alphabet. They should try to use words from the unit if possible. A student misses a turn if he/she can't remember the items, or add another letter.

4 Tell students to do some Internet research on one or more of these topics.

   ● What these early scientists discovered about electricity:

     ● Faraday

     ● Maxwell

     ● Kirchhoff

   Useful websites (at the time of writing): www.bbc.co.uk/history/historic_figures; http://inventors.about.com.

   ● Incandescent lamps will soon no longer be on sale in Europe. Why? What is going to replace these lamps? Why?

Note that a lot of the information will be in very complex English, but students should be able to record the basic details and report back in the next lesson.

4 THE COMPUTER

In this unit, the development of the computer is covered. Lesson 4.2 looks at the invention of the integrated circuit, or microchip, its advantages and its impact on society. At the same time, the use of computers in education is covered: Lessons 4.1, 4.3 and 4.4 guide students to a more efficient use of the Internet and computers in research.

Note that students will need access to a computer with an Internet connection for some exercises in this unit.

Skills focus

Reading

- identifying topic development within a paragraph
- using the Internet effectively
- evaluating Internet search results

Writing

- reporting research findings

Vocabulary focus

- computer jargon
- abbreviations and acronyms
- discourse and stance markers
- verb and noun suffixes

Key vocabulary

access (n and v)	index	register
browse	Intranet	search (n and v)
data	keyword	search engine
database	log in/log on	software
default	log off	technology
document	login (n)	username/ID
electronic	media	web page
exit (v)	menu	
hyperlink	password	

Abbreviations and acronyms

The *Computer Jargon Buster* on page 31 of the Course Book gives the meanings of many of these.

CAD	ISP	URL
CAL	LCD	USB
CAM	PDF	WAN
CIM	PIN	WWW
HTML	PPT	
HTTP	ROM	

4.1 Vocabulary

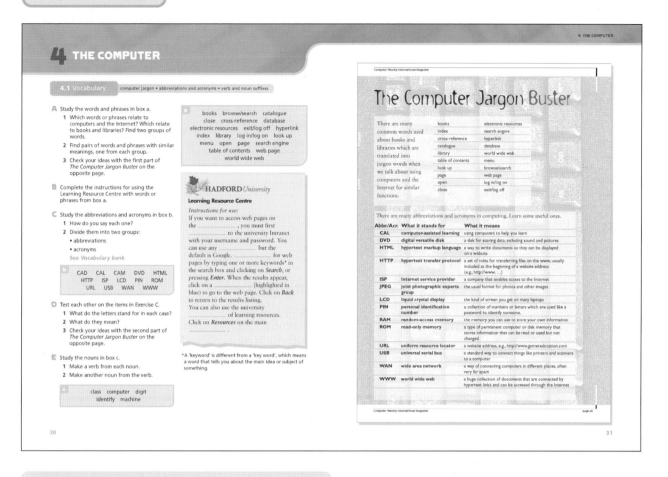

General note

If possible, hold this lesson in a room where there is a computer, or bring in a computer.

Read the *Vocabulary bank* at the end of the Course Book unit. Decide when, if at all, to refer your students to it. The best point is probably Exercise C, or at the very end of the lesson or the beginning of the next lesson, as a summary/revision.

Lesson aims

- gain fluency in the meaning, pronunciation and spelling of key computing terms, abbreviations and acronyms
- understand how verbs can be formed from nouns, and nouns from verbs, through the addition of suffixes

Introduction

Familiarize students with computer terminology using some or all of the following activities.

1 Using a computer or a picture of a computer as a starting point, elicit some or all of the following:

PC	*CPU (central*	*DVD*
laptop	*processing*	*USB port*
monitor	*unit)*	*accessory*
screen	*hard disk*	*printer*
desktop	*floppy disk*	*scanner*
icon	*program*	*CD burner*
keyboard	*database*	*Internet*
keys	*slot*	*email*
mouse	*CD*	*the web*

2 Ask students to suggest verbs used in computing. Elicit some or all of the following. A good way to do this is to open a program such as Word (in English) and look at the words and symbols on the toolbars.

switch on	*press*	*paste*
start up	*open*	*enter*
shut down	*close*	*delete*
log on/log off	*exit*	*insert*
click	*save*	*highlight*
double-click	*select*	*undo*
hold	*copy*	*print*

3 Ask students whether they normally use the library or the Internet to find information. Elicit the advantages and disadvantages of both. (There is so much emphasis on using computers nowadays, students often forget that there is a lot of information readily to hand in the library.)

Answers

Possible answers:

Library

Advantages	Disadvantages
easy to look things up in a dictionary or an encyclopaedia	books can be out of date
you can find information in your own language	the book may not be in the library when you want it
information is usually correct	most books can't be accessed from home (though this is now starting to change)

Internet

Advantages	Disadvantages
a lot of information from different sources	difficult to find the right key words
information is usually more up-to-date than books	difficult to know which results are the best
can be accessed from home	information is often not correct
you can quickly and easily get copies of books or journal articles not in your library	you may have to pay for the books/articles/information

Exercise A

Ask students to study the words in box a and elicit that they all relate to research.

Set for pairwork. Tell students to decide *and justify* the pairs they choose. If necessary, give an example: *index, search engine results*.

To help students understand what a database is, refer to ones they are familiar with in your college, e.g., student records, exam results, library catalogues, etc.

Students may argue that some terms are not exact equivalents, e.g., *catalogue/database*. Discuss any objections as they arise.

Answers

Model answers:

Common word or phrase for books and libraries	Word or phrase for Internet and electronic information
books	electronic resources
index	search engine
cross-reference	hyperlink
catalogue	database
library	world wide web
table of contents	menu
look up	browse/search
page	web page
open	log in/log on
close	exit/log off

Language note

Log in and *log on*: these two verbs are used a little differently. *Log in* is used when accessing a closed system such as a college Intranet. *Log on* is used for open systems such as the Internet in general, as in *You can log on to the Internet with a hand-held computer*. Note also that the related noun has now become one word (*login*). The opposite of *log in* is *log out*, while the opposite of *log on* is *log off*.

Exercise B

Set for individual work and pairwork checking. Ensure that students read *all* the text and have a general understanding of it before they insert the missing words.

Feed back by reading the paragraph or by using an OHT or other visual display of the text. Discuss alternative ideas and decide whether they are acceptable. Verify whether errors are due to using new words or to misunderstanding the text.

Answers

Model answers:

If you want to access web pages on the world wide web, you must first log in to the university Intranet with your username and password. You can use any search engine, but the default is Google. Browse/search for web pages by typing one or more keywords in the search box and clicking on *Search*, or pressing *Enter*. When the results appear, click on a hyperlink (highlighted in blue) to go to the web page. Click on *Back* to return to the results listing.

You can also use the university database of learning resources. Click on *Resources* on the main menu.

Exercise C

Set for pairwork. Feed back, eliciting ideas on pronunciation and confirming or correcting. Build up the two lists on the board. Establish that one group are acronyms, i.e., they can be pronounced as words: PIN = /pɪn/. The other group are abbreviations, i.e., they are pronounced as letters: HTTP = H-T-T-P. Drill all the abbreviations and acronyms. Make sure students can say letter names and vowel sounds correctly.

Elicit that words with normal consonant/vowel patterns are *normally* pronounced as a word and those with unusual patterns are *normally* pronounced with single letters. Refer to the *Vocabulary bank* at this stage if you wish.

> ### Methodology note
> Don't discuss the meaning at this point. This is covered in the next activity.

Answers
Acronyms: CAD /kæd/, CAL /kæl/, CAM /kæm/, PIN /pɪn/, ROM /rɒm/, WAN /wæn/.

Abbreviations: DVD, HTML, HTTP, ISP, LCD, URL (not pronounced /ɜːl/), USB, WWW.

Exercise D

1 Introduce the verb *stand for*. Elicit examples of common abbreviations and ask what they stand for. Set for pairwork. Tell students to pick out the ones they already know first. Next, they pick out the ones they are familiar with but don't know what they stand for – and guess.

2 Elicit the meanings without reference to the *Computer Jargon Buster* if possible.

3 Refer students to the *Computer Jargon Buster* to verify their answers. As a follow-up, elicit other common abbreviations from IT or electrical engineering.

> ### Language note
> If students don't use acronyms or initial abbreviations in their language, a discussion about the reasons for using them is useful. They will then know how to find the meaning of new ones when they meet them. You might point out that abbreviations can sometimes be longer than the thing they abbreviate! For example, world wide web is three syllables, whereas WWW is six. It evolved because it is quicker to write, but it is longer, and harder, to say. Note that WWW is frequently written in lower case letters (www), presumably because it is lower case in URLs.

> It is also possible to mix acronyms with abbreviations: for example, JPEG – J /peg/. Point out the field of ICT is developing at an incredible speed and new acronyms and abbreviations are constantly being created.

Exercise E

Set for individual work and pairwork checking. Feed back, highlighting the changes from noun form to verb in the case of *identity/identify* and *machine/mechanize*.

Answers
Model answers:

Noun 1	Verb	Noun 2
class	classify	classification
computer	computerize	computerization
digit	digitize	digitization
identity	identify	identification
machine	mechanize	mechanization

> ### Language note
> Both *~ise/~ize* (*~isation/~ization*) forms are acceptable in British English. American English usage is *~ize* (*~ization*).

Closure

Ask students whether they agree with the following statements.

1 Every college student must have a computer.

2 The college library uses a computer to help students find information.

3 College departments use computers to store research data.

4 Students can't do research without a computer.

5 College computers can access research data from other colleges and universities.

6 College computers can access research data from businesses and the media.

7 A personal computer can store information students think is important.

8 Computers can help us to talk with students from other colleges and universities.

9 Computers can help students access data from anywhere in the world.

10 A computer we can carry in our pocket can access worldwide data.

4.2 Reading

General note

Read the *Skills bank – Developing ideas in a paragraph* at the end of the Course Book unit. Decide when, if at all, to refer students to it. The best time is probably Exercise E, or at the very end of the lesson or the beginning of the next lesson, as a summary/revision.

Lesson aims

- prepare to read a text by looking at title, topic sentences
- understand the purpose of discourse markers and stance markers in the development of a topic

Introduction

Ask students how, where and why they use computers. They should answer in some detail with examples. Encourage them to use the vocabulary, abbreviations and acronyms from Lesson 4.1.

Exercise A

Set for general discussion. Allow students to debate differences of opinion. Encourage them to give examples if they can.

Answers

Possible answers:

1. It depends to some extent on the definition of 'computer'. The abacus is a kind of calculating device, so could be considered an early type of computer in that it is a tool for computation. It was invented around 2400 BC. However, the first digital computers were invented in the 1940s.

2. The diode, the semiconductor, the integrated circuit, the microprocessor – all these were key inventions and discoveries in the development of the computer.

Exercise B

1 Write the title of the reading text on the board. Discuss with the whole class, eliciting suggestions.

2 Set for pairwork and whole class feedback. Do not confirm or correct at this point.

3 Set for pairwork. Tell students to think of four or five questions with different *Wh~* question words:

What ...?

Where ...?

When ...?

Why ...?

How ...?

If you want, you could choose some questions to write on one side of the board.

Answers

Possible answers:

1 The development of the digital computer.

2 Accept any possible answers. Guide students to think about what technology the different generations of computers were based on. Don't give them the answers yet, but encourage them to think about vacuum tubes, diodes, semiconductors, microchips, etc.

3 Possible questions:

What were the three generations of computers?

What were their characteristics?

Where were they invented?

When were the first computers sold?

How many computers were manufactured?

etc.

Exercise C

1 Set for pairwork.

2 Set for pairwork and whole class feedback. Write the answers on the board.

Answers

Model answers:

1 One of the Colossus computers built in England during the Second World War to decipher German coded messages.

2 The IBM 1401 – one of the most important of the second-generation computers that was commercially produced.

3 The Apple 1 computer – one of the first small third-generation computers for personal use.

Exercise D

Set for individual work and pairwork checking. Feed back, trying to get consensus on each point, but do not actually confirm or correct. Preface your remarks with phrases like: *So most of you think ... You all agree/disagree that ...*

Point out to students that the use of plurals with countable nouns when making a generalizing statement implies *all*, e.g., *computers* means *all computers*. The truth may actually be better expressed with a limiting word, e.g., *most/some/many,* or with words which express possibility such as *may* or *seem*, or adverbs such as *sometimes, usually, often.*

Remind students to look back at these predictions while they are reading the text (Exercise F).

Exercise E

Review paragraph structure – i.e., paragraphs usually begin with a topic sentence which makes a statement that is then expanded in the following sentences. Thus, topic sentences give an indication of the contents of the paragraph. You may wish to refer students to the *Skills bank* at this point.

1 Write the topic sentences from the text on an OHT or other visual medium, or use Resource B from the additional resources section. Take the first sentence and identify the subject of the main clause with a box. This is the **topic.** For example:

In all fields, the $\boxed{\textit{impact of computers}}$ *has been enormous.*

What is the sentence saying about *the impact of computers*? The answer is: it *has been enormous.* Underline these words. These words constitute the comment which the sentence is making about the topic. Note that the initial prepositional phrase (acting as a sentence adverbial) simply provides more information about the topic: it is not the focus of the sentence. The focus of the sentence is on the **comment** being made. Thus a topic sentence consists of both a topic and a comment about the topic which is explained and expanded on in the rest of the paragraph.

Set the remaining sentences for individual work and pairwork checking.

2 Set for pairwork. Tell students that their analysis of the topic sentences may help them. Feed back with the whole class. Point out any language features which led them to draw their conclusions.

Answers

Possible answers:

1

	Topic	Comment
Para 1	the impact of computers	has been enormous.
Para 2	the development of the computer	started relatively recently
Para 3	The second-generation computers	were more advanced.
Para 4	The invention of the integrated circuit	signalled an important development.
Para 5	Integrated circuits	have brought many advantages.
Para 6	This new technology	had important consequences.

2

	Predicted content	Notes
Para 1	some examples of the impact of computers in different fields	the words *in all fields* point to the idea of an overview, or wide perspective in this paragraph
Para 2	more information about how computers developed initially	the word *recently* contrasts with *enormous* in the first paragraph, indicating that not only was the impact large but also the development was rapid
Para 3	characteristics of second-generation computers.	the words *second* and *more* link this paragraph with the previous one, indicating that the development is being looked at sequentially
Para 4	details of how integrated circuits were used in computers	the topic of this paragraph is integrated circuits rather than third-generation computers, suggesting that the focus will be on this component rather than computers as a whole
Para 5	details of the advantages of integrated circuits	the repetition of *integrated circuits* in the topic sentence links this paragraph to the previous one
Para 6	examples of these consequences	the word *this* links this paragraph to the previous one – it looks at the consequences of the technology mentioned there, i.e., the invention of the microchip

Exercise F

Set the reading. Tell students to read for good understanding. When everyone has read the text, discuss any vocabulary items that may have caused difficulties.

If you have previously written questions on the board, ask students to say which were answered. Then tell the same pairs as in Exercise B to discuss which of their questions were answered. Feed back with the whole class, asking a few pairs to say which of their questions were answered and which were not.

Exercise G

Set for individual work and pairwork checking. Feed back with the whole class, asking students to say which parts of the text deal with each statement. Ask students to say how the false statements in Exercise D could be changed to reflect the information in the text.

Exercise H

The purpose of this exercise is for students to try to identify the information structure of each paragraph and to see how a new step in the progression of ideas may be signalled by a rhetorical marker or phrase. Direct students' attention to the handwritten notes in the left margin of the text. Explain that the notes are key words which summarize (in the reader's own words) the ideas in the text. The notes are written next to the relevant parts of the text. A good idea is to make an OHT of the text and use a highlighter to indicate which are the relevant parts of the text. Point out that often (but not always) a new step in the development of ideas is shown by a rhetorical marker or a phrase. The development may be more information: in paragraph 4 we have *for example*. Or the development may be a contrast: in paragraph 6 we have *however*.

1 Set for pairwork. Tell students to decide on some similar key words for the ideas in the remaining four paragraphs and to write these words next to the appropriate part of the text. Feed back with the whole class, eliciting suitable key words for the left margin and using a highlighter or OHT pen to indicate the phrases or sentences in the text which correspond to the key words.

2 Set for individual work and pairwork checking. Feed back with the whole class, identifying the discourse and stance markers.

Answers

Possible answers:

1
   Para 2: early computers/characteristics/example of first-generation computer
   Para 4: microchips in third-generation computers/definition of microchip/characteristics
   Para 5: advantages of integrated circuits
   Para 6: consequences of integrated circuits/example/expansion/example

2
   Para 1: obviously, however
   Para 4: for example
   Para 5: in addition, obviously
   Para 6: however, for example

Answers

Possible answers for Exercise G:

	True/false/not mentioned	Possible rewording
Computers have had a big influence on the field of Electrical Engineering.	true – para 1, sentence 3	
The first computers used punched paper tape for input.	true – para 2, sentence 3	
Transistors were an immediate improvement on vacuum tubes.	false – para 3, sentence 3	Initially, transistors were not as reliable as vacuum tubes, but they soon improved.
Disk drives were in use before the invention of the microchip.	true – para 3, sentence 6	
Canada played an important role in the development of computers	not mentioned (it's false)	
In a microchip, the components are soldered to a printed circuit board.	false – para 4, sentence 4	The components of an integrated circuit are formed on a semiconductor surface.
It only became possible to manufacture computers commercially after the invention of the microchip.	false – para 3, sentence 6	Second-generation computers were manufactured commercially.
Applications of integrated circuits are limited to computers.	false – para 6, sentence 4	Integrated circuits are used in a wide range of electronic devices, such as mobile phones.

Language note

The relation of one sentence to the previous sentence is not always made explicit by rhetorical markers or phrases. In fact, overuse of markers is to be avoided.

If there is no marker or phrase, the relationship can be deduced usually by the position of the sentence in the paragraph, or by the meaning. For example, in the first, third and last paragraphs, the second sentences expand on the first sentences.

Closure

1 Divide the class into groups. Write the five topic sentences on strips, or photocopy them from the additional resources section (Resource 4B). Make a copy for each group. Students must put them into the correct order.

   Alternatively, divide the class into two teams. One team chooses a topic sentence and reads it aloud. The other team must give the information triggered by that topic sentence. Accept a prediction or the actual paragraph content. However, ask students which it is – prediction or actual. Note that in fact the article has six paragraphs, but that two of them are about integrated circuits.

Language note

There is no universal logic to the structuring of information in a text. The order of information is language-specific. For example, oriental languages tend to have a topic sentence or paragraph summary at the end, not the beginning, of the paragraph. Or students whose first language is Arabic might structure a particular type of discourse in a different way from native English speakers. So it is important for students to see what a native speaker writer would consider to be a 'logical' ordering.

2 Refer students back to the sentences in Exercise D. Students should find it easier to comment on these now that they have read the text.

3 Focus on some of the vocabulary from the text, including:

appliance	network (n)
assembly	reliability
consume	removable disk drive
equipment	solder (v)
handbuilt	storage
input (n)	store (v)
low-cost production	vacuum tube
mass production	
model (n)	

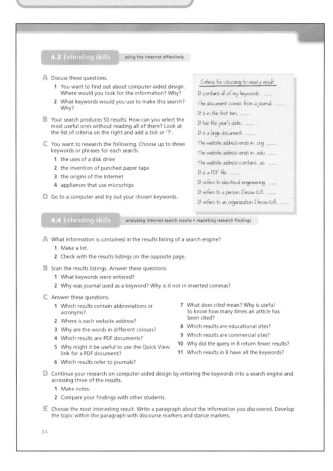

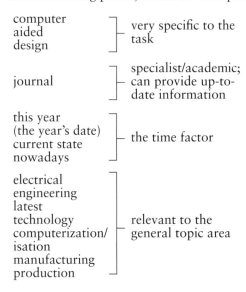

Put students in groups and ask them to compare how they normally use a computer to find information. Ask each group to produce a set of advice for using the Internet. Then, as a class, produce an accepted set of advice.

Key words to elicit: *search engine, keyword, website, web page, website address, search result, subject directory*

Note: Where the subject is a new one or a fairly general topic, it is a good idea to start first with a **subject directory** which evaluates sites related to the topic and collects them in one place. Some examples are:

Academic Info; BUBL LINK; INFOMINE; The WWW Virtual Library.

Exercise A

Write *computer-aided design* on the board.

1 Set for class discussion. Make sure students give reasons for their answers. Accept their answers at this stage.

2 Remind students that words in English often have more than one meaning, so care must be taken to get the desired result.

Answers

Possible answers:

1 In a current journal – very useful, as recent articles give the latest information, and many journals have a specialist/academic focus.

On the Internet – good if the correct keywords are used and a careful selection of results is made. Since it is a general topic, it would benefit from a search with a subject directory such as The WWW Virtual Library on http://vlib.org/.

In a textbook – useful if there is an up-to-date one, but books take time to publish, so even the latest may be out of date in these technologically fast-moving times.

2 In this list of possible keywords, the first three are obvious starting points; others are also possible.

computer aided design	very specific to the task
journal	specialist/academic; can provide up-to-date information
this year (the year's date) current state nowadays	the time factor
electrical engineering latest technology computerization/ isation manufacturing production	relevant to the general topic area

General note

Students will need access to a computer with an Internet connection. If computers are not available during the lesson, part of the lesson can be set for private study.

Lesson aim

● learn or practise how to use the Internet efficiently for research

Introduction

Brainstorm the uses of the Internet. Then brainstorm what the important factors to consider are when using the Internet. These should include:

● the search engines students use and why. Note that there are now a large number of search engines to suit different purposes. It is not necessarily a good idea to use Google exclusively.

● how to choose *and write* key words in their preferred search engine

● how they extract the information they want from the results

Exercise B

Set for pairwork. Remind students of the research topic.

Feed back, encouraging students to give reasons for their decisions. Emphasize that we only know what *might* be useful at this stage.

Establish that company sites often end in *.com*.

Answers

Model answers:

- ✓ It contains all of my keywords. *(but check that the meaning is the same)*
- ✓ The document comes from a journal. *(current information)*
- ? It is in the first ten. *(a web page can have codes attached to put it high in the list)*
- ✓ It has this year's date. *(current information)*
- ? It is a large document. *(size is no indication of quality)*
- ✓ The website address ends in .org *(because it is a non-profit organization)*
- ✓ The website address ends in .edu *(because it is an educational establishment)*
- ✓ The website address contains .ac *(because it is an educational establishment)*
- ? It is a PDF file. *(file type is no indication of quality)*
- ? It refers to electrical engineering. *(may not be relevant)*
- ? It refers to a person I don't know (of). *(may not be reliable)*
- ✓ It refers to an organization I know (of). *(reliable)*

Language note

PDF stands for *portable document format*. PDF documents look exactly like the original documents, and can be viewed and printed on most computers, without the need for each computer to have the same software, fonts, etc. They are created with Adobe Acrobat software.

Exercise C

Set for individual work and pairwork checking. Ask students to compare their choice of key words with their partner, and justify their choice.

Answers

Possible answers:

The following combinations will produce results provided the words in bold are included.

1. uses **disk drive** / removable disk drives / fixed computer drive
2. invention **punched tape** / punched paper tape / computer tape input
3. origins **Internet** / beginnings Internet / invention Internet
4. **appliances** containing **microchips** / devices using microchips / integrated circuit applications

Exercise D

Students should try out different combinations to discover for themselves which gives the best results.

Closure

Tell students to think of their own question for research, as in Exercise C, and find the best web page for the data by entering appropriate keywords.

Ask students to write their question on a piece of paper and sign it. Put all the questions in a box. Students pick out one of the questions at random and go online to find the best page of search results. From those results they can find the most useful web page. They should ask the questioner for verification.

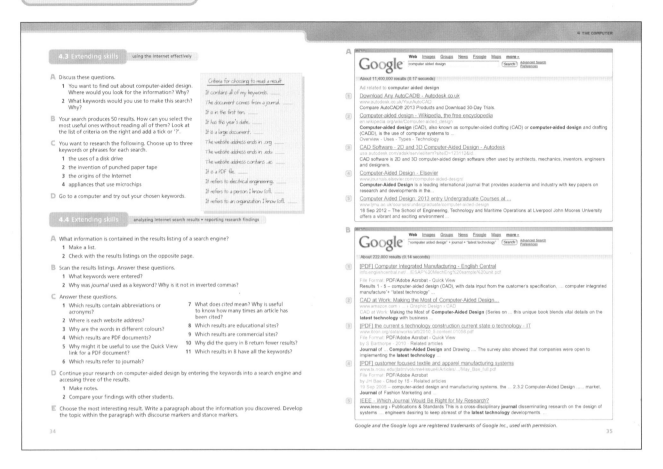

General note

Students will need access to a computer with an Internet connection. If computers are not available during the lesson, part of the lesson can be set for private study.

Lesson aims

- examine a page of Internet search results critically
- report Internet search findings in a short written summary

Introduction

Ask students what problems they had, what lessons they have learnt and what advice they can give from their Internet search experience in Lesson 4.3. Brainstorm the important factors when searching for information on the Internet and put them in order of importance.

Exercise A

Set for pairwork. Students should first make a list of information they expect to find in search engine results.

(They should do this before they look at the search engine results on the right-hand page.) They should then look at the page of results and identify any other information that is there.

Answers

Possible answers:

> number of results
> keywords used
> time taken
> title of document
> type of document
> quotations from the text with keywords highlighted
> date
> web address/URL

Exercise B

This is further reinforcement on keywords. Set for pairwork or whole class discussion.

Answers

Model answers:

> 1 A: "computer aided design"
>
> B: "computer aided design", journal, "latest technology"

2 Because journals give specialist/academic information which (in a recent issue) is up to date. Inverted commas are put round a phrase to indicate that it is all a meaningful lexical item. In Google, *journal* does not need them, as it is one word.

Exercise C

This detailed examination of the results should make students aware of the content, so that they can make an educated selection of a web page with useful information. Set for pairwork. Make sure that students are aware that PDF stands for 'portable document format'.

Answers

Model answers:

1 Acronyms/abbreviations:

Result A1: CAD

Result A2: CAD, CADD

Result A3: 2D, 3D

Result B1: PDF, CAD

Result B2: CAD

Result B3: PDF, IT

Result B4: PDF

Result B5: IEEE

Note: Students may identify further abbreviations in the website addresses, e.g., .org, .com, etc.

2 In green on the second line of each result.

3 Blue = titles and viewing information; green = website address; bold black = keywords.

4 Results B1, B3 and B4 (portable document format = viewed as a real text page).

5 In order to preview a PDF without having to download it, which may take a long time and use a lot of computer memory.

6 Results A4, B3, B4 and B5

7 The number of times an academic article has been cited means the number of times it has been referred to in later articles. It is a useful way of measuring how much impact or influence an article has had.

8 Results A5 and B4

9 Results A2, A3 and B2 are commercial sites. A1 is an advert related to the search. Note that results that are advertisements appear in a yellow box, and that other adverts related to the search often appear in a column on the right of the main results.

10 Query B returned fewer results because more search items were added. The more detailed a query, the more likely you are to find the kind of results you are looking for.

11 Results B3 and B4.

Exercise D

1 Set for individual work. Students should input the keywords again. They will not get exactly the same results page as here, but the results should be comparable. Tell them to take notes.

2 Set for pairwork. Feed back, getting students to tell the rest of the class about their most interesting findings. Encourage other students to ask questions.

Exercise E

Set for individual work. Students can complete it in class or for homework.

Closure

1 Focus on some of the vocabulary connected with using the Internet, including:

website
web address/URL
search engine
search results
input
keyword
key in
log in/log on
username
password
access

2 The importance of the care needed when selecting keywords can be demonstrated by a simple classroom activity. Tell the class you are thinking of a particular student who you want to stand up. Say (for example):

It's a man. (all the men stand up and remain standing)
He has dark hair. (only those with dark hair remain standing)
He has a beard.
He has glasses.
He's tall.
His name begins with A.
And so on.

When only one student remains, ask the class to list the minimum number of keywords necessary to identify only that student. Make sure they discard unnecessary ones. For example, if all students have dark hair, that is unnecessary.

3 Finding the keywords for familiar topics is another activity, done in groups. For example, they could:

● find their own college record (name, ID number or date of entry)

● find their last exam results (name, class, subject, date)

● find a book in the library about robots used in manufacturing (robot, manufacture, factory, etc.)

1 Work through the *Vocabulary bank* and *Skills bank* if you have not already done so, or as a revision of previous study.

2 Use the *Activity bank* (Teacher's Book additional resources section, Resource 4A).

   A Set the wordsearch for individual work (including homework) or pairwork.

   Answers

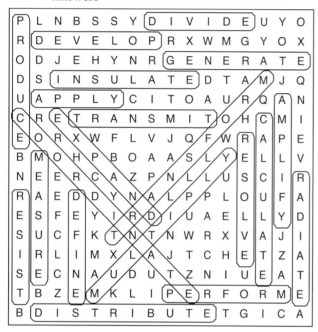

Verb	Noun	Verb	Noun
apply	application	insulate	insulation
amplify	amplification	measure	measurement
calculate	calculation	multiply	multiplication
coordinate	coordination	perform	performance
define	definition	produce	production
develop	development	radiate	radiation
distribute	distribution	resist	resistance
divide	division	resolve	resolution
expand	expansion	transform	transformation
generate	generation	transmit	transmission

   B Set for pairwork. Teach students how to play noughts and crosses if they don't know – they take it in turns to say the abbreviation or acronym, and what it stands for. If they succeed, they can put their symbol – a nought 0 or a cross **X** – in that box. If a person gets three of their own symbols in a line, they win.

3 Write the acronyms and abbreviations from the unit on cards, or photocopy them from the additional resources section (Resource 4C). Divide the class into two teams. A student selects a card and reads it correctly. (Speed is of the essence.) Alternatively, one team picks a card with an acronym or abbreviation; the other team gives the actual words.

You can follow this up by eliciting other acronyms and abbreviations from the students – in particular, common/useful ones from the field of Electrical Engineering.

4 Have a class debate: 'The invention of the computer has improved our lives in every way.' Ask two students to prepare an opening argument for and against.

Some points:

Students will presumably be able to come up with a range of points in favour of computers. They may need a little help with the disadvantages. Encourage them to think of the consequences (in brackets) of the following points:

- we can do more work in a day (rise in unemployment)
- we lead sedentary lives (a range of health disorders, e.g., heart attack)
- we use our body in repetitive, unusual ways that we are not used to, e.g., moving a mouse (health disorders, e.g., eye strain)
- we interact with other people less (psychological and social problems)
- we can access information that may not be good for us (pornography)
- people can access private information (cyber crime, e.g., fraud)
- computers can go wrong and lose data (need for hard copies)

5 Ask students to work in small groups to research and feed back to the group on some recent electrical devices that use computer technology. Three research questions could be:

   1 *Did the device already exist before the invention of the computer?*
   2 *How does this device use computer technology?*
   3 *How has computer technology improved the design of this device?*

If students are going to do research on the Internet, suggest that they type in *history* then their topic to get some potential texts. Alternatively, you can do this research before the lesson and print off some pages for students to work from.

Remind students that they can't possibly read everything they find, so they must use the topic sentences to decide if a paragraph is worth reading.

5 THE TELEVISION – FROM CRT TO LCD AND 3D

This unit looks at small electrical items and the technology behind different types of television set and screen. The first listening extract, from a lecture, gives an overview of the topic and looks at some examples of television technology and devices. The second listening extract is from a seminar about 3D televisions. This leads into work on two types of lens used in 3D technology: passive and active.

Skills focus

 Listening

- understanding 'signpost language' in lectures
- using symbols and abbreviations in note-taking

Speaking

- making effective contributions to a seminar

Vocabulary focus

- word sets: synonyms, antonyms, etc.
- the language of trends
- common lecture language

Key vocabulary

actually	deep	involved	rows
appliance	designed	item (n)	screen (n)
arguably	display (n)	kind (n)	setting
aspect	drop (n and v)	large	sharply
attached	economical	light (adj)	slightly
basically	expensive	low	slim
business	fall (v)	narrow	small
called	flat (adj)	obviously	steady
channel (n)	fundamentally	out of date	substance
clearly	gradual	picture (n)	thin
commercial	growth	place (n)	twisted
compact (adj)	heavy	possibly	type (n)
concerned	high	probably	unchanged
created	image	programme (n)	wide
crucial	immovable	recent	worsen
decline (n and v)	improve	resolution	
decrease (n and v)	increase (n and v)	rise (n and v)	

5.1 Vocabulary

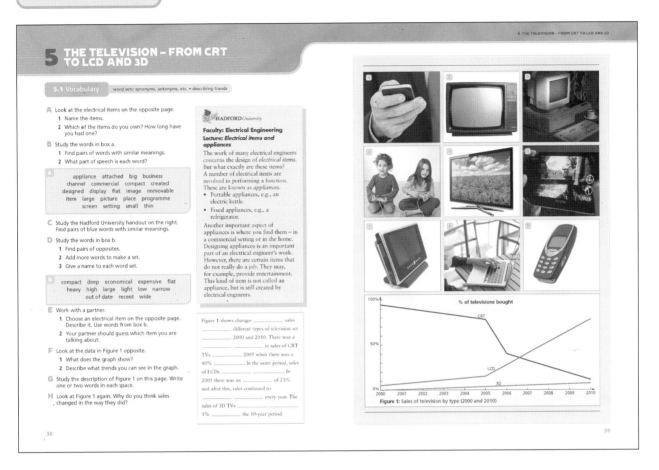

General note

Read the *Vocabulary bank – Vocabulary sets* and *Describing trends* at the end of the Course Book unit. Decide when, if at all, to refer your students to it. The best time is probably at the very end of the lesson or the beginning of the next lesson, as a summary/revision.

Lesson aims

- gain an understanding of lexical cohesion in texts through building word sets, synonyms and opposites/converses
- use appropriate language for describing trends

Introduction

Do some vocabulary revision from the previous units. For example:

1 Choose some words with different meanings in general and Electrical Engineering English (see Units 1 and 2). Ask students to say or write two sentences using each word with a different meaning. Some examples are: *ground, band, wave, series, resistance, field, charge, current, dish*, etc. If necessary, students can work with their dictionaries.

2 Choose some prefixes and suffixes (see Units 1 and 4). Write them on the board. Ask students to give the meaning of the affix and an example of a word.

3 Dictate some of the key vocabulary from Unit 3. Ask students to check their spellings (with a dictionary) and group the words according to their stress patterns.

Exercise A

Set both questions for pairwork discussion and whole class feedback. Do not comment or correct at this point. Students don't need to be able to identify the make/brand (although some may be able to do this) – just the name of the electrical item.

Elicit the general term *electrical items* and write it on the board. Ask for some other examples of electrical items and write these on the board under *electrical items* (e.g., *TV, video camera, game console, mobile phone*). Point out that the general term can be used instead of the more specific word to avoid repetition in a text – this happens to some extent in conversation but is particularly useful in written texts. For each type of electrical item there are also different *makes* (= usually the name of the company that makes the item) with *models* (= usually an item with a particular design or set of specifications) to suit different customers.

Language note

General words like *electrical items* are called hypernyms or superordinate terms. Words like *television* and *mobile phone* are called hyponyms or class members.

Answers

Model answers:

1

   1 A recent mobile phone: smartphone
   2 An old-fashioned CRT television
   3 An old desktop PC
   4 An old PlayStation
   5 A recent wide-screen flat LCD
   6 A new PlayStation model
   7 A recent portable television
   8 A new, small laptop
   9 An older model of mobile phone

2 Accept all reasonable answers.

Exercise B

The purpose of this exercise is to build sets of synonyms. This not only helps in understanding textual cohesion, but is useful for paraphrasing.

Set both questions for pairwork. Students should look for pairs of words/items. Tell them to use their dictionaries if necessary to check the grammatical information, and to note if they find other words with similar meanings.

Feed back with the whole class, building up a table on the board, and eliciting other words which can be used with the same meaning.

Answers

Model answers:
See table below.

Word 1	Part of speech	Word 2	Part of speech	Words with similar meanings/notes
appliance	n (C)	item	n (C)	object, device, product can also use *goods* for plural
attached	adj	immovable	adj	fixed
big	adj	large	adj	great, enormous
business	n (C)	commercial	adj	'business setting' is a noun+noun compound, while 'commercial setting' is an adjective+noun combination
channel	n (C)	programme	n (C)	TV station
compact	adj	small	adj	little
designed	adj	created	adj	made
display	n (C)	screen	n (C)	monitor
flat	adj	thin	adj	use with *screen* or *display*
picture	n (C)	image	n (C)	
place	n (C)	setting	n (C)	location, situation, environment

Exercise C

Set for individual work and pairwork checking. Feed back with the whole class. Discuss alternative ideas and decide whether they are acceptable. Check the meaning of any unknown words in the text (e.g., *entertainment*). Note that the blue words are general-purpose words frequent in academic contexts.

Answers

Model answers:

part	aspect
known as	called
concerns	involves
function	job

Exercise D

1 Set for pairwork. Feed back. Start the first column of the table as shown in the Answers section.

2 Do the first pair of words with the whole class as an example. Set the remainder for pairwork. Feed back, completing the second column of the table on the board.

3 Discuss with the whole class. Elicit a word or phrase which describes the whole set of words and add this to the table.

Answers

Possible answers:

Opposites	Other words	Word for set
high / low	good, poor	level (of resolution/ quality, etc.)
large / compact	big, small, little, bulky, portable	size (overall)
recent / out of date	modern, old, up to date, new	age
light / heavy	weighty	weight
wide / narrow	broad	size (horizontal from left to right)
flat / deep	thin, thick, slim	size (depth, i.e., horizontal in direction away from speaker)
expensive / economical	pricey, cheap, costly	price

Exercise E

Choose one of the items yourself and give a description (see Answers section below, asking students to identify which item you are talking about). Set the remainder for pairwork, telling students to use several of the categories in Exercise D for each item, adding other words or ideas if they need to.

Feed back as a class discussion, building the table in the Answers section if you wish.

Answers

Possible answers:

Item	Characteristics
recent mobile phone	compact, up to date, light, flat, expensive
old-fashioned TV	low screen resolution, large, out of date, heavy, deep (i.e., not flat)
old desktop PC	poor screen resolution, large, out of date, heavy, deep, not very portable
old PlayStation	poor quality, low screen resolution, out of date, heavy, relatively slow (operation)
recent TV screen	flat, light, high resolution, wide, modern, expensive (latest model), efficient (electrical consumption)
new PlayStation model	modern, thin, light, narrow, expensive, quick (operation)
recent portable TV	very compact, flat, up to date, light, small screen
new, small laptop	compact, up to date, light, small screen, flat screen, relatively cheap, portable
old model of mobile phone	poor-quality reception, large, old fashioned, heavy, bulky, relatively cheap

Exercise F

With the whole class, discuss what Figure 1 shows. Elicit some of the verbs and adverbs which students may need in order to discuss question 1. For example:

Go up	No change	Go down	Adverbs
rise increase grow improve	stay the same remain at … doesn't change is unchanged	fall decrease decline worsen drop	slightly gradually steadily significantly sharply dramatically

Note: These verbs are generally used in an intransitive sense when describing trends.

1 Discuss with the whole class. The answer to this question should be one sentence giving the topic of the graph.

2 Set for pairwork. Students should write or say a sentence about each type of TV. Feed back, eliciting sentences from the students. Write correct sentences on the board, or display the model answers on an OHT. Make sure that students notice the prepositions used with the numbers and dates.

Answers

Possible answers:

1 The graph shows changes in sales of different types of television sets between 2000 and 2010.

2 The percentage of CRT TVs sold <u>dropped</u> <u>steadily</u> from 96% in 2000 to 10% in 2010. It <u>fell</u> <u>significantly</u> from about 80% to 40% in 2005.

The percentage of LCDs sold <u>increased</u> <u>gradually</u> until 2005 and then <u>rose</u> <u>sharply</u> to 86% in 2010.

The percentage of 3D TVs sold <u>increased</u> <u>slightly</u> between 2000 and 2010.

Underline the verbs and adverbs. Ask students to make nouns from the verbs and adjectives from the adverbs. Alternatively, you could reproduce the table (minus the noun and adjective forms) on the board, on an OHT or on a handout. The incomplete table is reproduced in the additional resources section (Resource 5B) to facilitate this.

Verbs	Nouns	Adverbs	Adjective
rise	a rise	gradually	gradual
increase	an increase	sharply	sharp
grow	growth*	slightly	slight
improve	improvement	markedly	marked
fall	a fall	significantly	significant
decrease	a decrease	rapidly	rapid
drop	a drop	steeply	steep
decline	a decline	steadily	steady

*usually (but not always) uncountable in this sense

Return to the original answer sentences and ask students to make sentences with the same meaning, using the nouns and adjectives in place of the verbs and adverbs. Note that when using the noun + adjective, sentences can be made using *There was ...* or *showed*. Do one or two examples orally, then ask students to write the remaining sentences. Feed back.

Answers

Model answers:

The percentage of CRT TVs sold dropped steadily from 96% in 2000 to 10% in 2010.	There was a steady drop in the percentage of CRT TVs sold from 96% in 2000 to 10% in 2010.
It fell significantly from about 80% to 40% in 2005.	There was a significant fall from about 80% to 40% in 2005.
The percentage of LCDs sold increased gradually until 2005 and then rose sharply to 86% in 2010.	There was a gradual increase in the percentage of LCDs sold until 2005, and then a sharp rise to 86% in 2010.
The percentage of 3D TVs sold increased slightly between 2000 and 2010.	There was a slight increase in the percentage of 3D TVs sold between 2000 and 2010.

Exercise G

Set the text completion for individual work and pairwork checking. Feed back with whole class. Again, make sure that students notice the prepositions, especially the use of *by* to show the size of the increase.

Answers

Model answers:

Figure 1 shows changes <u>in</u> sales <u>of</u> different types of television set <u>between</u> 2000 and 2010. There was a <u>steady</u> <u>decrease</u> in sales of CRT TVs <u>until</u> 2005 when there was a 40% <u>drop</u>. In the same period, sales of LCDs <u>rose</u> <u>gradually</u>. In 2005 there was an <u>increase</u> <u>of</u> 23% and after this, sales continued to <u>rise</u> <u>significantly</u> every year. The sales of 3D TVs <u>increased</u> <u>by</u> 5% <u>over</u> the 10-year period.

Exercise H

Tell students to look at all the information on the right-hand page, i.e., the pictures of the TVs as well as Figure 1. They should be able to see *possible* reasons for the change in sales.

Set for pairwork. Feed back with the whole class. Encourage a discussion. If necessary, prompt students to think about the following areas: development of new technology, price, screen size and resolution, viewing pleasure, visual design, flat screen, etc.

Closure

In the box below are some important features of TVs which affect how well they sell. Ask students to work in small groups or pairs to:

- rank the features from most to least important when buying a TV
- discuss which of these features might be the chief reasons for the increase in sales of LCD TVs and the corresponding decrease for CRT TVs
  - price
  - screen size
  - screen resolution
  - brand
  - design and style
  - efficiency in terms of electrical consumption
  - how up to date the technology is

5.2 Listening

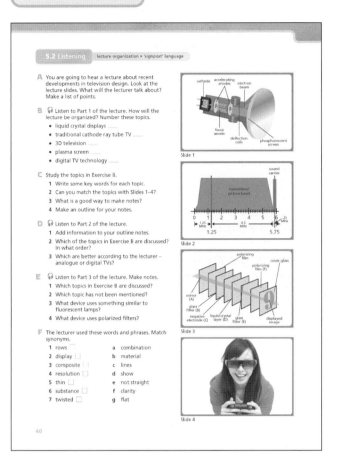

2 Remind students about preparing for a lecture. If
you wish, review Unit 1 *Skills bank – Making the
most of lectures.*

Exercise A

Remind students that when lecturers begin their talks,
they usually provide their listeners with an outline.
Remind/tell students about the *signpost language* which
speakers use at the beginning to list the areas they will
cover. On the board, build the table below, eliciting
suggestions from the students. Alternatively (or in
addition), you could refer to the *Skills bank* at this
point.

Sequencing words		Verbs
To start with, Firstly,		begin/start by ...ing discuss examine
Secondly, Then ... After that,	I'll	consider mention talk about
Finally,		look at define give a(n) outline/overview/definition/ summary of ... end/finish/conclude by ...ing

Refer students to the lecture slides. Set the exercise for
pairwork.

Ask students to feed back their possible lecture ideas to
the whole class using the signpost language on the
board to order their points. Accept any reasonable
ideas. One possibility is given below.

Language note

Speakers will usually avoid repeating words. So
they would be unlikely to say *To start with, I'll
start by ...* .

Answers

Possible answer:

To start with, the lecturer will look at cathode ray tube
TV sets and analogue signals transmitted via radio
waves. After that he/she will talk about new screens,
e.g., liquid crystal or plasma displays. He/she will finish
by looking at 3D TVs, which you watch wearing
special glasses.

General note

Read the *Skills bank – Signpost language in a
lecture* at the end of the Course Book unit. Decide
when, if at all, to refer students to it. The best time
is probably at the very end of the lesson or the
beginning of the next lesson, as a
summary/revision.

Lesson aims

• improve comprehension through understanding of
signposts and lexical cohesion
• deal with disorganization in lectures/fractured text

Further practice in:

• predicting content from own background
knowledge and from the lecture introduction
• using the introduction to decide the best form of
notes to use

Introduction

1 Review key vocabulary by writing a selection of
words from Lesson 5.1 on the board and asking
students to put the words in groups, giving reasons
for their decisions.

🎧 Exercise B

Tell students they are only going to hear the introduction to the lecture. Give students time to read the topics. Check that they understand the meaning. Remind them they will only hear the introduction once, as in a lecture. Tell them to listen out for the signpost language on the board. While they listen, they should number the topics from 1–5 in the order in which the lecturer will talk about them.

Play Part 1. Allow students to compare answers. Feed back. Ask students to say what signpost language they heard related to each topic. Confirm the correct answers.

Answers

liquid crystal displays – 3 (*Then we'll look at …*)

traditional cathode ray tube TV – 1 (*to start with, I'll look at …*)

3D television – 5 (*I'll finish by mentioning …*)

plasma screen – 2 (*Secondly, I'll examine …*)

digital TV technology – 4 (*After that I want to analyze …*)

Transcript 🎧 1.20

Part 1

Good morning, everyone. Shall we start? OK. Today we're going to look at television technology. Everyone nowadays, or nearly everyone, has a television set. In fact, many families have more than one. And, as you are probably aware, this is a very interesting time for television set design. After about 60 years of a more or less standard model based on the cathode ray tube, there are now several new types of television on the market. These take advantage of new technology in all sorts of ways, but particularly in terms of transmission and display.

So … er … let's see – yes – to start with, I'll look at a traditional cathode ray tube TV and how it works. Secondly, I'll examine the plasma screen – you may have heard of this but probably don't have one at home. Then we'll look at liquid crystal displays, or LCDs. After that, I want to analyze the changes which digital technology has brought to the field of television. I'll finish by mentioning one of the most exciting developments in this field – 3D television. I hope we have time to cover all these topics, so let's start straight away!

Exercise C

1 Set for pairwork. Divide the topics up among the pairs so that each pair concentrates on one topic. Feed back. Accept any reasonable suggestions.

2 Refer students to the lecture slides. Students should try to guess which of the topics each slide could refer to. Set for individual work and pairwork checking. Feed back but do not confirm or correct yet.

3 Elicit suggestions from the whole class. If you wish, refer students to Unit 1 *Skills bank*.

4 Set for individual work. Students should prepare an outline on a sheet of paper preferably using either numbered points (with enough space between the points to allow for notes to be added) or a mind map/spidergram (see example below).

Answers

Possible answers:

1 Some key words are:

liquid crystal displays – *flat, light, molecules, twisted, polarization, filters*

traditional cathode ray tube TV – *analogue, pixel, colour, intensity, horizontal, vertical, signal, bandwidth, frequency, channel, antenna, cable*

3D television – *glasses, images, lenses, polarized*

plasma screen – *cells, glass, gas, mercury, fluorescent lamp, phosphor, primary colours*

digital TV technology – *resolution, transmission, data*

2 Accept any reasonable answers with good justifications.

3/4 Example of spidergram:

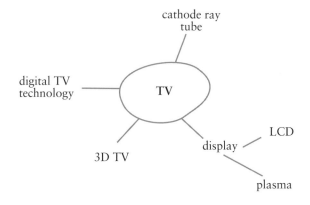

Methodology note

There is no need to teach all the words given in the model answers for question 1. However, if students suggest words that others do not know, it would of course be reasonable to check/clarify meanings of such words at this point.

🎧 Exercise D

Tell students to use their outline from Exercise C to take notes. Which topics do they expect to hear in this section?

Play Part 2. Put students in pairs to compare their notes and discuss the questions.

Feed back. When it becomes clear that the lecturer did not actually stick to the plan in the introduction, say that this happens very often in lectures. Lecturers are human! Although it is a good idea to prepare outline notes, students need to be ready to alter and amend these. Discuss how best to do this. One obvious way is to use a non-linear approach such as a mind map or spidergram, where new topics can easily be added.

After checking answers to questions 2 and 3, build a complete set of notes on the board as a spidergram, as in the example in the Answers section.

Answers

Possible answers:

1 Example notes:

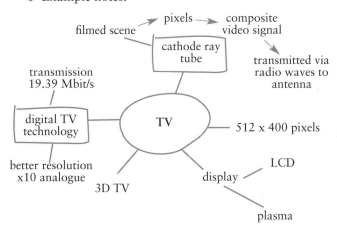

2 Discussed first: traditional cathode ray tube TVs; second: digital TV technology.

3 Digital TVs because of their better resolution.

Transcript 🎧 1.21

Part 2

Actually, the basics of analogue television transmission have been more or less standard for the last 60 years. A video camera films a scene at a rate of 30 frames per second. The camera then turns the picture into rows of individual dots, or picture elements, called *pixels*. Each pixel is given a colour and intensity. The rows of pixels are then combined with horizontal and vertical synchronization signals so the electronics inside a TV set will know how to display them. The final signal, containing the colour, intensity and position of each pixel, is known as a *composite video signal*. A TV signal requires 6 megahertz of bandwidth frequency when a sound signal is added – you can see an example in Slide 2. The tuner in your TV extracts the correct video signal from the waves transmitted to the antenna.

Fundamentally, the big problem with analogue TV is resolution. An analogue TV screen displays 525 lines of resolution every 30th of a second. That's something like 512 by 400 pixels. With digital transmission, TV channels carry a 19.39 megabit per second stream of digital data on a separate frequency from analogue signals. A digital TV can receive and decode much more data, and it follows that digital screens can display more pixels than a traditional analogue TV. Naturally, that makes a big difference. I saw a tennis match on a digital screen and it was just amazing – such detail! Anyway, er … to return to the main point, digital TVs offer a wide range of advantages over analogue TVs and will soon replace them completely.

🎧 Exercise E

Ask students what they expect to hear about in the next part. Refer students to their outline again. Give them time to read the questions. Note that the final part of the lecture will be heard in Lesson 5.3, but there is no need to tell them this at this point. Play Part 3. Set the questions for pairwork. Students should use their notes to help them answer the questions.

Feed back. Note that there is no need to build a set of notes on the board at this point – this will be done in Lesson 5.3. Ask students if they can remember what the lecturer was talking about when she lost her place (buying the wrong sort of TV monitor) and exactly what she said to indicate that she had lost her place (*Er … Where was I? Oh, yes.*).

Answers

Model answers:

1 Liquid crystal displays and plasma screens.

2 3D TVs.

3 Plasma screen.

4 LCD screen.

Transcript 🎧 1.22

Part 3

There are two main types of digital screens – the *liquid crystal display*, or LCD, and the *plasma screen*. Let's look first at plasma. A plasma display panel, or PDP, has a much flatter screen than a cathode ray tube television. The panel is made up of tiny plasma cells situated between two panels of glass. Each cell contains a mixture of gases and mercury, and acts rather similarly to a fluorescent lamp. When an electric current is applied, the cell emits light, and different cells can be made to emit light of different colours by changing the type of phosphors painted on the inside of the cell. Each pixel consists of three cells which emit the primary colours of light – red, green and blue. Varying the voltage of the signals to the cells allows us to see different colours on the screen.

LCDs are arguably very similar to plasma screens – they are also light and thin. But they are actually very different. What I mean is, they are based on very different technology, and it's essential that we understand this difference. The general public doesn't seem to understand this so they go and buy a new screen and get the wrong one for their needs, wasting money. Er … where was I? Oh yes. Perhaps the most important difference is that LCDs do not produce light of their own. They need a source of background light, which each pixel can block or allow to pass. A pixel of an LCD consists of a cell of liquid crystal, which is an unusual substance that consists of twisted molecules. They respond to an electric current by untwisting themselves. The amount they untwist depends on the voltage, and when they untwist, the amount of light that passes through the layer changes. In this way, the passage of light through each cell can be controlled electronically. In colour LCDs, each individual pixel consists of three cells with red, green and blue filters.

Exercise F

This gives further practice in identifying words and phrases used synonymously in a particular context.

Set for individual work and pairwork checking.

Answers

1 rows	c lines
2 display	d show
3 composite	a combination
4 resolution	f clarity
5 thin	g flat
6 substance	b material
7 twisted	e not straight

Closure

1 Check that students understand some of the concepts and vocabulary in the unit so far, including:

television set
cathode ray tube (CRT)
digital TV technology
transmission
display
plasma screen
liquid crystal display (LCD)
pixel
video signal
antenna
resolution
TV channels
digital data
phosphor
primary colours
synchronization
decode
polarizing filter

Note: Students will need their lecture notes from this lesson in Lesson 5.3.

5.3 Extending skills

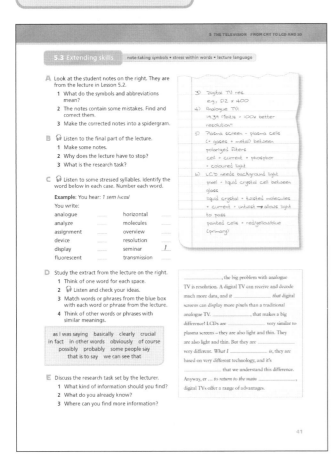

Lesson aims

- use symbols in note-taking
- understand and use lecture language such as stance adverbials (*naturally, arguably*), restatement (*what I mean is ...*) and other commentary-type phrases

Further practice in:

- stress within words
- asking for information
- formulating polite questions

Introduction

As in Unit 3, encourage students to ask you questions about the information in the lecture in Lesson 5.2 as if you were the lecturer. Remind them about asking for information politely. If they can't remember how to do this, you could tell them to revise the *Skills bank* for Unit 3.

Put students in pairs. Student A must ask Student B about the information in the lecture in Lesson 5.2 to help him/her complete the notes from the lecture. Then they reverse roles. Again, they can revise language for this in the *Skills bank* for Unit 3.

Exercise A

1 Revise/introduce the idea of using symbols and abbreviations when making notes. Ask students to look at the example notes and find the symbols and abbreviated forms. Do they know what these mean? If not, they should try to guess.

   If you wish, expand the table in the Answers section below with more symbols and abbreviations that will be useful for the students. There is also a list at the back of the Course Book for students' reference.

2 Ask students to tell you what kind of notes these are (linear and numbered). Set the question for pairwork. Students will need to agree what the notes are saying and then make the corrections.

3 Set for individual work. Feed back with the whole class and build the spidergram in the Answers section on the board.

Answers

Model answers:

1

Symbol/abbreviation	Meaning
res.	resolution
e.g.	(for) example
×	multiply
→	gives
M	mega
px	pixel
/	per
=	equals, the same as, is
×	times
+	and, plus
LCD	liquid crystal display

2 Suggested corrections:

> 3) <u>Analogue</u> TV res.
> e.g., 512 × 400
> 4) <u>Digital</u> TV:
> 19.39 Mbit/s = better resolution!!
> 5) Plasma screen – plasma cells (= gases + <u>mercury</u>) between <u>glass</u>
> cell + current + phosphor = coloured light
> 6) LCD needs background light
> pixel = liquid crystal cell between <u>polarized filters</u>
> liquid crystal = twisted molecules + current = untwist → allows light to pass
> painted cells = red/<u>green</u>/blue (primary)

3 Example notes:

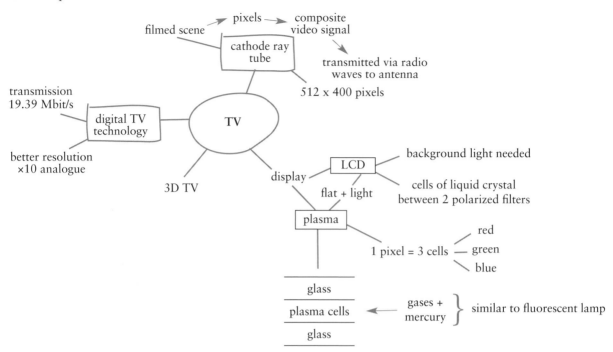

Language note

Some abbreviations are universal and some are personal. People often develop their own personal system of symbols and abbreviations. For example, *TV* for television is used by many people, but *res.* for 'resolution' is an example of a longer word abbreviated by the individual who wrote these notes.

🎧 Exercise B

Tell students they will hear the final part of the lecture. Give them time to read the questions. Tell them to take notes – there isn't really enough information in the lecture to complete the final leg of the spidergram.

Play Part 4. Put students in pairs to compare their notes and discuss the questions. Feed back. For question 2, ask students if they can remember the exact words used by the lecturer (*oh, dear … sadly, I see that we've run out of time.*).

Answers

Model answers:

1 Example notes: Stereoscopy – two images projected on the screen. The left eye of the viewer (wearing glasses) only sees one of these images and the right eye sees the other. The brain then combines them into a 3D image. Different sorts of glasses: coloured lenses, polarized lenses, 'active shutter' lenses.

2 Because there is no more time.

3 The research task is to find out about the technology behind the different types of glasses used for watching 3D TV.

Transcript 🎧 1.23

Part 4

Finally, let's quickly look at the idea of 3D television. As you probably know, 3D films in the cinema have been around for some time. There have been various technologies developed, but the more successful ones have used *stereoscopy*. Basically, two film cameras are needed, which take two similar but slightly different images, just as our eyes see an object from similar but different angles. Each image is directed to one eye only and our brain combines them in such a way that we see a three-dimensional object. The problem here is how to ensure that one eye only sees one of the images projected on the screen. This is solved by a pair of glasses that the viewer has to wear. However … oh, dear … sadly, I see that we've run out of time. This means that I'll have to ask *you* to do some research. I'd like you to find out about these different types of glasses and the technology behind them, that is, coloured, polarized and active shutter lenses. We'll discuss what you've found out next time I see you.

🎧 Exercise C

Remind students of the importance of stressed syllables in words (see the teaching notes for Unit 3.3, Exercise A). Play the recording, pausing after the first few to check that students understand the task.

Feed back, perhaps playing the recording again for each word before checking. Ideally, mark up an OHT of the words.

Answers

analogue	8
analyze	7
assignment	3
device	11
display	5
fluorescent	10
horizontal	9
molecules	2
overview	6
resolution	4
seminar	1
transmission	12

Transcript 🎧 1.24

1 'seminar
2 'molecules
3 a'ssignment
4 reso'lution
5 dis'play
6 'overview
7 'analyze
8 'analogue
9 hori'zontal
10 fluo'rescent
11 de'vice
12 trans'mission

🎧 Exercise D

This exercise gives students a chance to focus on some typical lecture language.

1 Set for pairwork. Students should try to think of a word for each of the blank spaces.

Note that they should *not* try to use the words from the box for this. Do not feed back at this point.

2 Tell students they will hear the sentences from the lecture and should fill in the missing words as they listen. There will be pauses at the end of each sentence but you will play the recording straight through without stopping (as a kind of dictation). Feed back with the whole class, playing the sentences again if necessary. Check the meanings and functions of the words and phrases. Point out the fixed phrases (in italics in the text) and

encourage students to learn these. Ask students to repeat the sentences for pronunciation practice, making sure that the stress and intonation are copied from the model.

3 Set for individual work and pairwork checking. Students should check in their dictionaries for meanings or pronunciations of words from the box that they don't know. Feed back, building the first two columns of the table in the Answers section on the board.

4 Elicit suggestions from the whole class for a third column: 'Other similar words'.

If you wish, students can practise saying the sentences in question 2 but this time with words from questions 3 and 4.

After completing Exercise D, students can be referred to the *Vocabulary bank – Stance* and the *Skills bank – Signpost language in a lecture* for consolidation.

Answers

Model answers:

1/2 *Fundamentally*, the big problem with analogue TV is resolution. A digital TV can receive and decode much more data, and *it follows that* digital screens can display more pixels than a traditional analogue TV. *Naturally*, that makes a big difference! LCDs are *arguably* very similar to plasma screens – they are also light and thin. But they are *actually* very different. *What I mean is*, they are based on very different technology, and it's *essential* that we understand this difference. Anyway, er … *to return to the main point*, digital TVs offer a range of advantages.

3/4

Word/phrase from the lecture	Words/phrases from the box	Other similar words/phrases
Fundamentally	basically	in essence, really
it follows that	we can see that	logically
Naturally	of course, obviously, clearly	certainly
arguably	probably, possibly, some people say	perhaps
actually	in fact	in reality
What I mean is	that is to say, in other words	or, by that I mean, to put it another way
essential	crucial	important
to return to the main point	as I was saying	going back to

Transcript 🎧 1.25

Fundamentally, the big problem with analogue TV is resolution.

A digital TV can receive and decode much more data, and it follows that digital screens can display more pixels than a traditional analogue TV.

Naturally, that makes a big difference!

LCDs are arguably very similar to plasma screens – they are also light and thin.

But they are actually very different.

What I mean is, they are based on very different technology, and it's essential that we understand this difference.

Anyway, er … to return to the main point, digital TVs offer a range of advantages.

Language note

There are three main categories of language here:

1 Stance markers. These are words or phrases that speakers use to show what they feel or think about what they are saying. Adverbs used like this are generally (though not always) positioned at the beginning of the sentence.

2 Phrases used to indicate a restatement. It is very important for students both to understand and to be able to use these, since speakers frequently need to repeat and explain their points.

3 Phrases used to show that the speaker has deviated from the main point and is now about to return to it. Again, this type of phrase is very common in lectures and discussions.

Exercise E

Remind students of the task set by the lecturer at the end of Part 4. Set the questions for pairwork discussion. Students should first list the sort of information they will need to find, then discuss and make notes on what they already know. Then they should compile a list of possible sources of information.

Feed back on all three questions with the whole class.

Answers

Possible answers:

1 Definitions, explanations and anything else that is relevant.

2 Answers depend on the students.

3 Internet, library, subject textbooks, encyclopedias, etc.

Closure

Play a version of the game 'Just a minute'. Put students in groups of four. Give them an envelope in which they will find topics written on slips of paper. Students take turns to take a slip of paper from the envelope and then talk for one minute on the topic. Encourage them to use as many of the words and phrases from Exercises C and D as they can. Each person should talk for up to a minute without stopping. If they can talk for one minute they get a point. If they deviate from their topic or can't think of anything more to say, they have to stop. The person who has the most points is the winner.

Suggestions for topics follow. Or if you prefer, you can use other topics unrelated to electrical engineering.

screen resolution
LCD technology
pixels
TV transmission
cathode ray tube TVs
plasma screens
analogue signals
digital data

5.4 Extending skills

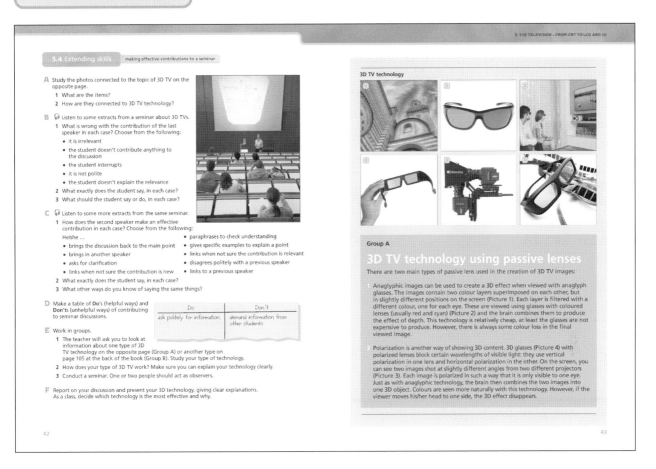

5.4 Extending skills making effective contributions to a seminar

A Study the photos connected to the topic of 3D TV on the opposite page.
 1 What are the items?
 2 How are they connected to 3D TV technology?

B 🎧 Listen to some extracts from a seminar about 3D TVs.
 1 What is wrong with the contribution of the last speaker in each case? Choose from the following:
   • it is irrelevant
   • the student doesn't contribute anything to the discussion
   • the student interrupts
   • it is not polite
   • the student doesn't explain the relevance
 2 What exactly does the student say, in each case?
 3 What should the student say or do, in each case?

C 🎧 Listen to some more extracts from the same seminar.
 1 How does the second speaker make an effective contribution in each case? Choose from the following:
   He/she ...
   • brings the discussion back to the main point
   • brings in another speaker
   • asks for clarification
   • links when not sure the contribution is new
   • paraphrases to check understanding
   • gives specific examples to explain a point
   • links when not sure the contribution is relevant
   • disagrees politely with a previous speaker
   • links to a previous speaker
 2 What exactly does the student say, in each case?
 3 What other ways do you know of saying the same things?

D Make a table of **Do's** (helpful ways) and **Don'ts** (unhelpful ways) of contributing to seminar discussions.

Do	Don't
ask politely for information	demand information from other students

E Work in groups.
 1 The teacher will ask you to look at information about one type of 3D TV technology on the opposite page (Group A) or another type on page 105 at the back of the book (Group B). Study your type of technology.
 2 How does your type of 3D TV work? Make sure you can explain your technology clearly.
 3 Conduct a seminar. One or two people should act as observers.

F Report on your discussion and present your 3D technology, giving clear explanations. As a class, decide which technology is the most effective and why.

42

3D TV technology

Group A
3D TV technology using passive lenses
There are two main types of passive lens used in the creation of 3D TV images:

Anaglyphic images can be used to create a 3D effect when viewed with anaglyph glasses. The images contain two colour layers superimposed on each other, but in slightly different positions on the screen (Picture 1). Each layer is filtered with a different colour, one for each eye. These are viewed using glasses with coloured lenses (usually red and cyan) (Picture 2) and the brain combines them to produce the effect of depth. This technology is relatively cheap, at least the glasses are not expensive to produce. However, there is always some colour loss in the final viewed image.

Polarization is another way of showing 3D content. 3D glasses (Picture 4) with polarized lenses block certain wavelengths of visible light: they use vertical polarization in one lens and horizontal polarization in the other. On the screen, you can see two images shot at slightly different angles from two different projectors (Picture 3). Each image is polarized in such a way that it is only visible to one eye. Just as with anaglyphic technology, the brain then combines the two images into one 3D object. Colours are seen more naturally with this technology. However, if the viewer moves his/her head to one side, the 3D effect disappears.

43

Lesson aims

- make effective and appropriate contributions to a seminar

Further practice in:

- speaking from notes
- reporting information

Introduction

Revise stance words and restatement/deviation phrases from the previous lesson. Give a word or phrase and ask students to give one with a similar meaning. Alternatively, give a sentence or phrase from the lecture in Lessons 5.2 and 5.3 and ask students to tell you the accompanying stance word or restatement phrase, e.g., _____ *(Fundamentally), the big problem with analogue TV is resolution.*

Exercise A

1 Tell students to look at the photos connected to 3D TV. Set for pairwork discussion. See possible answers below but don't give too much information at this stage, since students will be doing research on this technology later in the lesson.

2 Ask students to use what they know about 3D TV technology. Feed back, accepting any reasonable suggestions. Clearly the brief information in Part 4 of the lecture in Lesson 5.3 will be relevant here. Again, don't give too much information, since students will be finding out more for themselves later on.

Answers

Possible answers:

1 Two of the photos illustrate what a TV screen looks like for different 3D technology: *anaglyphic* (Photo 1) and *polarization* (Photo 3). The other photos show examples of types of glasses that viewers need to wear while watching 3D TV: *passive* glasses with coloured lenses (Photo 2) and with *polarized* lenses (Photo 4); and *active* glasses using shutter lens technology (Photos 5 and 6).

2 See information in Exercise E.

🎧 Exercise B

In this exercise, students will hear examples of how *not* to contribute to a group discussion.

1/2 Allow students time to read the questions. Tell them they will hear five extracts. They should choose a different answer for each one. Set for individual work and pairwork checking. Play all the extracts through once.

Play the extracts a second time, pausing after each one. Students should write down the actual words, as in a dictation, then check in pairs. When students have completed questions 1 and 2, feed back with the whole class, maybe building up columns 1 and 2 of the table in the Answers section on the board.

3 Set for pairwork discussion. Feed back, adding a third column to the table on the board.

Answers

Model answers (bottom of page):

Transcript 🎧 1.26

Extract 1

LECTURER: Right, Leila and Majed, what did you find out about 3D TVs?

LEILA: Well, first of all, we looked at the website 'How stuff works' to get an overview of the topic.

MAJED: I bought a new TV last week.

Extract 2

LECTURER: And what else did you do?

LEILA: We talked to my flatmate. He works for Sony.

MAJED: That was a waste of time!

Extract 3

LECTURER: Leila, can you give us an explanation of how passive lenses work in 3D technology?

LEILA: Well, yes, there are two different types of lens – coloured and polarized.

LECTURER: What do the rest of you think? Do you agree? Evie, what about you?

EVIE: Well, erm … I'm not sure really.

Extract 4

LECTURER: Majed, can you explain how the coloured lenses work?

MAJED: OK. Right, the screen shows two different images. Each image has a sort of coloured tint to it, and this corresponds to the colour of the lenses.

JACK: So it's anaglyphic.

Extract 5

LECTURER: What do you mean by 'anaglyphic', Jack?

JACK: I mean using coloured lenses for 3D television is an example of anaglyphic technology. That's what …

EVIE: Actually, it's called stereoscopy.

🎧 Exercise C

1/2 This time students will hear good ways of contributing to a discussion. Follow the same procedure as for 1 and 2 in Exercise B above. This time they need to listen for the second speaker.

Again, when students have completed 1 and 2, feed back with the whole class, maybe building up a table on the board. If you wish, students can look at the transcript at the back of the Course Book.

3 Ask the whole class for other words or phrases that can be used for the strategy and add a third column to the table as on next page.

	Contribution is poor because	Exact words	How to improve
Extract 1	it is irrelevant	Majed: I bought a new TV last week	say something relevant: for example, something about how they did their research
Extract 2	it is not polite	Majed: That was a waste of time!	use polite (tentative) language when disagreeing, e.g., *Actually, I'm not sure it was really very useful.*
Extract 3	the student doesn't contribute anything to the discussion	Evie: Well, erm … I'm not sure really.	be ready to contribute something when brought into the discussion by the lecturer or other students
Extract 4	the student doesn't explain the relevance	Jack: So it's anaglyphic.	the comment is relevant to the topic but he doesn't explain why. He should say, for example, what he said later after the lecturer asked him to explain (i.e., *it's an example of anaglyphic technology*)
Extract 5	the student interrupts	Evie: Actually, it's called stereoscopy.	she should wait until the speaker has finished

Transcript 🎧 1.27

Extract 6

LECTURER: Let's go back to this idea of wearing coloured glasses – what we call anaglyphic technology. First of all, tell us about the choice of colour for the lenses.

LEILA: Well, all the information we've read talked about blue and red lenses for the glasses. Didn't it, Majed?

MAJED: Yes. Those were the only colours they used – and it's a special type of blue called cyan.

Extract 7

MAJED: The picture on the screen shows two different images that have been filtered differently.

JACK: Sorry, I don't follow. Could you possibly explain how they are filtered?

MAJED : Well, basically they colour one image blue and one image red.

Extract 8

EVIE: I don't understand how we see a 3D object from these two images.

LEILA: Well, imagine the screen shows a banana. Our left eye sees the banana slightly differently from our right eye. For example, it will see a part of it that is hidden from our right eye. The two images on the screen correspond to these different views.

Extract 9

MAJED: Yes, the visual cortex of the brain combines these two images into the perception of a three-dimensional object.

JACK: If I understand you correctly, you're saying that our brain sees these two images and believes it is looking at one real object in space.

MAJED: Yes, that's correct.

Extract 10

LECTURER: This is all very interesting, isn't it?

EVIE: Yes, but if we just go back to the idea of 3D TV, this method of using coloured lenses in glasses is now rather old-fashioned.

LEILA: That's right!

Extract 11

JACK: I think the whole idea is silly. I mean, it would be really expensive. And anyway we can't sit at home watching TV wearing strange glasses!

MAJED: I'm not sure that's true. I think the 3D effect could be so effective that we might find normal TV a bit boring in comparison.

Answers

Model answers:

	Helpful strategy	Exact words	Other ways to say it
Extract 6	brings in another speaker	Leila: Didn't they, Majed?	What do you think, Majed?/What do you make of this, Majed?
Extract 7	asks for clarification	Jack: Sorry, I don't follow. Could you possibly explain …?	I don't quite understand. Could you say a bit more about …?
Extract 8	gives specific examples to explain a point	Leila: Well, imagine … For example, …	For instance, …
Extract 9	paraphrases to check understanding	Jack: If I understand you correctly, you're saying that …	So what you're saying is …
Extract 10	brings the discussion back to the main point	Evie: Yes, but if we just go back to …	Thinking about …/If we can go back to … for a moment, …
Extract 11	disagrees politely with a previous speaker	Majed: I'm not sure that's true. I think …	I don't think I agree with that. In my opinion …
Extract 12	links to a previous speaker	Leila: As Evie said earlier …	Going back to what Leila said a while ago …
Extract 13	links when not sure the contribution is new	Jack: I'm sorry. Has anybody made the point that …?	I don't know if this has been said already, but …
Extract 14	links when not sure the contribution is relevant	Evie: I don't know if this is relevant.	I'm not sure if this is a little off the point, but …

Extract 12

LECTURER: So what do you think is the most effective 3D TV technology available?

LEILA: As Evie said earlier, the idea of coloured glasses was popular some years ago.

Extract 13

LECTURER: Any other ideas?

EVIE: I'm sorry. Has anybody made the point that 3D TVs are really expensive. Maybe no one will buy one because of that.

LECTURER: Yes, actually. Jack did say that earlier, but it's an important point.

Extract 14

LECTURER: So any other points about 3D TV?

EVIE: I don't know if this is relevant but 3D technology might be more appropriate for computer games than for normal television.

LECTURER: Yes, that's interesting.

Exercise D

Set for group work. Tell students to brainstorm suggestions for more good and bad seminar strategies. They should think about what helps a seminar discussion to be successful. It may help to think about having seminar discussions in their own language, but they should also think about what is involved in having a seminar discussion in English. Aspects to consider include language, how to contribute to discussions and how to behave.

Feed back, making a list on the board.

Answers

Possible answers:

Do	Don't
prepare the topic beforehand	
ask politely for information	demand information from other students
try to use correct language	
speak clearly	mumble, whisper or shout
say when you agree with someone	get angry if someone disagrees with you
link correctly with previous speakers	
build on points made by other speakers	
make a contribution, even if you are not sure if it is new or relevant	stay silent, waiting for 'the perfect moment'
be constructive	be negative
give specific examples to help explain a point	be vague
listen carefully to what others say	start a side conversation
allow others to speak	dominate the discussion
paraphrase to check understanding	

Exercise E

Set students to work in groups of five or six. Give the groups a letter: A or B. Group As should look at the information about passive lenses (coloured and polarized) and Group Bs should look at the information about active shutter lenses.

In each group there should be one or two observers and three or four discussing. Groups should also appoint one person to take notes on the discussion, since they will have to present their explanation to another group. During the discussion, they will need to make sure they have understood how their type of glasses and the technology behind them work in creating 3D TV.

While students are talking, you can listen in and note where students may need help with language, and where particularly good examples of language are used.

The students acting as observers for the discussion should use a checklist of things to watch for. One observer can concentrate on poor contributions and the other on good contributions. Sample checklists are provided in the additional resources section (Resource 5C) – students simply mark in each cell whenever the behaviour occurs.

Exercise F

For this exercise, an A and a B group can join together to make one larger group. Alternatively, if the groups are already large, divide each group in half and send one half plus one observer to another group, so that the new groups consist of 50% As and 50% Bs.

Before the groups report on their discussion, remind them about speaking from notes (see Unit 1 *Skills bank*).

First, the observers should give an overview of how the seminar discussion went and should highlight especially good practice. They can also report on poor contributions, but this needs to be done carefully and constructively (possibly without mentioning names), so that individuals are not embarrassed or upset.

Then the person who took notes should present an explanation of their technology to the other group.

When both groups have presented their work, encourage students to compare the advantages and disadvantages of the various technologies. Decide together which is the most effective and why.

Finally, feed back to the whole class on what you heard as you listened in to the groups. Suggest improvements for words and phrases, and highlight good practice.

Closure

1 If you wish, refer students to the *Skills bank – Seminar language* for consolidation.

2 Focus on some of the vocabulary connected with research from Lessons 5.2 and 5.4. For example:

clarity
combination
composite
display
filter
flat
lens
lines
material
projector
resolution
rows
show (v)
shutter
straight
substance
thin
twisted

Extra activities

1 Work through the *Vocabulary bank* and *Skills bank* if you have not already done so, or as a revision of previous study.

2 Use the *Activity bank* (Teacher's Book additional resources section, Resource 5A).

A Set the wordsearch for individual work (including homework) or pairwork.

Answers

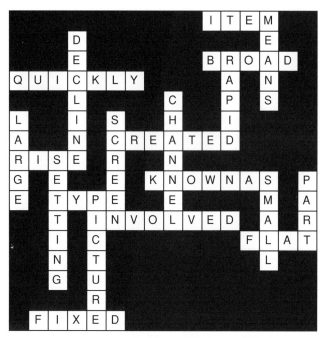

B Students should select any six words from the box (listed in *Students' words* column below). Call out words at random from the *Teacher's words* column, not forgetting to note which words you have called. Students cross out the antonym, if they have it on their card. When someone has managed to cross out all the words on his/her bingo card, he/she should call out *Bingo!* Check to see if all the words are correctly crossed out. If the student has made a mistake, they are out of the game. The first person to correctly cross out all the words on his/her bingo card is the winner.

An alternative is to put students in groups to play the game, with one student acting as the teacher. In this case, you will need to prepare a list of teacher's words for each group.

Students' words	Teacher's words
active	passive
cheap	expensive
easy	difficult
fall	rise
flat	deep
heavy	light
increase	decrease
large	compact
low	high
narrow	wide
recent	out of date
sharply	gradually
slightly	significantly
slow	rapid
twisted	straight
vertical	horizontal

3 Students can search for two examples of similar electrical items for sale on the Internet, particularly online shopping sites, and make a comparison of them, mentioning their technical specifications and other relevant criteria, e.g., price, style, make, etc. Students can present their findings to the whole class or in groups.

6 CONTROL SYSTEMS

Unit 6 looks at a field of Electrical Engineering known as *control systems*. It focuses on a very common feedback loop controller known as *PID*, which is central to control system design. Initially this is examined in Lesson 6.1 in the context of setting the temperature of a domestic oven, and discussed in more detail in the reading text of Lesson 6.2. Later on in the unit, another example of PID control is looked at: cruise control for cars.

Skills focus

Reading

- locating key information in complex sentences

Writing

- reporting findings from other sources: paraphrasing
- writing complex sentences

Vocabulary focus

- synonyms, replacement subjects, etc., for sentence-level paraphrasing

Key vocabulary

accelerator	input	regulate
adaptive	integral	response
brake	offset (n)	set (adj)
calculate	on-off control	significant
clutch	oscillation	solve
constant (n)	output	stable
contribution	overshoot (n)	supply (v)
control loop	parameters	switch (v)
cruise control	pedal (n)	system
damped	perfect	test (v)
derivative	possibility	tight
droop (n)	predict	trial (v)
eliminate	process (n)	tune (v)
exceed	programme (v)	underdamped
feedback (n)	proportional	unstable
fluctuate	rate (n)	variable
heater	reaction	widely

6.1 Vocabulary

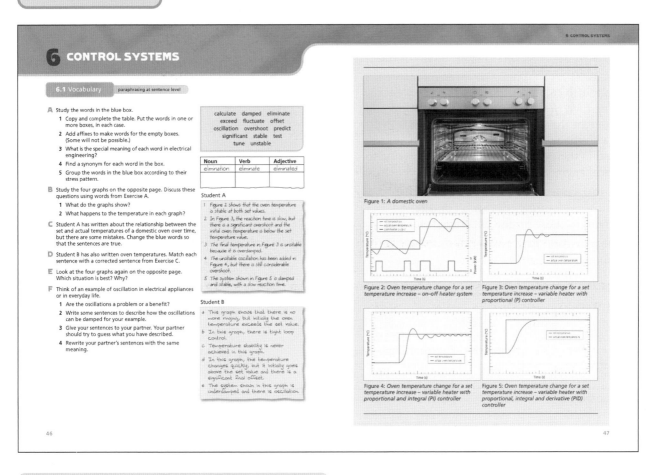

6 CONTROL SYSTEMS

6.1 Vocabulary — paraphrasing at sentence level

A Study the words in the blue box.
1 Copy and complete the table. Put the words in one or more boxes, in each case.
2 Add affixes to make words for the empty boxes. (Some will not be possible.)
3 What is the special meaning of each word in electrical engineering?
4 Find a synonym for each word in the box.
5 Group the words in the blue box according to their stress pattern.

B Study the four graphs on the opposite page. Discuss these questions using words from Exercise A.
1 What do the graphs show?
2 What happens to the temperature in each graph?

C Student A has written about the relationship between the set and actual temperatures of a domestic oven over time, but there are some mistakes. Change the blue words so that the sentences are true.

D Student B has also written oven temperatures. Match each sentence with a corrected sentence from Exercise C.

E Look at the four graphs again on the opposite page. Which situation is best? Why?

F Think of an example of oscillation in electrical appliances or in everyday life.
1 Are the oscillations a problem or a benefit?
2 Write some sentences to describe how the oscillations can be damped for your example.
3 Give your sentences to your partner. Your partner should try to guess what you have described.
4 Rewrite your partner's sentences with the same meaning.

calculate damped eliminate
exceed fluctuate offset
oscillation overshoot predict
significant stable test
tune unstable

Noun	Verb	Adjective
elimination	eliminate	eliminated

Student A
1 Figure 2 shows that the oven temperature is stable at both set values.
2 In Figure 3, the reaction time is slow, but there is a significant overshoot and the initial oven temperature is below the set temperature value.
3 The final temperature in Figure 3 is unstable because it is overdamped.
4 The unstable oscillation has been added in Figure 4, but there is still considerable overshoot.
5 The system shown in Figure 5 is damped and stable, with a slow reaction time.

Student B
a This graph shows that there is no more ringing, but initially the oven temperature exceeds the set value.
b In this graph, there is tight loop control.
c Temperature stability is never achieved in this graph.
d In this graph, the temperature changes quickly, but it initially goes above the set value and there is a significant final offset.
e The system shown in this graph is underdamped and there is oscillation.

Figure 1: A domestic oven

Figure 2: Oven temperature change for a set temperature increase – on-off heater system

Figure 3: Oven temperature change for a set temperature increase – variable heater with proportional (P) controller

Figure 4: Oven temperature change for a set temperature increase – variable heater with proportional and integral (PI) controller

Figure 5: Oven temperature change for a set temperature increase – variable heater with proportional, integral and derivative (PID) controller

46

47

General note

Read the *Vocabulary bank* at the end of the Course Book unit. Decide when, if at all, to refer students to it. The best time is probably at the very end of the lesson or the beginning of the next lesson, as a summary/revision.

Lesson aims

- paraphrase at sentence level using passives, synonyms, negatives, replacement subjects

Further practice in:

- affixes
- words with different meanings in general English
- stress within words
- word sets – synonyms, antonyms

Introduction

1 Revise affixes, e.g., *re~*, *de~*, *non~*, *photo~*, *multi~*, *~sis*, *~ify*, *~ical*, *~ion*, *~ular*. Do this by dividing the class into small groups. Give each group one affix. Allow three or four minutes. The group which can list the most words is the winner.

2 Revise words describing graphs (from Unit 5). Draw a line graph on the board. The line should rise and fall, sharply and gradually, and have a peak and a point where it levels off. Point to each part of the line and ask students to give you the appropriate verb and adverb. Alternatively, draw your own line graph and describe it. Students should try to draw an identical line graph from your description while you are talking.

Exercise A

1 Tell students to make a table with three columns and fifteen rows in their notebooks. Go through the example in the Course Book. Set the exercise for individual work and pairwork checking. Tell students to use their dictionaries if they need to check meanings, grammatical category, etc. Feed back with the whole class, building the first three columns of the table in the Answers section on the board. Ask students to say what general meanings they can give for the words.

2 Refer to the example (*eliminate*) in the Course Book. Ask students to suggest a form of *eliminate* which is an adjective (*eliminated*). Set for pairwork. Students should try to fill as many empty boxes as

possible with words with appropriate affixes. They should continue to use their dictionaries to check meanings and spellings. Note that it is possible to use the past/present participle of a verb as an adjective if there is no other possibility. Feed back with the whole class, checking meanings of the words added to the table.

3 Add a fourth column on the board and give it the heading *Electrical engineering meaning*. Underline or highlight the words as shown in the table below and, with the whole class, ask students to suggest (or find in their dictionaries) meanings specific to electrical engineering for these words.

4 Work in a similar way with the fifth column, *Electrical engineering synonym*. Limit the synonyms to those for the underlined words.

5 Set for pairwork. Feed back with the whole class, checking pronunciation.

Answers

Model answers:

1/2/3/4

Noun	Verb	Adjective	Electrical engineering meaning	Electrical engineering synonym
calculation	calculate	calculated	(v) work out using mathematics or arithmetic	(v) compute, work out, determine
damping	damp	damped	(adj) non-oscillatory	(adj) diminished, reduced, suppressed, non-fluctuating
elimination	eliminate	eliminated	(v) remove completely	(v) cancel, remove
excess	exceed	exceeded	(v) be greater or larger than a given amount	(v) better, overtake, pass
fluctuation	fluctuate	fluctuating	(v) change a lot in a regular way	(v) oscillate, change, alternate, swing
offset, offsetting	offset	offset	(n) a sustained difference between a set point and a controlled variable	(n) deviation, error, difference
oscillation	oscillate	oscillating	(n) frequent or regular increase or decrease in value	(n) fluctuation, ringing
overshoot	overshoot	overshot	(v) exceed a target value (as in a signal)	(v) go above/beyond, exceed
prediction	predict	predicted	(v) suggest what will happen based on evidence	(v) anticipate, forecast, infer, suppose
signification	signify	significant	(adj) important in meaning or effect	(adj) important, valid, powerful
stability	stabilize	stable	(adj) resistant to change of position or condition	(adj) steady, immovable, set
test	test	tested	(v) check by carrying out experiments	(v) analyze, experiment, investigate, verify
tuning	tune	tuned	(v) adjust for better functioning	(v) adapt, adjust, regulate, set
instability	destabilize	unstable	(adj) having a tendency to change/move away from a steady state	(adj) unsteady, erratic, changeable, vacillating, unpredictable

5

one syllable	damped, test, tune
Oo	offset (noun), stable
oO	exceed, offset (verb), predict
oOo	unstable

Ooo	calculate, fluctuate
ooO	overshoot
oOoo	eliminate, significant
ooOo	oscillation

Exercise B

1 Set for pairwork discussion. Students should refer to the words they have looked at in Exercise A to help describe what is shown in the graphs. Monitor but don't assist. Feed back with the whole class, checking that students can give the topic of the graphs, and the meanings of the vertical and horizontal axes. Elicit words which can be used from Exercise A (underlined below, including synonyms).

2 Set for pairwork discussion. Remind students about words they have already studied for describing trends in graphs. Feed back with the whole class, asking one or two students to describe the trend for each graph. Make sure that students use the present simple tense to talk about the behaviour of the temperature.

Answers

Model answers:

1 All four graphs show the relationship between set temperature and actual temperature of a domestic oven over time, when the set temperature is turned up. The left and right vertical axes represent temperature and oven heater power respectively, and the horizontal axis represents time. The graphs show <u>tests</u> with ovens operated by different control systems. In the first, the oven heater is only able to switch itself on and off. In the other three situations, the oven heater output is gradable, but in each case the control system uses different correcting parameters. This affects the way that oven temperature changes over time, with varying success in terms of effective performance. Note that the different types of controller will be discussed in later lessons.

2 In the first graph the temperature is <u>unstable</u> and <u>fluctuates</u> around both set temperatures. When the oven temperature is turned up, the oven heater is switched on until the set temperature is reached. Then the oven heater turns itself off, but the stored heat in the metal means that the temperature keeps on rising well above the set temperature. When the oven cools down below the set temperature, the heater is turned on again. This is an <u>unstable</u> system because it continues to <u>fluctuate</u> widely.

The second graph shows that when a higher temperature is selected, the oven heater increases its output in such a way that there is a quick rise in temperature up to the set value. However, the temperature <u>exceeds</u> the set value <u>significantly</u> and then <u>oscillates</u> around an <u>offset</u> value. This, too, is an unstable system.

In the third graph the control system of the oven performs in a similar way to that in the second graph, and shows a <u>significant</u> <u>overshoot</u>. However,

there is a fast reaction time and the <u>offset</u> has been <u>eliminated</u>. The system is <u>damped</u> so there is no <u>unstable</u> ringing.

In the final graph, the temperature rises rapidly, but there is no <u>overshoot</u> or <u>offset</u>, and there are no <u>fluctuations</u> in value. The system has been <u>tuned</u> to make it <u>stable</u>.

Exercise C

As well as requiring the use of antonyms, this exercise checks that students have understood the graphs in Exercise B. Set for individual work and pairwork checking. Feed back with the whole class. A good way to do this is to use an OHT with blanks for the blue words (see additional resources section, Resource 6B).

Answers

Model answers:

1 Figure 2 shows the oven temperature is <u>unstable</u> at both set values.

2 In Figure 3 the reaction time is <u>quick</u>, but there is a significant overshoot and the <u>final</u> oven temperature is below the set temperature value.

3 The final temperature in Figure 3 is unstable because it is <u>underdamped</u>.

4 The unstable oscillation has been <u>eliminated</u> in Figure 4, but there is still considerable overshoot.

5 The system shown in Figure 5 is damped and stable, with a <u>quick</u> reaction time.

Exercise D

Introduce the idea of paraphrasing – or restating. Elicit from the students the main ways to do this at sentence level, namely:

- using different grammar
- using different words
- reordering the information

Write these points on the board. Also make the point very strongly that a paraphrase is not a paraphrase unless 90% of the language is different. There are some words which must remain the same, but these are very few, and are likely to be words specific to the subject, such as *temperature*. It is best to try to use all three of the above strategies, if possible.

Students should look carefully at the corrected sentences from Exercise C and then compare them with the paraphrases. The first step is to identify which sentences match. Set for individual work and pairwork checking. It may be helpful for the students if you reproduce the corrected sentences from Exercise C and the sentences in Exercise D on strips of paper so that they can move them around. Both sets of sentences are reproduced in the additional resources section (Resource 6C) to facilitate this.

Feed back with the whole class. A good way to do this is to reproduce the sentences on OHTs, with each sentence cut into a separate strip. Lay the sentences on the OHP one at a time, as you agree what is the correct match.

Once the sentences are correctly paired, ask students to locate the parts of each sentence which seem to match. They will need to look at the overall meaning of each phrase, using what they know about the subject, to make sure that the phrases are similar. Set for pairwork. Feed back with the whole group, using the OHT strips and highlighting the matching parts with coloured pens.

Answers

Model answers:

1 Figure 2 shows the oven temperature is unstable at both set values.	c Temperature stability is never achieved in this graph.
2 In Figure 3 the reaction time is quick, but there is a significant overshoot and the final oven temperature is below the set temperature value.	d In this graph the temperature changes quickly, but it initially goes above the set value and there is a significant final offset.
3 The final temperature in Figure 3 is unstable because it is underdamped.	e The system shown in this graph is underdamped and there is oscillation.
4 The unstable oscillation has been eliminated in Figure 4, but there is still considerable overshoot.	a This graph shows there is no more ringing, but initially the oven temperature exceeds the set value.
5 The system shown in Figure 5 is damped and stable, with a quick reaction time.	b In this graph there is tight loop control.

A final step is to discuss in detail the changes that have been made. Students should refer to the list of types of changes you have written on the board. Look at each paraphrase with the class and ask students what changes have been made. Be specific about the types of vocabulary or grammar changes. For example, in the first answer above, the paraphrase uses passive, changes adjective (unstable) to noun (stability), uses negative adverb of frequency (never) for the negative adjective (*un*stable), and alters all vocabulary except for *temperature*.

Exercise E

Put students in pairs to discuss the four graphs, and which represents the best situation in terms of oven temperature control. Feed back with the whole group. If you wish, you could write some descriptive sentences on the board.

Answers

Model answer:

The last graph shows the best situation for temperature control because the oven temperature rises quickly when the set temperature is changed, does not overshoot the required value and rapidly stabilizes at exactly the set value. The other situations are all problematic in some way and may result in the food being undercooked or overcooked.

Exercise F

1/2 Set for individual work. Suggest the following examples if students are stuck:

- a washing machine
- alternating current
- loudspeakers
- a pendulum clock
- an old car driving over a bumpy road

3 Set for pairwork. Go round and check what students have written, giving advice if necessary.

Sample answer for 'washing machine':

The device has internal shock-absorbers, which should mean that it doesn't oscillate significantly. However, with use, oscillations can develop and become a problem. They can be noisy, cause the device to become unstable and move around, and may result in it breaking down. The oscillations can be damped by checking that the device is on a level surface. An anti-vibration pad can be put under the device's legs. In addition, the internal screws can be tightened and the shock-absorbers checked for wear.

4 Set for individual work or for homework. Tell students to try to follow the advice for paraphrasing in Exercise D, i.e., to reorder the information and to change vocabulary and grammar as far as possible. You may wish to refer students to the *Vocabulary bank* at this point to provide a reminder for grammar structures to use.

Sample answer for 'washing machine':

There are shock-absorbers inside this device and these are designed to eliminate any problematic oscillations. Nevertheless, when it has been used for some time, oscillations may occur resulting in noise, instability of position, and ultimately cause the device to stop working. This may be due to uneven horizontal positioning, which needs to be checked. Placing the legs of the device on an anti-vibration pad can help the problem. Otherwise, the device needs to be opened and the shock-absorbers and internal screws checked.

Closure

Discussion:

1 Why are graphs useful and what kind of information can be presented in a graph?

2 Can students think of other electrical items that use a type of control similar to that shown in the graphs?

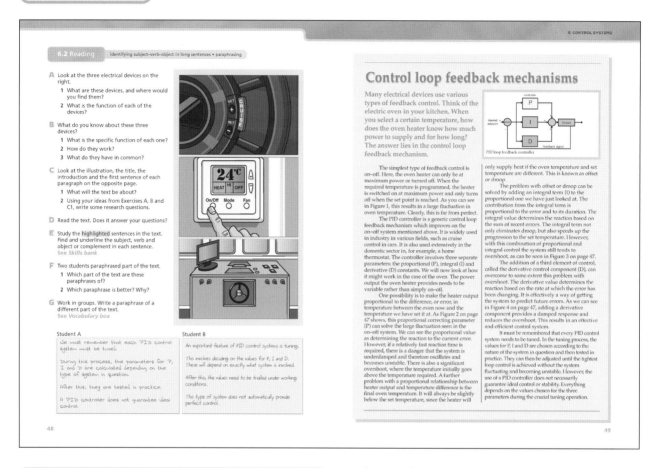

General note

Read the *Skills bank* at the end of the Course Book unit. Decide when, if at all, to refer students to it. The best time is probably after Exercise E, or at the very end of the lesson or the beginning of the next lesson, as a summary/revision.

Lesson aims

- identify the kernel SVO/C of a long sentence

Further practice in:

- research questions
- topic sentences
- paraphrasing

Introduction

Remind the class about techniques when using written texts for research. Ask:

What is it a good idea to do:

- *before reading?* (think of research questions)
- *while you are reading?* (look for topic sentences)
- *after reading?* (check answers to the research questions)

What words in a text signal the development of a topic in a new direction? (markers showing contrast such as *but, however, at the same time, on the other hand*, etc.)

If you wish, refer students to Unit 4 *Skills bank*.

Exercise A

1/2 Set for general discussion. Feed back with the whole class. Accept any reasonable answers.

Answers

Model answers:

1 Photo 1: a vehicle cruise control system

Photo 2: a home thermostat

Photo 3: a ship's automatic steering system

2 A vehicle cruise control system: to drive a vehicle at a set speed

A home thermostat: to keep the temperature of the rooms of a house stable

A ship's automatic steering system: to keep the set direction of a ship constant

Exercise B

1/2/3 Set for pairwork discussion. Feed back with the whole class. Give answers to question 1. Accept any reasonable comments for questions 2 and 3. Try to guide students so they realize that all three devices use some sort of feedback control system. However, do not go into too much detail here since the answers will come later in the unit in the reading and writing sections.

Answers

Model answers:

1 A vehicle cruise control system keeps your car's speed stable automatically, without the driver having to intervene. A home thermostat maintains the temperature of your house at a set value. A ship's automatic steering system holds the course of the ship steady and requires no human intervention once set.

Exercise C

1 Set for individual work. Elicit ideas, but do not confirm or correct.

2 Set for individual work and pairwork checking.

Exercise D

Set for individual work. Feed back with the whole class.

Exercise E

Draw a table with the headings from the Answers section on the board. If you wish, students can also draw a similar table in their notebooks. Explain that in academic writing, sentences can seem very complex. This is often not so much because the sentence structure is highly complex in itself, but because the subjects and objects/complements may consist of clauses or complex noun phrases. Often the verb is quite simple. But in order to fully understand a text, the grammar of a sentence must be understood. Subject + verb + object or complement is the basic sentence structure of English. Students need to be able to locate the subjects, main verbs and their objects or complements.

Elicit from the students the subject, main verb and object for the first sentence. Ask students for the *head word* of each subject, main verb and object (underlined in the table in the Answers section). Write them in the table on the board. Using high-speed questioning, get students to build the whole phrase that constitutes the subject/main verb/object/complement.

Example 1:

As we can see in Figure 4, <u>adding</u> a derivative component <u>provides</u> a damped <u>response</u> and <u>reduces</u> the <u>overshoot</u>.

What is this sentence about? = adding

What does adding do? = it provides and it reduces

What does it provide? = a response

What does it reduce? = the overshoot

Write these head words in the table on the board. Then elicit the remaining words and add to the table:

Adding what exactly? = a component

What sort of component? = a derivative component

Give me more information about the response = a damped response

Ask students to identify the subordinate clause in the sentence of Example 1 (*As we can see in Figure 4*). Point out that this part contains information which is extra to the main part of the sentence. The sentence can be understood quite easily without it.

Example 2:

This example shows how to deal with *is* + complement.

A further <u>problem</u> with a proportional relationship between heater output and temperature difference <u>is</u> the final <u>temperature</u>.

What is this sentence about in general? = a problem

More particularly? = a problem with a proportional relationship

A relationship between what? = between heater output and temperature difference

What's the main verb in this sentence? = is

So what is the problem? = the final temperature

The idea is that students should be able to extract something which contains the kernel even if it does not make complete sense without the full phrase.

Set the remainder of the exercise for individual work followed by pairwork checking. Finally, feed back with the whole class.

You may wish to refer students to the *Skills bank – Finding the main information*.

Answers

Model answers (on next page):

Subject	Verb	Object/complement
The PID <u>controller</u>	<u>is</u>	a generic control loop feedback <u>mechanism</u> which attempts to improve on the on–off system mentioned above.
this proportional correcting <u>term</u> (P)	<u>can solve</u>	the big <u>fluctuation</u> seen in the on–off system.
A further <u>problem</u> with a proportional relationship between heater output and temperature difference	<u>is</u>	the final <u>temperature</u>.
the <u>system</u> still	<u>tends to overshoot</u>	
The <u>addition</u> of a third element of control	<u>can overcome</u>	this <u>problem</u> with overshoot.
<u>adding</u> a derivative component	<u>provides</u> (and) <u>reduces</u>	a damped <u>response</u> the <u>overshoot</u>

Exercise F

Set for individual work and pairwork checking. Make sure that students identify the original phrases in the text first before looking at the paraphrases.

Feed back with the whole class. A good way to demonstrate how Student A's text contains too many words from the original is to use an OHT and highlight the common words in colour. (A table giving the sentences plus commentary is included in the additional resources section – Resources 6D and 6E.) Check that students are able to say which parts of the paraphrase match with the original, and which structures have been used.

Answers

1 The first part of the final paragraph (paragraph 7).

2 Student B's paraphrase is better, because it uses fewer words from the original text and uses different sentence structures.

Language note

It is important that students understand that when paraphrasing, it is not sufficient to change a word here and there and leave most of the words and the basic sentence structure unchanged. This approach is known as 'patch-writing' and is considered to be plagiarism. It is also important when paraphrasing not to change the meaning of the original – also quite hard to do.

Exercise G

Refer students to the *Vocabulary bank* at this stage. Review paraphrasing skills with the whole class before starting this exercise.

Divide the text into parts. For example, long paragraphs can be divided into two (though of course you should not use the first part of paragraph 7). Paragraph 2 could be kept as one part since it is short. Paragraph 4 is quite long so it could be divided into three parts, giving a total of thirteen different parts for this text. Give each section to different students to work on. Alternatively, you could choose one part of the text for all students to work on, for example the second part of paragraph 7. This can be done in class or, if you prefer, as individual work/homework.

If students are doing the work in class in groups or pairs, a good way to provide feedback is to get them to write their paraphrase on an OHT. Show each paraphrase (or a selection) to the class and ask for comments. Say what is good about the work. Point out where there are errors and ask for suggestions on how to improve it. Make any corrections on the OHT with a different coloured pen.

Closure

1 Divide the class into two teams. Write the seven topic sentences from the reading text on strips, or photocopy them from the additional resources section (Resource 6F). One team chooses a topic sentence and reads it aloud. The other team must give the information triggered by that topic sentence. Accept only the actual paragraph content.

2 Dictate the following to the class:

Think of an example of a device which:

… needs to be tuned regularly.

… fluctuates with the time of day.

… is heavily damped.

… fluctuates with temperature.

… doesn't need to be tested before it is switched on.

… eliminates the need for manual calculations.

… oscillates regularly.

… fluctuates with movement.

Students work in pairs to think of a device which fits the description. The first pair to find a device for each category are the winners. If students are finding it difficult, put the following answers up on the board (but in mixed-up order).

1 Diesel-engine trucks

2 A solar panel's output

3 The paper cone of a loud speaker

4 Resistance in a wire

5 A typical household appliance

6 A calculator

7 A pendulum

8 Your heart

Feed back with the whole class.

6.3 Extending skills

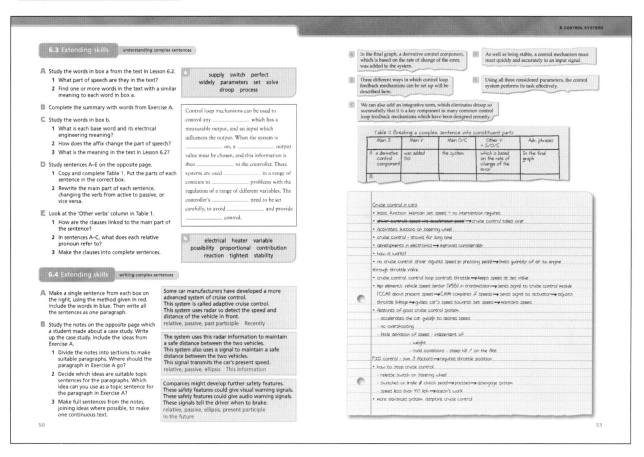

Lesson aims

- study sentence structure in more detail
- identify the main information in:

  an active sentence

  a passive sentence

  a complex sentence with participles

  a complex sentence with embedded clauses

Further practice in:

- vocabulary from Lesson 6.2

Introduction

Ask students to see how many phrases or compound nouns they can make with the word *control*. Tell students to brainstorm a list in pairs. Feed back with the whole class.

Possible answers: *control bus, control channel, control chart, control input, control instruction, control interval, control layer, control line, control memory, control problem, control rod, control scene, control structure, control surface, control system, control transformer.*

Exercise A

Ask students to study the words in the box and to find the words in the text. Set for individual work and pairwork checking. Tell students *not* to use their dictionaries to begin with but to use what they know to guess meanings and parts of speech. If necessary, they should use dictionaries when checking in pairs. Deal with any common problems with the whole class.

Answers

Model answers (paragraph numbers are given in brackets):

Word	Part of speech	Similar meaning
supply (1)	v (T)	provide (3)
switch (2)	v (T)	turn(ed) (2)
perfect (2)	adj	ideal (7)
widely (3)	adv	extensively (3)
parameters (3)	n (C)	constants (3)
set (4)	v (T) and past participle used as adjective to modify noun, e.g., 'set temperature'	programmed (2)
solve (4)	v (T)	overcome (6)
droop (4,5)	n (U)	offset (4,5)
process (7)	n (C)	operation (7)

105

Exercise B

Set for individual work and pairwork checking. Students should make use of all the words they have discussed in Exercise A (i.e., the synonyms as well as the words in the box). Feed back with the whole class.

Answers

Model answers:

Control loop mechanisms can be used to control any process/operation which has a measurable output, and an input which influences the output. When the system is switched/turned on, a set/programmed output value must be chosen, and this information is then supplied/provided to the controller. These systems are used widely/extensively in a range of contexts to solve/overcome problems with the regulation of a range of different variables. The controller's parameters/constants need to be set carefully, to avoid offset/droop and provide perfect/ideal control.

> **Language note**
>
> The use of words as synonyms often depends on the context. For example, although the base meanings of *offset* and *droop* are not exactly synonymous, they could both be used in the final sentence of the summary text with very little difference in meaning.

Exercise C

Set for pairwork. Feed back with the whole class. Note that not all the base words have specifically electrical engineering meanings. Tell students to explain the meaning in electrical engineering terms as far as possible.

Answers

Model answers (paragraph numbers are given in brackets):

Word	Base and meaning	Effect of affix	Meaning in text
electrical (1)	electron (n, C) – a particle carrying a charge	~*ical* = adjective ending	powered by electricity
heater (1)	heat 1. (v, T) – to raise the temperature (of something) 2. (n, U) – quality of being hot	~*er* = something that performs the action of the verb	electrical device providing heat
variable (3)	vary (v, T) – to change something	~*able* = adjective ending	can be varied, changeable
possibility (4)	possible (adj) – describes something that can or might happen	~*ity* = makes noun	option
proportional (3)	proportion (n, U) – the relationship of one quantity to another	~*al* = adjective ending	related by a constant ratio
contribution (5)	contribute (v, T + I) – to be one of the causes of something	~*ion* = makes noun	portion added
reaction (6)	react (v, I) – to behave in a particular way	~*ion* = makes noun	performance, behaviour
tightest (7)	tight (adj) – in a small space (of time)	~*est* = superlative form	quickest reaction time possible
stability (7)	stable (adj) – steady	~*ity* = noun ending	lack of fluctuations

Exercise D

1 Copy the table headings from the Answers section onto the board and complete the example with the students. Tell them that when they look at the 'Other verbs' column they may well find several, and should number each verb and subject/object/complement section separately. Point out that the order of each part of the sentence is not reflected in the table: the table is just a way to analyze the sentences.

Set the rest of the sentences for individual work and pairwork checking. Feed back with the whole class. Draw their attention to the 'main' parts of the sentence: it is very important in reading that they should be able to identify these. Notice also that the main parts can stand on their own and make complete sentences.

2 Set for individual work. If the clause is active it should be changed to passive, and vice versa.

Answers

Model answers:

1 See table below.

2 Possible answers:

A The engineer added a derivative control component to the system.

B I/the author will describe three (different) ways (to set up control loop feedback mechanisms).

C A(n) (integrative) term can also be added.

D An input signal must be reacted to quickly and accurately (by a control mechanism).

E The task is performed effectively (by the control system).

Exercise E

This exercise involves looking carefully at the dependent clauses in sentences A–E.

1 Say that these clauses have special ways to link them to the main part of the sentence. Do this exercise with the whole class, using an OHT of the table in Exercise D, and a highlighter pen to mark the relevant words. (A version of the table without underlining is included in the additional resources section – Resource 6G.) Go through the clauses, asking students what words or other ways are used to link the clauses to the main part of the sentence.

2 Set for individual work and pairwork checking. Students should look at each sentence and identify the antecedents of the relative pronouns. You could ask them to use a highlighter pen or to draw circles and arrows linking the words.

3 Students must be able to get the basic or kernel meaning of the clause. Take sentence A as an example and write it on the board. Point out that the relative pronouns and other ways of linking these clauses to the main clause will need to be changed or got rid of. Students should aim to write something that makes good sense as a complete sentence. They can break a sentence into shorter sentences if necessary.

Set the remaining clauses for individual work. Feed back with the whole class. Accept anything that makes good sense.

	Main subject	Main verb	Main object/complement	Other verbs + their subjects + objects/complements	Adverbial phrases
A	a derivative control component	was added (to)	the system.	which* is based on the rate of change of the error	In the final graph
B	Three different ways	will be described		in which control loop feedback mechanisms can be set up	here.
C	We	can (also) add	an integrative term	1. ... which eliminates droop so successfully 2. ... that it is a key component in many common control loop feedback mechanisms 3. ... which have been designed	recently.
D	a control mechanism	must react (to)	an input signal.	As well as being stable, ...	quickly accurately
E	the control system	performs	its task	Using all three considered parameters, ...	effectively.

*underlined text = means by which dependent clause is joined to main clause

Answers

1 See table in Exercise D above. Sentences A–C use relative clauses. D and E use participle clauses (*As well as being stable*; *Using*).

2 A *which* = the derivative control component

   B *which* = ways

   C 1. *which* = the integrative term

   2. *which* = control loop feedback mechanisms

3 Possible answers:

   A A derivative control component is based on the rate of change of the error.

   B Control loop feedback mechanisms can be set up in three different ways.

   C 1. An integrative term eliminates droop (so) successfully.

   2. An integrative term is a key component in many common control loop feedback mechanisms.

   3. Many common control loop feedback mechanisms have been designed (recently).

   D A control mechanism must (also) be stable.

   E The control system uses all three considered parameters.

Language note

A dependent clause contains a verb and a subject and is a secondary part of a sentence. It is dependent because it 'depends' on the main clause. A main clause can stand by itself as a complete sentence in its own right (usually). A dependent clause always goes with a main clause and cannot stand by itself as a sentence in its own right.

Dependent clauses are typically joined to main clauses by certain types of words: for example, relative pronouns (e.g., *who*, *which*, etc.), linking adverbials (e.g., *if*, *when*, *before*, *although*, *whereas*, etc.), words associated with reporting speech (e.g., *that*, a *Wh~* word such as *what* or *why*), and so on.

Some dependent clauses are non-finite, that is, they don't have a 'full verb' but a participle form (e.g., *having finished*, *opening*) and the subject may not be stated.

For more on this, see a good grammar reference book.

Closure

Write the following underlined beginnings and endings of words on the board or dictate them. Ask students to give the complete word. Accept alternatives and other parts of speech.

<u>elec</u>(trical)

<u>hea</u>(ter)

(vari)<u>able</u>

<u>poss</u>(ibility)

(pro)<u>portional</u>

(contri)<u>bution</u>

<u>reac</u>(tion)

<u>tigh</u>(test)

(sta)<u>bility</u>

(para)<u>meters</u>

<u>off</u>(set)

<u>swi</u>(tch)

(sup)<u>ply</u>

(pro)<u>cess</u>

6.4 Extending skills

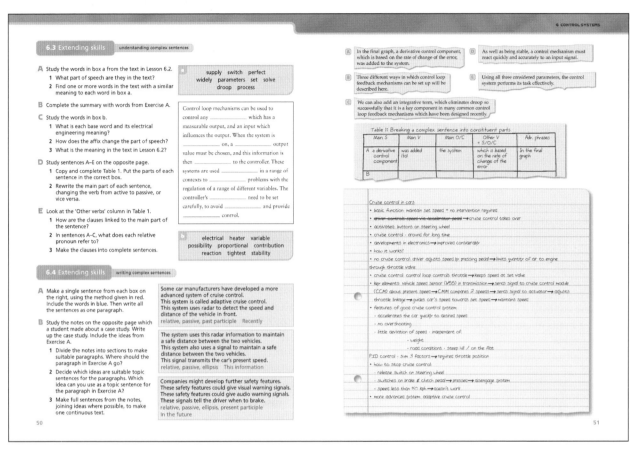

Lesson aims

- write complex sentences:
  with passives
  joining with participles
  embedding clauses
  adding prepositional phrases

Further practice in:

- writing topic sentences
- expanding a topic sentence into a paragraph

Introduction

Ask students to think about and discuss the following questions:

1 What devices use cruise control?

2 How does it work?

Exercise A

Set for individual work and pairwork checking. If necessary, do the first box with the whole class. Make sure students understand that they should write the three sentences as a continuous paragraph.

Feed back with the whole class. Accept any answers that make good sense. Point out where the phrases in blue act as linkers between the sentences to make a continuous paragraph.

Answers

Possible answer:

Recently, a more advanced system called adaptive cruise control has been developed, which uses radar to detect the speed and distance of the vehicle in front. This radar information, together with a signal that transmits the car's present speed, is used to maintain a safe distance between the two vehicles. In the future, further safety features might be developed which could give visual and audio signals, telling the driver when to brake.

Exercise B

In this exercise, students are required to use all they have practised about sentence structure as well as revise what they know about topic sentences and paragraphing.

Set for pairwork. Do not feed back after each question but allow students to work through the questions, proceeding to write up the whole text. They will need to decide where the best place will be for the paragraph in Exercise A, and should also add this to their text. Students can change the wording and add extra phrases to help the flow of the text, as long as the sense remains the same.

If possible, pairs should write their text on an OHT.

Select two or three OHTs for display and comment by the whole class. Make any corrections on the text yourself with a coloured pen. Alternatively, circulate the transparencies to other pairs to correct and comment on. These pairs then display the corrected work and explain why they have made the corrections.

Answers

Possible answers:

1/2 Paragraph divisions are given below, with the possible topic sentences underlined and in bold. Note that other answers may be possible.

- **basic function: maintain set speed = no intervention required**
- ~~driver controls speed via accelerator pedal~~ → cruise control takes over
- activated: buttons on steering wheel
- cruise control – around for long time
- developments in electronics → improved considerably

- **how it works?**
- no cruise control: driver adjusts speed by pressing pedal → limits quantity of air to engine through throttle valve
- cruise control: control loop controls throttle → keeps speed at set value

- **key elements:** vehicle speed sensor (VSS) in transmission → sends signal to cruise control module (CCM) about present speed → CMM compares 2 speeds → sends signal to actuator → adjusts throttle linkage → guides car's speed towards set speed → maintains speed

- **features of good cruise control system:**
  ○ accelerates the car quickly to desired speed
  ○ no overshooting
  ○ little deviation of speed – independent of:
    – weight
    – road conditions – steep hill / on the flat
- PID control – sum 3 factors → required throttle position

- **how to stop cruise control:**
  ○ release switch on steering wheel
  ○ switches on brake & clutch pedal → pressed → disengage system
- speed less than 40 kph → doesn't work

- **more advanced system: adaptive cruise control**
  (= controlling idea for the paragraph from Exercise A)

3 <u>The basic function of cruise control in a car is to maintain the speed that has been set by the driver, without any intervention required from him or her.</u> Instead of the driver controlling the car's speed via the accelerator pedal, cruise control takes over when buttons, usually located on the steering wheel, are activated. Cruise control has been around for a long time, but developments in electronics have meant these systems have improved considerably over the years.

<u>How exactly does the cruise control system work?</u> Normally, the driver adjusts his or her speed by changing the position of the accelerator pedal, which regulates the quantity of air that the engine takes in through the throttle valve. When cruise control is switched on, a control loop takes over the throttle and keeps the car's speed at the set value.

<u>There are several key elements in a cruise control system.</u> Firstly, there is a vehicle speed sensor (VSS), which is located in the transmission. Secondly, this sensor sends a signal to the cruise control module (CCM) with information about the car's present speed. Thirdly, the CCM compares this information with the set speed and sends a signal to the actuator, which adjusts the accelerator linkage to guide the car's speed towards the set speed and then maintain it.

<u>A good cruise control system has several features.</u> It accelerates the car quickly to the desired speed without overshooting. It then keeps that speed with little deviation, independently of weight and road conditions, such as when the car is going up a steep hill or travelling on the flat. Most systems use PID control, calculating each of the three factors and summing them to obtain the required throttle position.

<u>Cruise control can be stopped in several ways.</u> There is a release switch on the steering wheel, as well as switches mounted on the brake and clutch pedals which disengage the system when pressed. In addition, the system doesn't work at speeds of less than 40 kph.

<u>Recently, a more advanced system called adaptive cruise control has been developed, which uses radar to detect the speed and distance of the vehicle in front.</u> This radar information, together with a signal that transmits the car's present speed, is used to maintain a safe distance between the two vehicles. In the future further safety features might be developed which could give visual and audio signals, telling the driver when to brake.

Closure

Give students some very simple three- or four-word SVO/C sentences from the unit (or make some yourself) and ask them to add as many phrases and clauses as they can to make a long complex sentence. Who can make the longest sentence?

For example:

A control mechanism can create an efficient system.

→ **A control** loop feedback **mechanism**, consisting of proportional, integral and derivative parameters, that has been accurately tuned by an experienced electrical engineer **can create an efficient system** which provides tight loop control and does not overshoot, become unstable or have any offset … (42 words)

Extra activities

1 Work through the *Vocabulary bank* and *Skills bank* if you have not already done so, or as a revision of previous study.

2 Use the *Activity bank* (Teacher's Book additional resources section, Resource 6A).

   A Set the wordsearch for individual work (including homework) or pairwork.

Answers

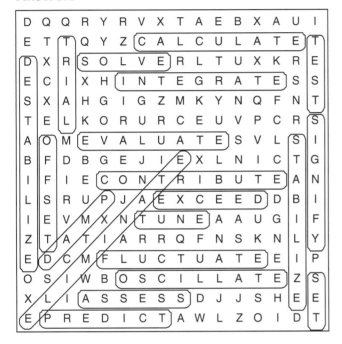

Verb	Noun
assess	assessment
calculate	calculation
contribute	contribution
damp	damping
destabilize	instability
eliminate	elimination
evaluate	evaluation
exceed	excess
fluctuate	fluctuation
integrate	integration

Verb	Noun
offset	offset
oscillate	oscillation
predict	prediction
signify	signification
solve	solution
stabilize	stability
set	setting
test	test
trial	trial
tune	tuning

Answers

B Students work in pairs or small groups and try to think of word pairs. They should be able to explain the meaning.

Alternatively, photocopy (enlarged) the words from the additional resources section (Resource 6H) and cut up into cards. Put the A and B words into separate envelopes. Put students into groups of four. Make one set of A and one set of B words for each group. Give one pair in each group the A words and the other pair the B words. Each pair takes it in turns to pick a word from their envelope. The other pair must try to find a word from their own envelope which can go with it.

Accept all reasonable word pairs.

Possible pairs are:

A	B
accelerator	pedal
brake	pedal
clutch	pedal
car	manufacturer
cruise	control
domestic	sector
electric	heater
electric	oven
electrical	devices
feedback	control
perfect	tuning
power	output
radar	detection
reaction	time
road	conditions
safe	distance
safety	features
set	value
steering	wheel
warning	signals

7 ELECTRIC POWER GENERATION, TRANSMISSION AND DISTRIBUTION

In this unit, we look at how electric power is generated in various kinds of power station, how it is transmitted across long distances, and how it is delivered to customers. Initially the focus is on the generation of electricity using wind turbines. Then the first listening extract, from a lecture, looks at a range of issues involved in the power transmission process, including energy loss, voltage choices and the role that transformers play in this. The second listening extract is from a seminar in which the distribution of electrical energy is discussed.

Skills focus

Listening
- understanding speaker emphasis

Speaking
- asking for clarification
- responding to queries and requests for clarification

Vocabulary focus
- compound nouns
- fixed phrases from electrical engineering
- fixed phrases from academic English
- common lecture language

Key vocabulary
See also the list of fixed phrases from academic English in the *Vocabulary bank* (Course Book page 60).

alternating current	generate	pylons
balancing	generation	renewable resource
blackout	grid	resistance
blade	hydroelectric power	safe
conductor	imbalance	safety
construction costs	load (n and v)	single-phase
copper	location	socket
demand (n)	neon	solar power
direct current	network (n)	sustainable
distribute	nuclear power	three-phase
distribution	offshore	transformer
efficiency	pollution	transmission
efficient	power line	transmit
energy loss	power station	turbine

7.1 Vocabulary

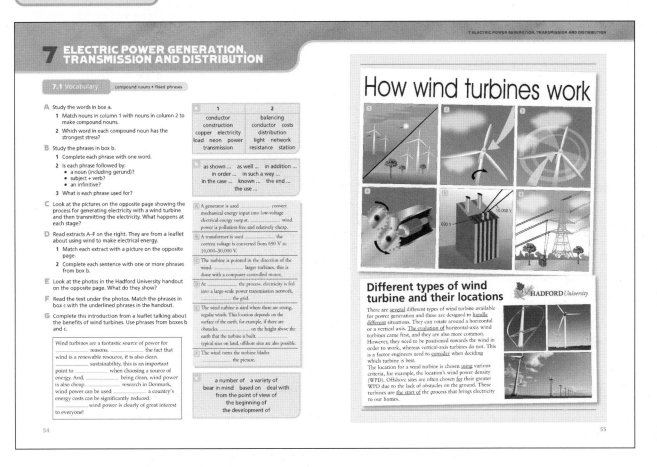

General note

Read the *Vocabulary bank* at the end of the Course Book unit. Decide when, if at all, to refer your students to it. The best time is probably at the very end of the lesson or the beginning of the next lesson, as a summary/revision.

Lesson aims

- understand and use some general academic fixed phrases
- understand and use fixed phrases and compound nouns from the discipline

Introduction

1 Revise some noun phrases (noun + noun, adjective + noun) from previous units. Give students two or three minutes to make word stars with a base word, trying to find as many possible combinations as they can (preferably without having to look at dictionaries).

For example:

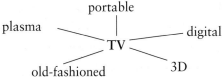

Other base words which could be used are *disc, phone, current*. If they are stuck for ideas, tell them to look back at previous units.

2 Introduce the topic of the lesson by looking at the various ways electricity is being used in the classroom where you are teaching. Discuss what students know about where the electricity comes from and how the electricity gets to the socket. What different stages in the process are they aware of?

Exercise A

Set for individual work and pairwork checking. Feed back with the whole class, making sure that the stress pattern is correct. Ask students to suggest other fixed phrases which could be made using the words in column 2.

Answers

Model answers:

conductor re'sistance
con'struction costs
copper con'ductor
electricity distri'bution
'load balancing
neon 'light
'power station
trans'mission network

Exercise B

1/2 Set for individual work and pairwork checking. Feed back with the whole class, building the first three columns of the table in the Answers section on the board.

3 Add the fourth column with the heading 'Use to …'. Give an example of the kind of thing you are looking for, i.e., a phrase which can describe why you would choose to use this fixed phrase. Elicit suggestions from the students to complete the table, supplying the information yourself if students don't know the answer. If students are not sure about the meaning of some of the phrases, give them some example sentences and tell them that you will look further at how they are used shortly. Leave the table on the board, as you will return to it.

Answers

Phrase	Followed by …		Use to …
as shown	in/by	noun/gerund	indicate a diagram or table
as well	as	noun/gerund	add information
in addition	to	noun/gerund	add information
in order	to	infinitive	give the purpose for doing something
in such a way	that*	subject + verb	give the result of doing something
in the case	of	noun/gerund	mention something
known	as	noun	give the special name for something
the end	of	noun	refer to the end of something
the use	of	noun	refer to the use of something

*as to is also possible after *in such a way*, although in this exercise, one word is required

Exercise C

Set for pairwork. Students should try to identify what each picture represents. One pair can describe each picture to the whole class. On the board, build up as many key words to describe the process as students can come up with. If students don't know some important words, tell them they will meet them shortly.

Answers

Answers depend on the students.

Exercise D

Explain that the information from the leaflet goes with the pictures they have just discussed. Each extract (A–F) goes with one picture. Students should first read the extracts, checking in the dictionary words they can't guess. They should not pay attention to the spaces at this point.

1 Set for pairwork. Feed back with the whole class. Add to the board any key words which might have been useful in Exercise C.

2 Set for individual work. Refer back to the table in Exercise B, which will help students to choose the correct phrase. Feed back with the whole class.

Answers

Model answers:

Picture	Extract
1	E The wind turbine is sited where there are strong, regular winds. This location depends on the surface of the earth, for example, if there are obstacles, as well as on the height above the earth that the turbine is built. In addition to typical sites on land, offshore sites are also possible.
2	C The turbine is pointed in the direction of the wind. In the case of larger turbines, this is done with a computer-controlled motor.
3	F The wind turns the turbine blades as shown in the picture.
4	A A generator is used in order to convert mechanical energy input into low-voltage electrical energy output. The use of wind power is pollution-free and relatively cheap.
5	B A transformer is used in such a way that the current voltage is converted from 690 V to 10,000–30,000 V.
6	D At the end of the process, electricity is fed into a large-scale power transmission network, known as the *grid*.

If you wish, ask students to return to the table in Exercise B and write one sentence for each of the fixed phrases to show their meaning. If you can put this into the context of an electrical process which students are very familiar with, such as electrolysis or making an electromagnet, so much the better.

Exercise E

Introduce the photos of the different wind turbines.

Set for pairwork discussion. Feed back with the whole group, making sure that students understand what wind turbines are and what they do. Do not correct or confirm students' views of the content at this point.

> **Subject note**
>
> In 1888 Charles F Brush built the world's first automatically operated wind turbine in Cleveland, Ohio. It was over 18 metres tall, weighed over 36 tons and had a 12kW dynamo.

Exercise F

Set for individual work and pairwork checking. Students should use their dictionaries if they are not sure of the meaning of the phrases. Note that some phrases can be used for the same thing – it is a good idea to use a different word to avoid repetition. Ask students to say which sort of wind turbine is shown in each photo.

Answers

Model answers:

There are (*several*) <u>a number of</u> different types of wind turbine available for power generation and these are designed to (*handle*) <u>deal with</u> (*different*) <u>a variety of</u> situations. They can rotate around a horizontal or a vertical axis. (*The evolution of*) <u>The development of</u> horizontal-axis wind turbines came first, and they are also more common. However, they need to be positioned towards the wind in order to work, whereas vertical-axis turbines do not. This is a factor engineers need to (*consider*) <u>bear in mind</u> when deciding which turbine is best.

The location for a wind turbine is chosen (*using*) <u>based on</u> various criteria, for example, the location's wind power density (WPD). Offshore sites are often chosen (*for*) <u>from the point of view of</u> their greater WPD due to the lack of obstacles on the ground. These turbines are (*the start of*) <u>the beginning of</u> the process that brings electricity into our homes.

> **Language note**
>
> The fixed phrases here are used in a situation which describes a series of chronological stages. However, the same words can be used when writing or talking in more general abstract academic terms, for example, when introducing an essay or lecture or piece of research. This use of these words will be covered later in the unit.

Exercise G

Set for pairwork. Feed back with the whole class.

Answers

Model answers:

Wind turbines are a fantastic source of power for <u>a number of/a variety of</u> reasons. <u>In addition to/as well as</u> the fact that wind is a renewable resource, it is clean. <u>From the point of view of</u> sustainability, this is an important point to <u>bear in mind</u> when choosing a source of energy. And, <u>in addition to/as well as</u> being clean, wind power is cheap. <u>As shown by</u> research in Denmark, wind power can be used <u>in such a way that</u> a country's energy costs can be significantly reduced. <u>The development of</u> wind power is clearly of great interest to everyone!

Closure

Tell students to cover the text and then describe:

- the typical main stages of electricity generation using wind turbines
- different types of wind turbine and their location
- some advantages of wind power

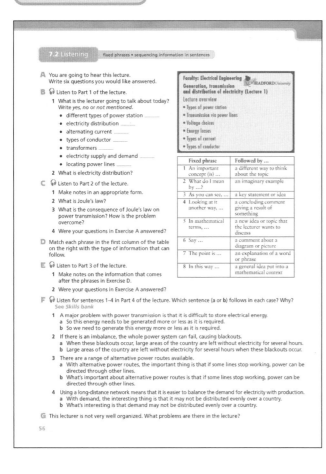

Lesson aims

- improve comprehension through recognition of fixed phrases and what follows them in terms of words/type of information
- understand how information can be sequenced in different ways within a sentence, e.g., for emphasis (see *Skills bank*)

Further practice in:

- understanding fractured text

General note

Read the *Skills bank – 'Given' and 'new' information in sentences* at the end of the Course Book unit. Decide when, if at all, to refer students to it. The best time, as before, is probably at the very end of the lesson or the beginning of the next lesson, as a summary/revision. Alternatively, use the *Skills bank* in conjunction with Exercise F.

Introduction

Review key vocabulary by writing a selection of words from Lesson 7.1 on the board and asking students to put them into phrases of two or more words.

Exercise A

Remind students about preparing for a lecture. If you wish, review Unit 1 *Skills bank – Making the most of lectures*. Remind students that, when they begin their talks, lecturers usually provide their listeners with an outline in order to aid comprehension. Elicit from the students the kinds of signpost words lecturers might use (e.g., *To start with, … , Firstly, … , I'll begin/start by …ing,* etc.). If necessary, refer students to Unit 5.

Refer students to the lecture slide. Tell them to look at the title and bullet points and to list ideas/make questions for each bullet point. At this stage do not explain any words from the slide, or allow students to check in their dictionaries, as the meanings will be dealt with in the lecture. Set the exercise for pairwork.

Feed back with the whole class: ask several students to read out their questions. Write some of the questions on the board.

🎧 Exercise B

Tell students they are going to hear the introduction to the lecture – not the whole thing. Give students time to read questions 1 and 2. Remind them they will only hear the recording once. Play Part 1. Allow students to compare their answers.

Feed back. Confirm the correct answers. Note that 'types of conductor' is mentioned on the slide, but not in the introduction, so we have no idea if this will be covered or not.

Answers

Model answers:

1

different types of power station	yes
electricity distribution	no
alternating current	yes
types of conductor	not mentioned
transformers	yes (by inference)
electricity supply and demand	yes
locating power lines	no

2 Electricity distribution is the transfer of electric energy from local substations to commercial and domestic customers, i.e., it comes after the transmission process.

Transcript 🎧 2.1

Part 1

Good morning, everyone. What I'm going to talk about today is *electric power transmission*: how electric power is carried from the power stations that generate it, to substations situated near towns and cities. This is only part of the process. What I mean is that from these substations, electricity is then distributed to individual customers in private houses, or factories and commercial buildings. This is the end of the distribution process. But this second step is known as *electricity distribution*, and is quite a different field in many ways from transmission. Plus, transmission and distribution lines are usually owned and operated by different companies. So I will deal with it later – I mean, in a future lecture.

Today, I want to look at how electricity is transmitted through high-voltage transmission networks, known as the *grid*. We will also look at a number of different types of current that can be used when transmitting electrical energy, including three-phase alternating current. Energy loss is a big problem here, so I want to show you a variety of ways that energy companies use to try to reduce this. We will then look at different sorts of generating power plants, and how supply and demand for electricity needs to be balanced. Bearing in mind that an imbalance can cause a major regional blackout, this is a very important area.

So, er … in my next lecture, we'll look at the location of power lines that make up the grid – overhead and underground. Today, however, let's start by looking at electrical transmission.

🎧 Exercise C

Refer students to the title on the lecture slide ('generation, transmission and distribution of electricity'). Ask students to suggest an appropriate type of notes. The key idea here is that we are talking about a type of *process*, which should instantly trigger the idea of a flowchart (see Unit 1).

Give students time to read the questions. Play Part 2.

Put students in pairs to compare their diagrams and discuss the questions. With the whole class, ask students how many answers to their questions in Exercise A they heard.

Build the flowchart from the Answers section on the board, at the same time checking the answers to questions 2 and 3.

Answers

Model answers:

2 Joule's law states that energy loss in a resistive conductor is proportional to the square of the current running through it and to its resistance, i.e., $P = I^2 \times R$.

3 The consequence of Joule's law is the problem of significant energy losses. To minimize these losses, electrical energy should be transmitted at high voltages when travelling long distances. This is achieved by using transformers to step up the voltage when leaving the power station, and then step down the voltage when arriving at the distribution substation and at the destination where the electricity is required.

4 Answers depend on students' questions.

Transcript 🎧 2.2

Part 2

The important thing about power transmission is the use of very high voltages. Joule's law states that energy losses in a power line are directly proportional to the square of the current passing through it. If the current is halved, the energy lost will be quartered. In other words, increasing the voltage in the line reduces the current, and this in turn reduces energy losses. So high voltages are used in order to keep losses to a minimum.

However, generating plants produce electricity at a relatively low voltage – between 3 and 30 kV. This voltage is increased using a step-up transformer to between 200 and 1200 kV for transmission over long distances to make it efficient from the point of view of costs. But we cannot use this sort of voltage in our homes, so, at substations, step-down transformers take the voltage back to a lower level for distribution. At the point of use, the electricity is transformed to an even lower voltage in such a way that it is suitable for commercial and domestic users.

117

These different steps in regulating the voltage level are the best way to keep the transmission process efficient and cheap, as well as safe.

Exercise D

Explain that these are common phrases in an academic context such as a lecture. Knowing the meaning of the phrases will help a lot with comprehension. Make sure students understand that the items in the second column are not in the correct order.

Set for individual work and pairwork checking. Tell students to check in a dictionary the meaning of any words they don't know. They should be able to guess the meanings of the phrases, even if they don't actually know the phrases.

Feed back with the whole class, completing the first two columns of the chart in the Answers section for Exercise D on the board. (Alternatively, make an OHT or other visual medium from Resource 7B in the additional resources section.) Once the 'Followed by …' column is completed, this will act as a predictive support for Part 3 of the lecture.

🎧 Exercise E

1 Tell students that in the next part of the lecture they will hear the phrases in Exercise D. They know now what *type* of information is likely to follow. Now they must try to hear what *actual* information is given. If you wish, photocopy the table in the additional resources section (Resource 7B) for students to write their answers on.

Do the first one as an example. Play the first sentence and stop after *'alternating current'*. Ask students: *What is the important concept?* (Answer: *'three-phase alternating current'*.)

Play the rest of the recording, pausing briefly at the points indicated by a // to allow students to make notes. Put students in pairs to check their answers.

Feed back with the whole class, asking questions based on the words in the 'Followed by …' column. For example:

After phrase number 2, what is the word or phrase that is explained?

After phrase number 3, what is the diagram that is commented on?

2 Refer back to students' questions in Exercise A. Discuss with the whole class whether they heard any answers to their questions.

Answers

1 Model answers (see below):

2 Answers depend on students' questions.

	Fixed phrase	Followed by …	Actual information (suggested answers)
1	An important concept (is) …	an idea or topic that the lecturer wants to discuss	three-phase alternating current
2	What do I mean by …?	an explanation of a word or phrase	there are three separate power lines running in parallel
3	As you can see, …	a comment about a diagram or picture	the AC graph
4	Looking at it another way, …	a different way to think about the topic	the characteristics of the voltage values in the graph
5	In mathematical terms, …	a general idea put into a mathematical context	each phase differs by 6⅔ ms
6	Say …	an imaginary example	electric power needs to be transmitted over very long distances
7	The point is …	a key statement or idea	transmitting direct current is cheaper for very long distances
8	In this way …	a concluding comment giving a result of something	direct current can offer an efficient alternative

Transcript 🎧 2.3

Part 3

Now, an important concept in electric power transmission is three-phase alternating current. // As you know, single-phase alternating current fluctuates. But in some situations it is useful to have a current with constant power and this is actually possible from a three-phase alternating current system. What do I mean by three-phase? Well, instead of only one power line with alternating current, there are three separate power lines running in parallel. // As you can see in the graph I'm handing out now, in each curve the current phase is shifted one-third of the cycle, so one curve is running a third of a cycle behind the second one, which is behind the third one. This is *three-phase alternating current* and it offers constant power. // Looking at it another way, if you consider the horizontal axis in the graph, we can see that the sum of the three voltages is always zero, and that the difference in voltage between any two phases oscillates as an alternating current. In mathematical terms, since a full cycle lasts 20 milliseconds in a 50 Hertz grid, each of the three phases differs by 6⅔ milliseconds.

However, three-phase alternating current is not the only option. Say, for example, electric power needs to be transmitted over very long distances. It is cheaper to use direct current than alternating current because fewer losses and lower construction costs are involved. // The point is that transmitting direct current is cheaper for very long distances – and by this I mean 600 kilometres or more – even though there are extra costs associated with converter stations at each end of the line. // In this way direct current can offer an efficient alternative when transmitting electric power over the length of a country or continent.

Subject note

The graph mentioned that shows three-phase alternating current would look like this:

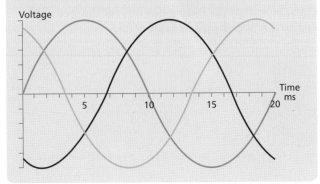

🎧 Exercise F

The purpose of this exercise is to look at how information tends to be structured in sentences. It also requires very close attention to the listening text.

Before listening, allow students time to read through the sentences. In pairs, set them to discuss which sentence (**a** or **b**) they think will follow the numbered sentences.

Play Part 4 all the way through. Students should choose sentence **a** or **b**. Put them in pairs to check and discuss why **a** or **b** was the sentence they heard.

Feed back with the whole class. Deal with sentences 1 and 2 first. Tell students that all the sentences are correct, but sentence **a** 'sounds better' when it comes after the first sentence. This is because of the way that sentences go together and the way in which information is organized in a sentence. Draw the table on the next page on the board. Show how the underlined words in the second sentence have been mentioned in the first sentence. In the second sentence, the underlined words are 'old' or 'given' information. When sentences follow each other in a conversation (or a piece of writing), usually the 'given' information comes in the first part of a sentence.

Now look at sentences 3 and 4. These are different. The normal choice would be the **a** sentences. However, here the speaker wanted to emphasize the idea of 'important' and 'different'. So a *Wh~* cleft sentence structure was used, which changes the usual order of information. Show this on the table as overleaf. This 'fronting' of information has the effect of special focus for emphasis.

Language note

In English, important information can be placed at the beginning or at the end of a sentence. There are two types of important information. The first part of the sentence contains the topic and the second part contains some kind of information or comment about the topic. Usually the comment is the more syntactically complicated part of the sentence.

Once a piece of text or a piece of conversation (i.e., a piece of discourse) has gone beyond the first sentence, a 'given'/'new' principle operates. Information which is 'given', in other words that has already been mentioned, goes at the beginning of the sentence. Normally speaking, information which is new goes at the end of the sentence. So in the second sentence of a piece of discourse, an aspect of the comment from the previous sentence may become the topic. Thus the topic of the second sentence, if it has already been mentioned in the previous sentence, is also 'given'. Of course, the given information may not be referred to with exactly the same words in the second sentence. Other ways to refer to the given information include reference words (*it, he, she, this, that, these, those,* etc.) or vocabulary items with similar meanings.

Information structure is covered in the *Skills bank* in the Course Book unit.

First sentence	Second sentence	
	Given information	New information
1 A major problem with power transmission is that it is difficult to store <u>electric energy.</u>	a So this <u>energy</u> …	… needs to be generated more or less as it is required.
2 If there is an imbalance, the whole power system can fail, causing <u>blackouts</u>.	a <u>When these blackouts occur</u> …	… large areas of the country are left without electricity for several hours.
		Given information	New information
3 There are a range of <u>alternative power routes</u> available.	normal order	a With <u>alternative power routes,</u> …	… that if some lines stop working, power can be directed through other lines.
	special focus	b What's <u>important</u> about alternative power routes is …	… that if some lines stop working, power can be directed through other lines.
4 Using a long-distance network means that it is easier to balance <u>the demand for electricity</u> with production.	normal order	a With <u>demand,</u>	… the <u>interesting</u> thing is that it may not be distributed evenly over a country.
	special focus	b What's <u>interesting</u> is …	… that demand may not be distributed evenly over a country.

Further examples of different ways to 'front' information and more practice will be given in Lesson 7.3.

Transcript 🎧 2.4

Part 4

Now … er … let's see … oh dear, I see we're running short of time … but perhaps I should say something about load balancing.

A major problem with power transmission is that it is difficult to store electric energy. So this energy needs to be generated more or less as it is required. This idea of matching supply and demand creates all sorts of problems. If there is an imbalance, the whole power system can fail, causing blackouts. When these blackouts occur, large areas of the country are left without electricity for several hours. This sort of failure can be avoided by joining electric transmission networks together in nationwide or continent-wide grids.

There are two main benefits of this sort of grid. First, there are a range of alternative power routes available. What's important about alternative routes is that if some lines stop working, power can be directed through other lines. In this way it can still arrive at the required destination. Second, using a long-distance network means that it is easier to balance the demand for electricity with production. What's interesting is that demand may not be distributed evenly over a country. Imagine one region is experiencing extremely hot weather. Demand for electricity will increase because everyone is using air-conditioning. There may not be enough electricity produced locally to satisfy this demand, so transmitting electrical energy from another part of the country will help ensure that system failure does not occur.

In this way we can see that creating wide power grids covering large areas makes a lot of sense. However, there is more to load balancing than simply moving electricity from one area of the grid to another. Demand can increase at certain times of day throughout the whole grid, and these variations of load need to be carefully planned for. This is done by using a combination of different types of electric power stations.

Now … oh dear, I was going to mention the different sorts of power station that exist and their advantages and disadvantages, but … ah … I see that time is moving on. So instead, I'm going to …

Exercise G

Set for pairwork discussion. Feed back with the whole class. Note that the lecture has not yet finished. The last part will be heard in Lesson 7.3.

Answers

Model answers:

Types of conductor were not covered in the introduction, but the topic is on the lecture slide.

The lecturer is running out of time.

The lecturer has not had time to talk about different sorts of power station and their advantages and disadvantages.

Closure

Ask students to find out the voltage and different types of plug and socket for the ten countries listed below and report back next lesson.

Australia

China

Denmark

Great Britain

India

Israel

Italy

Japan

North America

South Africa

7.3 Extending skills

Lesson aims

- extend knowledge of fixed phrases commonly used in lectures
- give sentences a special focus (see *Skills bank*)

Further practice in:

- stress within words

Introduction

As in Units 3 and 5, tell students to ask you questions about the information in the lecture in Lesson 7.2 as if you were the lecturer. Remind them about asking for information politely. If they need to revise how to do this, tell them to look back at the *Skills bank* for Unit 3.

🎧 Exercise A

Remind students of the importance of stressed syllables in words (see the teaching notes for Unit 3, Lesson 3, Exercise A). Play the recording, pausing after the first few words to check that students understand the task.

Feed back, perhaps playing the recording again for each word before checking. Ideally, mark up an OHT or other visual medium of the words. Finally, check students' pronunciation of the words.

Answers

alternating	7
conductor	10
demand	8
distribution	3
energy	11
generation	2
imbalance	9
network	5
power	12
pylons	4
station	6
transmission	1

Transcript 🎧 2.5

1. trans'mission
2. gener'ation
3. distri'bution
4. 'pylons
5. 'network
6. 'station
7. 'alternating
8. de'mand
9. im'balance
10. con'ductor
11. 'energy
12. 'power

🎧 Exercise B

Write these words on the board and ask students to say what symbols you can use for them when taking notes. Put the symbols on the board.

invented, leads to*	→
or	/
is, means, equals	=
increase	⇑
decrease	⇓
therefore, so	∴
and	&
a list	numbers or bullet points
for example	e.g.
depend on (each other)	⇔

*the arrow has a wide range of possible meanings, including *made, produced, did, causes, results in*, etc.

122

Tell students they will hear the final part of the lecture. Ask them to read the notes through. Remind them also to listen for their research task. Play Part 5.

Put students in pairs to compare their symbols. Feed back with the whole class, if possible using an OHT or other visual medium of the notes. Discuss acceptable alternatives, e.g., *step up & down* instead of *step up / down*.

Answers

Model answers:

1

   1   Transmitting energy $\rightarrow$ some energy loss

        Transformer $\rightarrow$ step up / down $=$ reduce loss

        ⇑ voltage $=$ ⇓ current $=$ ⇓ loss

        ∴ long distances $=$ high voltage

        & high voltage $\rightarrow$ thinner conductors $=$ cheaper

        BUT:

        • Too thin $\rightarrow$ weak $=$ extra costs, e.g., supports / pylons

        • Too high voltage $\rightarrow$ not safe

        Transformer $=$ 2 coils & core

        1st winding $\rightarrow$ magnetic flux in core $\rightarrow$ different voltage in 2nd winding

        2nd voltage ⇔ no of turns in winding

  2 They must research the distribution of electricity to customers.

Transcript 🎧 2.6

Part 5

The fact of the matter is, transmitting electricity always involves some sort of energy loss due to resistance. I'm going to finish with some comments about voltage-regulating transformers – in other words, how the voltage in power lines is stepped up and stepped down during the transmission process in order to reduce losses. As we have seen, for a given amount of power, it's raising the voltage that reduces current and resistive losses. This is why long-distance transmission uses high voltages – not to mention the fact that high voltages also mean that thinner copper conductors can be used, which reduces costs.

However, there is a limit to how high the voltage can be made, and how thin the conductors can be. The reason for this is that there are physical limits and financial considerations. Let's take overhead power lines as an example. If the conductor is made too thin, it has difficulty supporting itself on a purely mechanical level. So extra supports, or pylons, are needed, as well as more pole insulators,

maintenance, et cetera. It's all these extra costs that make the transmission of electricity much more expensive. Plus there's the fact that higher voltages have consequences in terms of safety – so this is another important limitation.

You've probably heard of how transformers work to regulate voltage, with two coils turned around a ferromagnetic core? Please take another look at the diagram I gave out earlier in the lecture. The varying current in the primary winding creates a varying magnetic flux in the core, and this in turn creates a varying magnetic field, which induces a voltage in the secondary winding. And this second voltage depends on the number of turns in the winding. It's these basic principles that all transformers follow. But, in practice, they are very flexible electrical devices. Let me put it another way. Transformers can range from tiny items found in small electrical devices such as microphones, to huge, incredibly heavy units used to interconnect sections of a continental power grid. Their use in transmission substations is what interests us today – for stepping up and stepping down the voltage of power lines as they cross the country.

Oh, I almost forgot to mention your research topics. OK, well, what comes after the transmission process is distribution of electricity to customers. So I'd like you to find out how this takes place and what are the main features of electricity distribution.

Exercise C

Set for pairwork. Feed back with the whole class. If necessary, play the relevant sections again. Ask for other phrases which have similar meanings, particularly from Lesson 7.3, and also from Unit 5. Build the table in the Answers section on the board. Accept any suitable words or phrases with similar meanings.

Answers

Model answers:
See table on next page.

Language note

The phrases in the table on the next page are appropriate in speaking. Many are not suitable for written language, for which different phrases which should be used.

Exercise D

Students need to decide which word(s) should receive the particular focus and then try to rewrite the sentences. Depending on the class, they can work in pairs or individually first.

Use	Fixed phrase	Other phrases
to introduce a new topic	You've probably heard of …	Now, an important concept is …
to emphasize a major point	The fact of the matter is, …	Actually, … In fact, … The point is that …
to add points	Not to mention the fact that … Plus there's the fact that …	also, and, too, as well
to finish a list	et cetera	and so on
to give an example	Let's take …	For example, … e.g., … Let's look at an example of this. For instance, …
to restate	Let me put it another way. In other words, …	What I mean is … That is to say, … By that I mean … To put it another way, …

Feed back with the whole class. Take each sentence in turn. Ask for suggestions as to which aspect could receive special emphasis (actual words are underlined below). Accept any reasonable answers. If you wish, replay Part 5 of the lecture for students to check their answers. Note that:

- sentences 1, 3 and 4 use an *It* construction to give the special focus
- sentence 2 introduces a new, general word (often found in academic contexts) followed by *is* plus a *that* clause
- sentence 5 uses a *Wh~* cleft sentence already seen in Lesson 7.2

Answers

Model answers:

1 <u>Raising the voltage</u> reduces current and resistive losses. (*It*)

  It's raising the voltage that reduces current and resistive losses.

2 The voltage value is <u>difficult to set</u> because there are <u>physical limits and financial considerations</u>. (*Two sentences. First = 'It'; Second = 'The reason'*)

  It's difficult to set the voltage value. The reason for this is that there are physical limits and financial considerations.

3 The transmission of electricity is much more expensive because of <u>all these extra costs</u>. (*It*)

  It's all these extra costs that make the transmission of electricity much more expensive.

4 All transformers follow <u>these basic principles</u>. (*It*)

  It's these basic principles that all transformers follow.

5 The distribution of electricity to customers <u>comes after</u> the transmission process. (*What*)

  What comes after the transmission process is the distribution of electricity.

After completing Exercises C and D, students can be referred to the *Vocabulary bank* and the *Skills bank* for consolidation and preparation for Exercise E.

Exercise E

Set the initial preparation for individual work. Students can refer to their notes in Lesson 7.2 (Exercises C and E) or the notes for completion in Lesson 7.3 (Exercise B). They should think about how they can use the phrases they have looked at, and ways of giving special focus/emphasis. (Note: They should not write out exactly what they are going to say in complete sentences and then read!)

Put students in pairs to give their oral summaries to each other, preferably pairing students who have chosen different sections to summarize.

Go around the class noting any problems or especially good examples of language use. You may wish to choose one or two individuals to give their summary to the whole class.

With the whole class, feed back any language or other difficulties which you noticed.

Exercise F

1 Set for pairwork. Review the advantages of wind power mentioned in the leaflet in Lesson 7.1: it's renewable, clean and cheap. Students should first try to think of other advantages, and then any disadvantages, making two lists. They should then decide the order of priority of the points in the lists.

2 Put the pairs in groups of four to present their points to each other.

  This activity links to the seminar activity in Lesson 7.4 (E and F), where the students analyze the advantages and disadvantages of other types of power station.

Closure

Dictate some words for which students have learnt note-taking symbols or abbreviations, such as *and, minus, approximately, less than, results in, therefore, because, etc., as, since, for example*. Students should write the symbol or abbreviation.

Remind them of the list of symbols and abbreviations at the back of the Course Book.

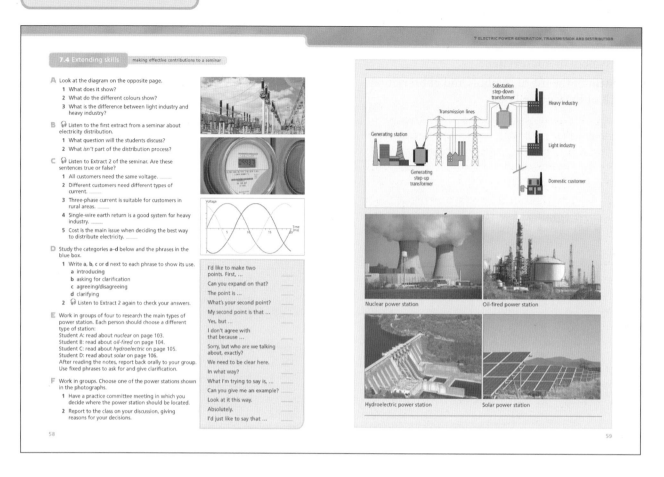

7.4 Extending skills · making effective contributions to a seminar

A Look at the diagram on the opposite page.
1 What does it show?
2 What do the different colours show?
3 What is the difference between light industry and heavy industry?

B Listen to the first extract from a seminar about electricity distribution.
1 What question will the students discuss?
2 What *isn't* part of the distribution process?

C Listen to Extract 2 of the seminar. Are these sentences true or false?
1 All customers need the same voltage. ___
2 Different customers need different types of current. ___
3 Three-phase current is suitable for customers in rural areas. ___
4 Single-wire earth return is a good system for heavy industry. ___
5 Cost is the main issue when deciding the best way to distribute electricity. ___

D Study the categories a–d below and the phrases in the blue box.
1 Write a, b, c or d next to each phrase to show its use.
a introducing
b asking for clarification
c agreeing/disagreeing
d clarifying
2 Listen to Extract 2 again to check your answers.

E Work in groups of four to research the main types of power station. Each person should choose a different type of station:
Student A: read about *nuclear* on page 103.
Student B: read about *oil-fired* on page 104.
Student C: read about *hydroelectric* on page 105.
Student D: read about *solar* on page 106.
After reading the notes, report back orally to your group. Use fixed phrases to ask for and give clarification.

F Work in groups. Choose one of the power stations shown in the photographs.
1 Have a practice committee meeting in which you decide where the power station should be located.
2 Report to the class on your discussion, giving reasons for your decisions.

I'd like to make two points. First, ... ___
Can you expand on that? ___
The point is ... ___
What's your second point? ___
My second point is that ... ___
Yes, but ... ___
I don't agree with that because ... ___
Sorry, but who are we talking about, exactly? ___
We need to be clear here. ___
In what way? ___
What I'm trying to say is, ... ___
Can you give me an example? ___
Look at it this way. ___
Absolutely. ___
I'd just like to say that ... ___

Nuclear power station
Oil-fired power station
Hydroelectric power station
Solar power station

58   59

Lesson aims

- make effective contributions to a seminar:

  using pre-organizers – *I'd like to make two points; I don't agree with that because ...*

  responding to queries by clarifying – *What I'm trying to say is ... Look at it this way ...*

Introduction

Revise phrases from the previous lessons. Give a word or phrase and ask students to give one with a similar meaning. Ask for phrases from the previous lesson which can be used to:

- introduce a new topic
- emphasize a major point
- add a point
- finish a list
- give an example

Exercise A

Set for pairwork discussion. Feed back.

Answers

Possible answers:

1/2 It shows the generation (black) of electricity at a power station, and the transmission (blue) and distribution (green) of electricity to customers.

3 Light industry is a manufacturing activity producing small- to medium-sized goods, e.g., furniture, for customers and is often situated near residential areas. Heavy industry, usually situated outside residential areas, involves the production of large-scale products, e.g., ship building.

Exercise B

Allow students time to read the two questions. Play Part 1 once only. Check answers in pairs. Feed back with the whole class.

Answers

Model answers:

1 Who are the different customers in the electrical distribution process and what are their electricity requirements?

2 Transmission up to the substation with its step-down transformer is not part of the distribution process. Also the wiring inside the house, from the electricity meter to the sockets, is not part of the distribution process.

Transcript 🎧 2.7

Extract 1

Now, as we know, the distribution of electricity comes after the electric power has been transmitted to the substations and the voltage reduced using step-down transformers. Distribution involves supplying electricity to all the different customers who need it – and that includes you and me at home as well as here at university. However, don't forget, we are not talking about the retail of electricity – in other words, how it is sold. So the distribution process stops at the electricity meter. Once a customer is connected, the measurement and pricing of electricity is another matter entirely. Now … what sorts of customer are there and what sorts of electricity do they need? Let's have some ideas.

🎧 Exercise C

Allow students time to read the questions. Play Extract 2 straight through once while they mark the answers true or false. Check in pairs and/or with the whole class. Check any unknown vocabulary, such as *printing press*.

Answers

1	false	Factories need high voltage compared to residential customers.
2	true	
3	false	Three-phase alternating current is necessary for factories with heavy machinery.
4	false	Single-wire earth return is good for rural areas.
5	false	Cost is one of two key factors to consider; the other is safety.

Transcript 🎧 2.8

Extract 2

(Note: the underlining relates to Exercise D)

JACK: Well. <u>I'd like to make two points. First,</u> different customers need electricity at different voltages.

LEILA: <u>Can you expand on that</u>, Jack?

JACK: Sure, Leila. Factories and heavy industries need around 50 kV.

LEILA: So?

JACK: So <u>the point is</u> that that's very different from the sort of voltage we need in our homes – that's around 240 V.

LECTURER: OK. So, <u>what's your second point</u>, Jack?

JACK: I was coming to that! <u>My second point is that</u> different customers need different kinds of current.

LEILA: <u>Yes, but</u> that's not important. They can all use the same alternating current if necessary.

MAJED: Well, <u>I don't agree with that</u>, Leila, <u>because</u> from what I've read, some customers need a three-phase service – which is how electricity is transmitted over the grid.

EVIE: <u>Sorry, but who are we talking about, exactly?</u> What sorts of customers are these?

LEILA: Yes, <u>we need to be clear here.</u> We certainly don't need three-phase alternating current in our homes. That would be ridiculous!

EVIE: <u>In what way?</u>

LEILA: Well, you only need three-phase current if you've got heavy equipment.

EVIE: I don't get that. Some people have big equipment in their homes too.

LEILA: <u>What I'm trying to say is,</u> only factories with big machinery need three-phase current. For the other customers, single-phase is enough.

EVIE: I still don't understand. <u>Can you give me an example,</u> Leila?

LEILA: OK. <u>Look at it this way.</u> A printing press is a really big piece of machinery. It needs three-phase alternating current at 50 kV. But light industry and residential customers don't need so much electrical power. Single-phase is enough for them.

MAJED: Yes, and single-phase is much cheaper to deliver. So it's much more suitable.

LECTURER: <u>Absolutely.</u> Cost and safety are the key factors when deciding what is the best way to distribute electricity.

MAJED: Yes, and <u>I'd just like to say that</u> I've read about a system called *single-wire earth return* – that's S-W-E-R for short – and this can be used for rural distribution. It's really cheap to set up so makes sense when there are only a few customers spread over a wide area.

🎧 Exercise D

Check the meaning of 'introducing' phrases. This means a phrase to use before your main statement to announce that you are going to say something. It may also signal how much you are going to say, or how important you think what you are going to say is.

1 Set for individual work and pairwork checking. Feed back.

2 Play Part 2 from Exercise C. Ask students to tell you to stop when they hear each phrase (underlined in the transcript above). Check what kind of phrase they think it is. Get students to repeat the phrase to copy the intonation.

If you wish, ask students to suggest other phrases that could be used in the same way.

Answers

Model answers:

I'd like to make two points. First, …	a
Can you expand on that?	b
The point is …	d
What's your second point?	b
My second point is that …	a
Yes, but …	c
I don't agree with that because …	c
Sorry, but what are we talking about, exactly?	b
We need to be clear here	d
In what way?	b
What I'm trying to say is, …	d
Can you give me an example?	b
Look at it this way.	d
Absolutely!	c
I'd just like to say that …	a

Exercise E

With the whole class, revise asking for information. Remind students of the questions used by the lecturer in Unit 5, Lesson 3 (see Unit 5 *Skills bank*). Remind students also about reporting information to people (see Unit 3 *Skills bank*).

Set students to work in groups of four. Each student should choose one type of power station and turn to the relevant page to make notes on the information. When everyone is ready, they should feed back to their group, giving an oral report on the information. It's important that they do not simply read aloud the information, but use it to inform their speaking.

Alternatively, the research activity can be done as a 'wall dictation' as follows. Use Resource 7C in the additional resources section. Make large A3 (or A4)

size copies of the information about power stations (one type of station per page) and pin the sheets on the classroom walls. Each student should leave his/her seat and go to the wall to find the information he/she needs. Students should not write anything down; instead they should read and try to remember the information. Then they return to their group and tell them the information. If they forget something, they can go back to the wall to have another look.

Circulate, encouraging students to ask for clarification and to use the appropriate phrases when giving clarification. Note where students are having difficulty with language and where things are going well. When everyone has finished, feed back to the class on points you have noticed while listening in on the discussions.

Exercise F

Move on from Exercise E to this simulation. Encourage students to make this as realistic as possible by encouraging them to get into their roles in the committee. This might work better if you get them to imagine that they are making decisions for their country or local area, if this is appropriate.

Alternatively, you could have a 'pyramid discussion'. Choose one location for the whole class to debate and put students in pairs to discuss whether it is a good choice for their area or country. After a short while, the pair should join together with another pair. This group of four should then come to an agreement. The group of four should then join another group of four. One or two people from each group of eight should then present the decision and the reasons for the decision to the class. It will help their presentation if they use visual aids such as charts or diagrams. Finally, the whole class should try to reach agreement on which location should be chosen, taking a vote if necessary.

Remind students about agreeing and disagreeing, and about good and bad ways to contribute to seminar discussions (refer to Unit 5 if necessary).

While the representatives are presenting their group decisions, you should occasionally interrupt with a wrong interpretation so that students are forced to clarify their statements. Or you could ask for clarification.

Closure

Discuss other sources of electric power, such as wave, tidal, geothermal (e.g., from geysers), biofuel (e.g., ethanol fuel from sugarcane). Ask students to *describe* and *evaluate* the characteristics of each source according to the following:

- location
- logistics
- cost
- environment
- sustainability
- set-up
- maintenance
- pollution
- safety

Extra activities

1 Work through the *Vocabulary bank* and *Skills bank* if you have not already done so, or as a revision of previous study.

2 Use the *Activity bank* (Teacher's Book additional resources section, Resources 7A).

   A Set the crossword for individual work (including homework) or pairwork.

Answers

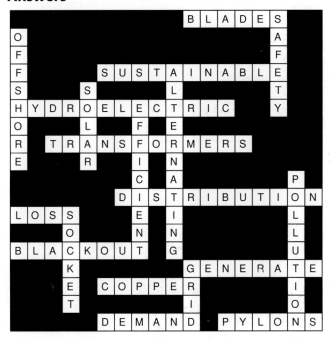

   B Make some statements about what you're going to do after the class and ask students to transform them into *Wh~* cleft sentences. For example:

   I'm going to have a coffee after the class.

   → *What you're going to do after the class is have a coffee.*

   I might go to a film tonight.

   → *What you might do tonight is go to a film.*

   Put students in pairs to practise.

8 TELECOMMUNICATIONS

This unit covers the topic of telecommunication. First the history of telecommunication is looked at briefly, focusing on the main inventions and developments. Then the processes involved in telecommunication are analyzed in more detail: key stages, elements and related devices. Examples of the main applications of telecommunication are given, including radio broadcasting and the mobile phone. Finally, the influence that telecommunication has had on the world is considered.

Skills focus

Reading
- understanding dependent clauses with passives

Writing
- paraphrasing
- expanding notes into complex sentences
- recognizing different writing types/structures:
  - outline/research report
  - description of an object
  - description of cause and effect
  - description of a process
- planning written assignments
- composing written assignments

Vocabulary focus

- synonyms
- nouns from verbs
- definitions
- common 'direction' verbs in written assignment titles (*compare, describe*, etc.)

Key vocabulary

adopt	fixed-line phone	radio
amplitude modulation	frequency modulation	receiver
application	impact (n)	shield (n and v)
breakthrough	information	signal (n)
broadcast (n and v)	isolate	smoke signals
carrier wave	line (n)	SMS text message
characteristic	medium	supply (n and v)
coaxial cable	message	surround (v)
communicate	mobile phone	telegraph
convert (v)	modulation	transcribe
demonstrate	network (n and v)	transfer (n and v)
deterioration	operate	transform
development	physical channel	transmit
device	point-to-point	transmitter
duplex (adj)	process (n and v)	wave (n)
element	provide	website
fibre-optic cable	purpose	wireless (adj)

8.1 Vocabulary

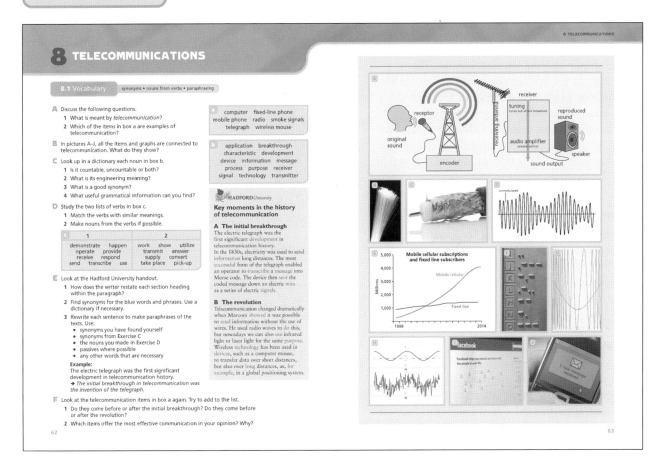

Lesson aims

- extend knowledge of synonyms and word sets (enables paraphrasing at word level)
- make nouns and noun phrases from verbs (enables paraphrasing at sentence level)

Further practice in paraphrasing at sentence level with:

- passives
- synonymous phrases
- negatives
- replacement subjects

Introduction

Revise ways of paraphrasing sentences. Write the following sentences from Unit 6 on the board and ask students to say what changes have been made in the paraphrased sentences.

Original sentence: *The unstable oscillation has been eliminated.*

Paraphrase: *There is no more ringing.*

(answer: passive to active, use of synonyms, replacement subject)

Original sentence: *The oven temperature is unstable.*

Paraphrase: *Temperature stability is not achieved in the oven.*

(answer: active to passive, adjective to noun, positive to negative)

Exercise A

Set for pairwork or class discussion. Accept any reasonable answers.

131

Answers

Possible answers:

1 Telecommunication concerns the transmission of messages over long distances.

2 All are examples of telecommunication, except for the computer and the wireless mouse. The computer, in itself, does not communicate with anyone else. However, if it has an Internet connection, then it does become part of a telecommunication system. Although a wireless mouse sends data to a computer, it is not over a long distance and so is not usually considered an item of telecommunication.

Exercise B

Set for pairwork discussion. Feed back with the whole class. Give answers but do not go into detail about exactly what they are, or the role they play in telecommunication. This will be dealt with in the reading text in Lesson 8.2.

Answers

Possible answers:

A the process of radio broadcasting: original sound is captured by a receptor and then encoded and transmitted between two antennae. The receiver tunes and amplifies the signal and reproduces it through a speaker.

B fibre-optic cables: a multi-fibre cable with a plastic cover.

C a coaxial cable: the central copper core is surrounded by a dielectric insulator, a metallic shield and mesh, and a plastic jacket for outside insulation.

D amplitude modulation of a radio wave: there is a varied strength of the transmitted signal – the amplitude is varied but the frequency remains constant.

E graph of mobile phone and fixed-line subscribers: the number of mobile phone users has increased rapidly and overtaken the number of fixed-phone lines subscribers.

F the Morse code alphabet: each letter and number is made up of a series of long or short signals

G frequency modulation of a radio wave: the amplitude of the signal is constant, but the frequency varies.

H deterioration of an analogue signal due to noise: the theoretical perfect resolution of the analogue signal is subject to distortion. Unwanted random addition (noise) has degraded the signal resolution.

I social networking sites: Facebook and Twitter have exploded in popularity over the last decade.

J text messaging: it is estimated that more than 20 billion SMS messages are sent every day.

Exercise C

Set for pairwork. You may wish to divide the work up between different pairs. For question 4 (useful grammatical information), tell students to look out for words that can have the same form when used as a noun or verb, nouns that can be only singular or only plural, nouns that change their meaning when used as U or C, etc.

Feed back, building up the table in the Answers section on the board.

Note: Exact synonyms can be difficult to find for some technical terms, e.g., see *technology* in the table below.

Answers

Model answers:
See table on next page.

Exercise D

Set for individual work and pairwork checking. Make sure students understand that they should find a verb in column 2 with a similar meaning to one of the verbs in column 1.

Feed back with the whole class, discussing the extent to which the verbs are exact synonyms, and if not, identifying any differences in meaning.

Answers

Model answers:

Verb	Noun	Verb	Noun
demonstrate	demonstration	show	
happen		take place	
operate	operation	work	
provide	provision	supply	supply
receive		pick up	
respond	response	answer	answer
send		transmit	transmission
transcribe	transcription	convert	conversion
use	use, usage	utilize	utilization

Exercise E

This is an exercise in paraphrasing based on word- and sentence-level techniques. As well as finding their own synonyms from memory and using the synonyms already discussed in Exercises C and D, students will use noun phrases in place of verb phrases as a technique in paraphrasing. Students should also make passive sentences wherever they can.

1 Set for individual work. Feed back with the whole class.

2 Set for individual work and pairwork checking.

3 Set for pairwork; pairs then check with other pairs. Alternatively, tell some students to write their answers on an OHT or other visual medium for discussion by the whole class.

Word	C/U	Meaning in electrical engineering	Synonym	Useful grammatical information
application	C	1. a specific use to which something (e.g., a theory, computer program, etc.) is put 2. in computing, a computer program with a user interface	service, use (in computing and plural: software)	with preposition: *application of* (a rule)/ *application to* (a situation)
breakthrough	C	a major achievement or success in technology that permits further progress	discovery, invention, step forward	common phrase: *a major/significant breakthrough*
characteristic	C	the qualities or features of something that belong to it, making it recognizable	attribute, feature, property	usually plural: *the characteristics of fibre-optic cables*
development	C/U	1. a significant event or change in a process [C] 2. the process of making a design better or more advanced [U]	change, event progress, evolution	C or U depends on use: C = *significant developments have been made …* U = *the development of telecommunication …*
device	C	an object invented for a particular function, often for measuring or recording information in some form	item, object, appliance, machine	
information	U	1. a collection of data or facts 2. in computing, data that is processed, stored or transmitted	facts, figures, news	uncountable, i.e., *how much information …?*; *a lot of information.* Can be found as countable in fixed expressions, e.g., *a piece of information,* (where *a piece of* quantifies the uncountable noun)
message	C	a set of transmitted data, usually communicated over some sort of network	communication [C]	
process	C	1. a series of operations, bringing about a result 2. in computing, a computer program or an instance of a program running concurrently with other programs	procedure, development	
purpose	C	The reason for which something is done or made	function, task, object, aim	
receiver	C/U	a device, such as a part of a radio, television set or telephone, that receives incoming signals and converts them to perceptible forms, such as sound or light	detection, device	
signal	C	an impulse or a varying electric quantity, such as voltage, current or electric field strength, representing coded information	impulse, data	
technology	C/U	scientific knowledge used in a practical way to create methods, devices and systems	(the application of) scientific knowledge and know-how, theory, methods	C or U depends on use: C = *cheaper technologies need to be developed* U = *a lot of recent technology uses the computer*
transmitter	C	an electronic device that generates and amplifies a carrier wave, modulates it with a meaningful signal derived from speech or other sources, and radiates the resulting signal from an antenna	sender, broadcaster	

Answers

Model answers:

1 A The initial breakthrough = the first significant development

B The revolution = (telecommunications) dramatically changed

2 Possible synonyms (including synonyms from Exercises C and D):

A The initial breakthrough

The electric telegraph was the first significant (*development*) <u>event</u> in telecommunication history. In the 1830s, electricity was used to send (*information*) <u>news</u> long distances. The most (*successful*) <u>effective</u> form of the telegraph enabled an operator to (*transcribe*) <u>convert</u> a (*message*) <u>communication</u> into Morse code. The device then (*sent*) <u>transmitted</u> the coded message down an electric (*wire*) <u>conducting cable</u> as a series of electric (*signals*) <u>impulses</u>.

B The revolution

Telecommunication changed dramatically when Marconi (*showed*) <u>demonstrated</u> it was possible to (*send*) <u>transmit</u> information without the use of wires. He used radio waves to (*do*) <u>achieve</u> this, but nowadays we can also (*use*) <u>utilize</u> infrared light and laser light for the same (*purpose*) <u>function</u>. Wireless (*technology*) <u>methods</u> has been used in (*devices*) <u>items</u>, such as a computer mouse, to transfer data over short distances, but also over (*long*) <u>considerable</u> distances, as, (*for example*) <u>for instance</u>, in a global positioning system.

3 Possible paraphrases:

A The initial breakthrough

The initial breakthrough in telecommunication was the invention of the telegraph.

It was during the first half of the 19th century that data could be transmitted far away using electricity.

In the most effective telegraph, a communication was converted into Morse code.

The transcribed data was transformed into long and short electrical impulses which were then transmitted along a length of conducting cable.

B The revolution

The wireless revolution in telecommunication took place when it was discovered that a conducting cable was not necessary to communicate data.

In Marconi's experiments, a communication was carried over radio waves; however, other means, such as infrared light and laser light, can be utilized today.

An example of an electrical item based on wireless theory is a remote mouse, which can send data just a few metres. Global positioning systems, on the other hand, can send data many hundreds of kilometres.

Exercise F

Set for pair or small group discussion. Feed back with the whole class. Accept any reasonable suggestions.

Answers

Possible answers:

Other examples of telecommunication devices that can be added are: TV, Internet, two-way radio, drum beats, semaphore towers and global positioning systems.

1 Before the breakthrough: smoke signals, drum beats, semaphore towers.

Between the breakthrough and the revolution: telegraph, first fixed-line phones.

After the revolution: later models of fixed-line phones and the remainder of the devices.

2 Accept any reasonable opinions here.

Closure

Organize students to work in pairs or small groups to put the devices in order of importance – first, for them personally, and second, for society as a whole. Then ask students to present their views.

8.2 Reading

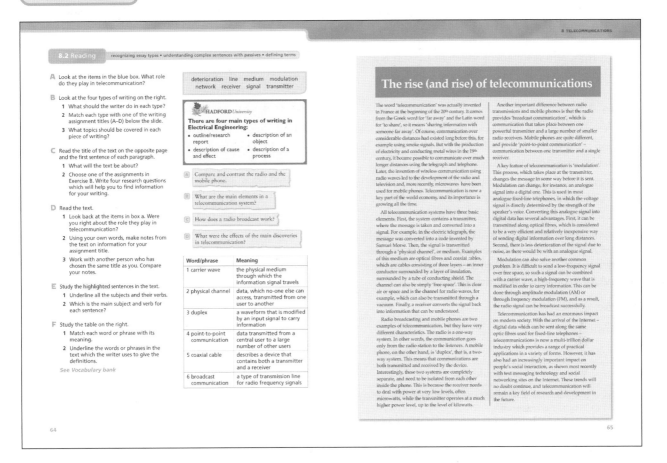

General note

Read the *Vocabulary bank* and *Skills bank* at the end of the Course Book unit. Decide when, if at all, to refer students to them. The *Vocabulary bank* section *Understanding new words: using definitions* is relevant to Lesson 8.2; the *Skills bank* will be more relevant to Lessons 3 and 4.

Lesson aims

- understand different types of writing
- interpret writing assignment titles
- find the main information in a passive clause
- understand internal definitions (see *Vocabulary bank*)

Further practice in:

- reading research
- finding the kernel of a long sentence

Introduction

With the whole class, discuss how to use written texts as sources of information when composing an answer for a writing assignment. Ask students:

1 *How can you choose useful sources?* (to get an idea of whether a text might be useful, survey the text, i.e., look at the title, look at the beginning and the end and the first line of each paragraph; in other words, skim-read to get an approximate idea of the text contents)

2 *If you decide that a text is going to be useful, what is it a good idea to do …*

- *… before reading?* (think of questions related to the writing assignment, to which you would like to find some answers)

- *… while reading?* (identify useful parts of the text; make notes **in your own words**)

- *… after reading?* (check answers to the questions)

Exercise A

Set the question for pairwork discussion with whole class feedback. Record responses from the class, e.g., on the board, but do not confirm or correct at this stage as answers are contained in the reading text later on in this lesson, and feedback is given in Lesson 8.2 Exercise D.

Exercise B

1 Refer students to the lecture slide. Discuss this question with the whole class. Build up the table in the Answers section on the board.

2 Set for pairwork. Feed back with the whole class. Ask the class to say which are the key words in each title that tell you what type of writing it is.

3 Set for pairwork. Feed back using the second table in the Answers section, discussing with the whole class what topics will need to be included in each essay. Add the notes in the third column.

Answers

Possible answers:

1

	What the writer should do
Outline/research report	• understand the purpose for doing this outline/research • list briefly the most important points of something • select according to length constraints • order for clear presentation
Description of an object (involves compare and contrast)	• according to the purpose, give a clear, detailed explanation so that it can be recognized and/or drawn • start with a central feature and relate everything to it • do by straight description or by comparing to a standard or familiar object • then use these aspects as the basis for paragraphing
Description of cause and effect	• according to the purpose, list the important causes and effects • give reasons • emphasize the causes, the effects or both • look behind the surface structure at the how and why, not just what/who/when
Description of a process	• according to the purpose, give a clear, detailed description of the steps of the process • give a reason for each step • state the outcome of each step, where applicable • explain each component as and when it enters the process

Key words are underlined:

Type of writing	Question	Topics
Outline/research report	B <u>What are the main elements</u> in a telecommunication system?	• description of topic: What is a telecommunication system? • subheading for each main element • list basic operation/function of each element
Description of an object	A <u>Compare and contrast</u> the radio and the mobile phone.	• similarities between radio and mobile phone • differences between radio and mobile phone
Description of cause and effect	D <u>What were the effects</u> of the main discoveries in telecommunication?	• subheading for each main discovery in chronological order • explanation of each discovery • list of effects of each discovery
Description of a process	C <u>How</u> does a radio broadcast <u>work</u>?	• subheading for each step of the process in order • description of what happens at each step • explanation of the link between one step and the next

Exercise C

1 Set for individual work. Feed back with the whole class. Accept all reasonable answers.

2 If necessary, remind students of the purpose of research questions and do one or two examples as a class. Set for individual work and pairwork checking. Feed back, getting good research questions for each writing assignment topic on the board.

Answers

Possible answers:

1 The title of the piece suggests that the text will look at the increasing importance of telecommunication in the world.

Paragraph 1 is going to look at the history of telecommunication.

Paragraph 2 will explain what all telecommunication systems have in common.

Paragraph 3 will compare and contrast two telecommunication devices.

Paragraph 4 is going to look at further differences between these devices.

Paragraph 5 will be about the concept of 'modulation' and what it does.

Paragraph 6 will discuss another advantage of using modulation.

Paragraph 7 will conclude by summarizing the impact of telecommunication on society.

2 Answers depend on students.

Exercise D

Set for individual work then pairwork comparison/checking. If you wish, students can make notes under the headings in the 'Topics' column of the table in Exercise B above. Encourage students to make notes in their own words.

Answers

Model answers:

1

Item	Role in telecommunication
deterioration	a problem when transmitting analogue signals, whereby signals become weaker and distorted due to the influence of 'noise'
line	a metal conducting wire, used in some telecommunication systems, e.g., fixed-line phones
medium	a general term for the physical channel through which signals are transmitted, e.g., wires, fibre-optic cables, free space
modulation	a process at the transmitter in which the signal is changed in some way to make it more efficient to transmit
network	a general term to describe the transmitters and receivers in a telecommunication system
receiver	a device that picks up a transmitted signal and converts it into useable, understandable information
signal	the data that is sent through the telecommunication system
transmitter	a device that converts the message into a signal and transmits it over the physical channel

2/3

Possible notes:

A *Compare and contrast the radio and the mobile phone.*

- Similarities:
  - both are examples of telecommunication
  - both have basic elements: transmitter/medium/receiver
  - both use wireless technology
  - both use free space as the physical channel

- Differences:
  - radio = broadcast communication; mobile phone = point-to-point communication
  - radio = one-way system (communication in one direction only); mobile phone = duplex (transmitter + receiver)

B *What are the main elements in a telecommunication system?*

- Telecommunication system: a way of communicating with people who are far away
- Transmitter:
  - message taken
  - message converted to signal
  - signal modulated, e.g., analogue to digital / combined with carrier wave (AM/FM modulation)
- Physical channel: message travels to receiver via, e.g.,
  - atmosphere (sound)
  - optical fibres
  - cable
  - free space (radio waves)
- Receiver: signal converted back into understandable information

C *How does a radio broadcast work?*

- Message (voice/music) taken
- Message converted to signal
- Signal passed to transmitter (in radio station)
- Transmitter modulates low-frequency signal
- Combines signal with high-frequency carrier wave (AM/FM)
- Powerful transmitter broadcasts radio waves
- Large number of small, low-power radio receivers pick up signal
- Receiver converts radio wave signal to audio sound

D *What were the effects of the main discoveries in telecommunication?*

- Originally: smoke signals
- Discovery of electricity + conducting metal wires:
  - telegraph and telephone invented – used Morse code
  - communication over longer distances possible
- Discovery of wireless transmission with radio waves:
  - radio and television invented
  - telephones became more efficient: reliable, cheaper, clearer sound
- Discovery of digital signals + optical fibres
  - more efficient, less deterioration of signal, clearer signal, faster transmission
  - Internet became possible
- Overall effect of developments in telecommunication
  - opened up a wide range of practical applications
  - changed people's social interaction

Exercise E

Set for individual work and pairwork checking. Students could copy out the sentences in their notebooks and then underline all the verbs and subjects.

Feed back with the whole class, building up the table in the Answers section on the board. Point out that each sentence has two verbs, which indicates that each sentence has two *clauses*. This means that the sentences are complex. (A simple sentence has only one main verb and subject.) To enable students to identify which is the 'main' part of the sentence (in bold in the table below), ask how the two clauses are 'joined' and add the joining words (here: a location word, two relative pronouns and a conjunction). The main part of the sentence is linked to the *dependent* part with these words.

Check understanding of the passives in each case by asking how each clause and sentence could be rephrased with an active verb, e.g.,

1 The system contains a transmitter, which takes the message and converts it into a signal.

2 Finally, a receiver converts the signal into information that people can understand.

3 This process, which takes place at the transmitter, changes the message in some way before the system sends it.

Answers

Possible answers:

	Joining word	Subject	Verb	Object/ complement
1		the <u>system</u>	contains	a <u>transmitter</u>*
	where	the <u>message</u>	is taken (is) converted	into a <u>signal</u>
2		a <u>receiver</u>	converts	the <u>signal</u> back into information
	that		can be understood	
3		This <u>process</u>	changes	the <u>message</u>
	which		takes place	at the transmitter
	before	it	is sent	

*the underlined noun is the head word of the noun phrase

Refer to Unit 7 *Skills bank* for a note on information structure.

Language note

The choice of whether to use an active or a passive construction often depends on how the writer wants to structure the information or whether the agent is important or not. Refer to Unit 7 *Skills bank* for a note on information structure.

Exercise F

Set for individual work and pairwork checking. In question 2, tell students to look for the actual words used and the punctuation, grammar and vocabulary devices which are used to indicate meanings.

Feed back with the whole class, pointing out the structures given in the third column of the table for question 2 in the Answers section. If you wish, refer students to the *Vocabulary bank – Understanding new words: using definitions*.

Answers

1

Word/phrase	Meaning
1 carrier wave	a waveform that is modified by an input signal to carry information
2 physical channel	the physical medium through which the information signal travels
3 duplex	describes a device that contains both a transmitter and a receiver
4 point-to-point communication	data, which no-one else can access, transmitted from one user to another
5 coaxial cable	a type of transmission line for radio frequency signals
6 broadcast communication	data transmitted from a central user to a large number of other users

2 Model answers:

Word/phrase	Actual words giving the meaning	Punctuation/vocab/structure
carrier wave	… , a high-frequency wave that is modified in order to carry information	word/phrase followed by a comma + noun + *that*
physical channel	… , or medium.	word/phrase followed by a comma + *or* + synonym / definition
duplex	… , that is, a two-way system. This means that communications …	word/phrase followed by a comma + *that is* + comma + definition; *This means* + definition
point-to-point communication	… – communication between one transmitter and a single receiver.	word/phrase followed by a dash + definition
coaxial cable	… which are cables consisting of three layers …	word/phrase followed by a comma + *which are* + a definition using present participle
broadcast communication	…, which is communication that takes place between one powerful transmitter and a large number of smaller …	word/phrase followed by a comma + *which is* + noun + defining relative clause (using *that* as relative pronoun)

Closure

In the article it is claimed that developments in telecommunication have changed the way that people interact socially. Ask students to discuss what sort of social interaction they have, and compare it with what their parents' generation had (or, say, 50 years ago).

Students should work in small groups and make a list of differences between the generations. Feed back, building up a list of differences on the board.

Ask students if they think these changes have been generally positive, or not, and why. Again, this could be done in groups. Then feed back with the whole class, encouraging full participation in the discussion.

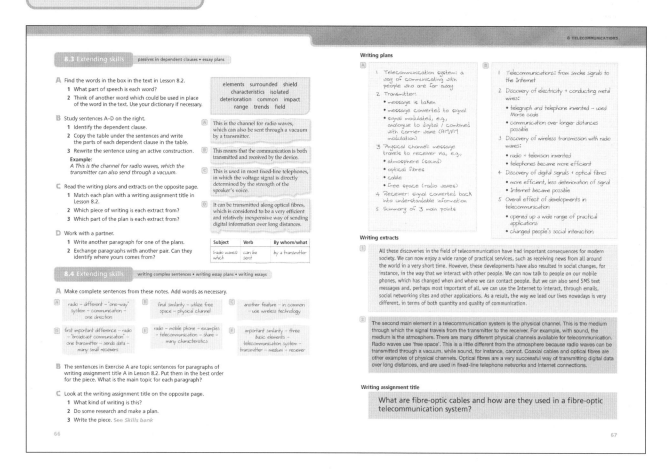

Lesson aims

- find the main information in a passive dependent clause
- recognize appropriate writing plans for different types of writing

Further practice in:

- vocabulary from Lesson 8.2

Introduction

Choose about 10–15 words from the previous unit which you think that students should revise. Write them in a random arrangement and at different angles (i.e., not in a vertical list) on an OHT (or other visual medium) or on the board. Allow students two minutes to look at and remember the words, and then take them away. Students should write down all the words they can remember.

Exercise A

Set for individual work and pairwork checking. Feed back with the whole class.

Answers

Model answers (paragraph numbers are given in brackets):

Word	Part of speech	Other word
elements (2)	n (C)	components
surrounded (2)	adj	enclosed
shield (2)	n (C)	protection n (U)
characteristics (3)	n (C)	features
isolated (3)	adj	separated
deterioration (5)	n (U)	degeneration
common (6)	adj	frequent
impact (7)	n (C)	influence
range (7)	n (C)	selection, variety
trends (7)	n (C)	movements, tendencies
field (7)	n (C)	area

140

Exercise B

Set for individual work and pairwork checking. Make sure that students can correctly identify the main clause, the dependent clause and the linking word. Do the first transformation with the class to check that they know what to do. Note that they do not need to rewrite the main clauses. Also, if no agent is given they will need to supply one themselves.

Answers

Model answers:

1/2

Main clause	Linking word	Dependent clause		
		Subject	Verb	By whom/what
A This is the channel for radio waves	which	(radio waves) which*	can be sent	by the transmitter
B This means	that	the communication	is transmitted (is) received	by the device
C This is used in most fixed-line telephones	in which	the voltage signal	is determined	by the speaker's voice
D It can be transmitted along optical fibres	which	(the process of transmitting digital data along optical fibres) which*	is considered ...	

* note that in A and D, the relative pronoun is the subject of the dependent clause. In C it is not the subject – instead, the subject is *the voltage signal*

3 A This is the channel for radio waves, which a transmitter can also send through a vacuum.

B This means that the device both transmits and receives the communication.

C This is used in most fixed-line telephones, in which the speaker's voice directly determines the voltage signal.

D It can be transmitted along optical fibres, which experts consider to be a very efficient and relatively inexpensive way of sending digital information over long distances.

Exercise C

Tell students to look back at the writing assignment titles in Lesson 8.2. You may also need to remind them of the topics which you decided are suitable for the task.

Set all three questions for individual work and pairwork checking. Feed back with the whole class. Ask students to say what aspects of the plans and the extracts enabled them to be identified. Check that students can match the parts of the extracts with the corresponding parts of the essay plan.

Answers

Model answers:

1 Plan A = assignment title B: *What are the main elements in a telecommunication system?*

   Plan B = assignment title D: *What were the effects of the main discoveries in telecommunication?*

2 Extract 1 = plan B

   Extract 2 = plan A

3 Extract 1 = plan B, point 5: **Overall effect of developments in telecommunication**: opened up a wide range of practical applications; changed people's social interaction.

   Extract 2 = plan A, point 3: **Physical channel: message travels to receiver** via, e.g., atmosphere (sound); optical fibres; cable; free space (radio waves)

Language note

Topic sentences are not always the first sentence of a paragraph. Sometimes, the first sentence of a paragraph links with the previous paragraph, and the topic is given in the second sentence.

Exercise D

Remind students about writing topic sentences. Set for pairwork. Even students who chose one of these two assignment titles in Lesson 8.2 should refer to the model writing plans/notes in the Course Book. In all cases, students should write using their own words, i.e., paraphrase the ideas in the text.

If you wish, you could ask some students – perhaps those who finish early – to write their paragraphs on an OHT or other visual medium for all the class to look at. Comment on the extent to which students have managed to paraphrase, whether they have successfully covered the point in the plan, and whether their topic sentence is supported well by the sentences that follow.

Closure

Ask students to finish the following sentences as quickly as possible.

Telecommunication is …

A carrier wave is …

The physical channel is …

'Duplex' means …

Morse code is …

Coaxial cables are …

'Modulation' means …

An example of modulation is …

Point-to-point communication means …

A transmitter is …

8.4 Extending skills

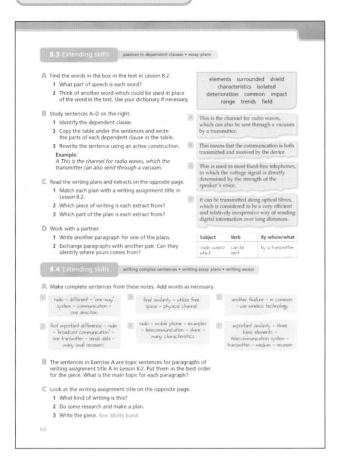

Lesson aims

- expand notes into complex sentences
- make a plan for a writing assignment
- compose a piece of writing

Further practice in:

- writing topic sentences
- expanding a topic sentence into a paragraph
- writing complex sentences with passives
- identifying the required type of writing

Introduction

Remind students about complex and compound sentences – that is, sentences with more than one clause. Remind students that academic texts typically consist of sentences with several clauses. Give the following simple sentences (or make your own) and ask students to add some more clauses to them:

Telecommunication means transmitting messages.

Wireless technology resulted in important changes.

Telecommunication requires a physical channel.

Digital signals are more efficient than analogue signals.

Telecommunication has changed the way we interact.

Exercise A

Set for individual work and pairwork checking. Remind students that they should try to make sentences in a good 'academic' style. Also remind them to use passives where necessary/possible, and to look out for ways of making dependent clauses, such as relative pronouns, linking words, etc. They will also need to pay attention to making correct verb tenses.

Feed back with the whole class.

Answers

Possible answers:

A The radio is also different because it is a 'one-way' system, which means that communication is only in one direction.

B The final similarity is that both devices utilize free space as their physical channel.

C Another feature that they have in common is that they both use wireless technology.

D However, the first important difference between them is that radio is an example of 'broadcast communication', where one transmitter sends data to many small receivers.

E The radio and the mobile phone are both examples of telecommunication, so they share many characteristics.

F One important similarity is that they both have the three basic elements of any telecommunication system, which are a transmitter, a medium and a receiver.

Exercise B

Set for individual work. Feed back with the whole class. Point out how this description text (compare and contrast) is organized by discussing all the similarities first and then all the differences. (See *Skills bank* for an alternative approach to comparison.)

If you wish, you could take this exercise further, asking students to build on the topic sentences by suggesting what ideas could follow the topic sentence in each paragraph. For this, they will need to refer to ideas in the text. Ideas for some of the paragraphs would need to be researched further. A web search is a good place to start for this. For example (at the time of writing): www.howstuffworks.com

Answers

Model answers:

Topic sentences	Paragraph topic
E The radio and the mobile phone are both examples of telecommunication, so they share many characteristics.	introduction
F One important similarity is that they both have the three basic elements of any telecommunication system, which are a transmitter, a medium and a receiver.	similarity: three basic elements
C Another feature that they have in common is that they both use wireless technology.	similarity: wireless technology
B The final similarity is that both devices utilize free space as their physical channel.	similarity: free space
D However, the first important difference between them is that radio is an example of 'broadcast communication', where one transmitter sends data to many small receivers.	difference: 'broadcast communication' vs. 'point-to-point communication'
A The radio is also different because it is a 'one-way' system, which means that communication is only in one direction.	difference: 'one-way' vs. 'duplex'

Exercise C

Discuss question 1 with the whole class. Set the research and planning (question 2) for group work, and the writing for individual work (this could be done at home). Students can do web searches to find more information.

Answers

1 Model answer:

This writing assignment is a combination of two types of writing: 'Description of an object' and 'Description of a process'.

2 Possible plan for writing:

- Introduction: description of a fibre-optic cable, i.e.,
  - glass core
  - cladding: optical material
  - plastic coating
  - thousands of fibres in one cable
  - jacket protection
- Two main types:
  - single-mode fibres – transmit infrared laser light
  - multi-mode fibres – transmit infrared light
- Key stages of the process:
  - transmitter encodes light signal
  - light travels through core, reflecting off mirror cladding
  - optical receiver detects signal using photocell or photodiode
  - receiver decodes light signal into electrical signal
  - electrical signal sent to TV, phone or computer

- Problem:
  - some deterioration of signal – impurities in glass
  - optical regenerator placed along cable – boosts degraded light signals

Closure

Ask students if they can remember a word from the unit …

	Example(s)
beginning with *trans*	transcribe, transfer, transform, transmit, transmitter
beginning with *sh*	shield
ending with *h*	breakthrough, telegraph
ending with *t*	adopt, convert, development, element, impact, point, transmit
with four syllables	modulation, application, communicate, development, information, isolated
with five syllables	characteristic, communication
with six syllables	deterioration
with seven syllables	telecommunication
which is a verb	broadcast, convert, demonstrate
which is an uncountable noun	information
which is an adjective	isolated, surrounded, duplex
which goes together with another word	coaxial cable, fibre-optic, fixed-line, frequency modulation, amplitude modulation, physical channel, text message, one-way
which is difficult to pronounce	deterioration (students' answers will vary)

Accept all reasonable answers.

Extra activities

1 Work through the *Vocabulary bank* and *Skills bank* if you have not already done so, or as a revision of previous study.

2 Use the *Activity bank* (Teacher's Book additional resources section, Resource 8A).

   A Set the wordsearch for individual work (including homework) or pairwork. Establish that some of the words are uncountable in the context in which they are used in the unit, although some can be countable in other contexts.

   Answers

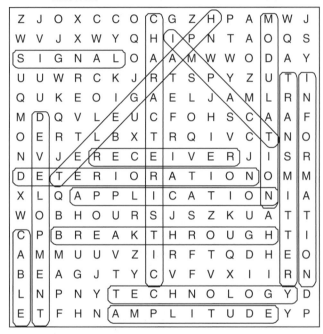

   B Set the spelling exercise for individual work and pairwork checking. If students are having difficulty, give them the first letter of the word.

   Answers

Jumbled word	Correct spelling
axocali bleac	coaxial cable
rebif-tocip caleb	fibre-optic cable
dexif-niel nehop	fixed-line phone
ncquerefy ludoonimat	frequency modulation
bolime honep	mobile phone
lacyhips nechanl	physical channel
komes gaslins	smoke signals
detulipam taludmooni	amplitude modulation
rericar veaw	carrier wave
lexpud	duplex

3 Check word stress by writing the following words on the board *without* stress markings. Students have to mark the stress and pronounce the words correctly.

   'amplitude
   a'dopt
   'carrier
   su'rrounded
   'duplex
   trans'mit
   'element
   'optic
   modu'lation
   'impact
   'network
   su'pply
   'channel
   'process
   'website

4 Remind students of how to give definitions (see Lesson 8.2). Then select five or six familiar electronic devices (e.g., mp3 player, laptop, mobile phone, digital camera, flat-screen TV, radio) and ask students to think of definitions (e.g., it's something that you use to listen to music; you need this when you want to take a photo; etc.).

This can also be done the other way round by giving the definitions and asking students to guess the word; once they get the idea, students can come up with items, questions and definitions themselves. Other forms for definitions can include:

   This is a website where ...
   This is a programme which ...
   If you want to ... , you need to ...

Other categories which can be used to practise both the language of definition and general scientific and cultural knowledge include:

- popular websites
- familiar places in the town or college where the students are studying
- well-known electronic brands
- computer software
- famous people

An alternative is *The Weakest Link* TV quiz show format, e.g., *What 'A' is a well-known brand of computer?* (Apple.)

9 SIGNAL PROCESSING

This unit focuses on analogue and digital signal processing. First we look at different types of signal and how and why they are processed. Filters and processors are covered for both analogue and digital signals. We then look at some applications of signal processing, including *active noise control* and *speech recognition technologies*.

Skills focus

 Listening

- using the Cornell note-taking system
- recognizing digressions in lectures

Speaking

- making effective contributions to a seminar
- referring to other people's ideas in a seminar

Vocabulary focus

- fixed phrases from electrical engineering
- fixed phrases from academic English

Key vocabulary

See also the list of fixed phrases from academic English in the Vocabulary bank (Course Book page 76).

amplitude	extract	processing
analogue	extraction	radar
barrier	filter (n and v)	random noise
cancellation	frequency domain	rarefaction phase
code (v)	hold (v)	sample (v)
compression phase	image	scanner
conversion	independent variable	smooth out
convert (v)	interference	soundproof (v)
dependent variable	low-pass filter	speech recognition
digital photo	noise-cancelling	stereo (n and adj)
digitization	periodic wave	trace (n)
discrete value	pick-up (n)	verification
echo (n)	plot (v)	voice recognition
editing	pressure wave	
equalization	process (v)	

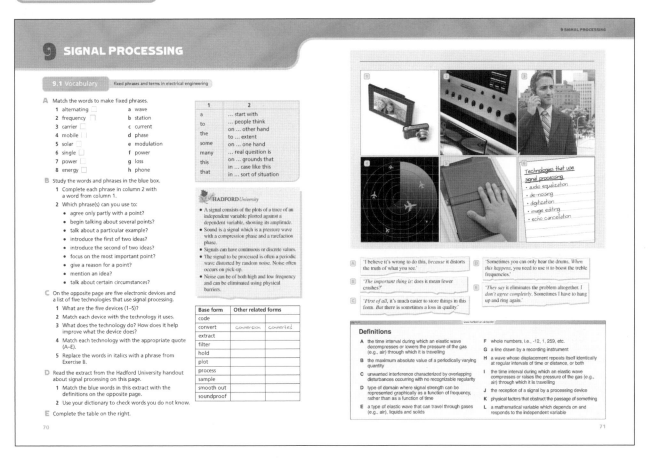

General note

Read the *Vocabulary bank* at the end of the Course Book unit. Decide when, if at all, to refer your students to it. The best time is probably at the very end of the lesson or the beginning of the next lesson, as a summary/revision.

Lesson aims

- understand and use some fixed phrases/compound nouns from electrical engineering
- understand and use some fixed phrases from academic English

Introduction

Introduce the topic for the unit. Ask students to say what the differences are between an analogue and a digital signal, and write their answers on the board. Ask if they can think of any examples of analogue and digital signals in everyday life. Do not say at this stage whether they are right or not, since the answers will be given in the first listening text in Lesson 9.2.

Exercise A

This gives revision of some compound noun phrases (noun + noun, adjective + noun) connected with electrical engineering from previous units.

Set for individual work or pairwork. Check that students remember the meanings and that they can pronounce the compounds with the main stress on the correct word. Accept any reasonable alternatives which apply to the topic of electrical engineering. Ask students to make sentences with the compounds.

Answers

Model answers:

1 alternating	'current*	adj + n
2 'frequency	modulation	n + n
3 'carrier	wave	n + n
4 mobile	'phone	adj + n
5 solar	'power	adj + n
6 single	'phase	adj + n
7 'power	station	n + n
8 'energy	loss	n + n

* when contrasted with *direct* (current), the adjective not the noun takes the primary stress

147

Exercise B

Set for individual work and pairwork checking. Point out that some of the words in the first column of Table 1 must be used more than once. Feed back with the whole class.

Answers

Model answers:

to start with	to begin talking about several points
many/some people think	to mention an idea
on the other hand	to introduce the second of two ideas
to some extent	to agree only partly with a point
on the one hand	to introduce the first of two ideas
the real question is	to focus on the point which the writer/speaker thinks is the most important
on the grounds that	to give a reason for a point
in a case like this	to talk about a particular example
in this/that sort of situation	to talk about certain circumstances

Exercise C

1/2/3 Set for pairwork discussion.

4   Set for individual work and pairwork checking.

5   Set for individual work. Check with the whole class, asking students to read out the quotation with the alternative phrase inserted in place of the original words in italics.

Answers

Model answers:

1/2/3

1 is a digital photograph in a modern digital frame – image editing can enhance the image by eliminating unwanted elements.

2 is a modern stereo system – audio equalization can create a more balanced sound.

3 shows a person having a conversation using a mobile phone – echo cancellation can make the telephone conversation easier to follow.

4 is an aircraft radar screen – de-noising can make it easier to see other aircraft.

5 shows a scanner scanning a sketch or painting – digitization can make a copy of an image for safe storage, while taking up less space than the original. Image editing can enhance the image as in 1.

4

1 (image editing): quote A

2 (audio equalization): quote D

3 (echo cancellation): quote E

4 (de-noising): quote B

5 (digitization): quote C

5

A *because*	... *on the grounds that* it distorts the truth of what you see.
B *The important thing is:*	The real question is: does it mean fewer crashes?
C *First of all*	*To start with*, it's much easier to store things in this form.
C *But*	*On the other hand*, there is sometimes a loss in quality.
D *When this happens*	*In a case like this*, you need to use it to boost the treble frequencies.
E *They say*	*Many/Some people think* it eliminates the problem altogether.
E *don't agree completely*	*agree to some extent*.

Exercise D

This exercise gives some key terms related to signal processing.

Set students to read the handout extract first and ask them to discuss in pairs which of the blue words they know and which are new to them. Feed back with the whole class, to establish how much is known. Where students give correct explanations, tell them they are right, and where they are wrong also tell them, but do not give the right answer at this point.

Set questions 1 and 2 for individual work and pairwork checking. Feed back with the whole class, checking the meaning of other possibly unknown words. In particular, make sure students know *elastic wave* and *disturbance*.

The words will be used throughout the unit, so don't worry too much about practice at this point. However, for extra practice at this point if you wish, set students to work in pairs. One student should shut the book. The other student should say one of the words for the first student to explain. Then change over.

Answers

Model answers:

trace	G	a line drawn by a recording instrument
dependent variable	L	a mathematical variable which depends on and responds to the independent variable
amplitude	B	the maximum absolute value of a periodically varying quantity
pressure wave	E	a type of elastic wave that can travel through gases (e.g., air), liquids and solids
compression phase	I	the time interval during which an elastic wave compresses or raises the pressure of the gas (e.g., air) through which it is travelling
rarefaction phase	A	the time interval during which an elastic wave decompresses or lowers the pressure of the gas (e.g., air) through which it is travelling
discrete values	F	whole numbers, i.e., –12, 1, 259, etc. (Also known as 'integers'.)
periodic wave	H	a wave whose displacement repeats itself identically at regular intervals of time or distance, or both
random noise	C	unwanted interference characterized by overlapping disturbances occurring with no recognizable regularity
pick-up (n)	J	the reception of a signal by a processing device
frequency	D	type of domain where signal strength can be represented graphically as a function of frequency, rather than as a function of time
barriers	K	physical factors that obstruct the passage of something

Exercise E

Set for individual work. Tell students to use their dictionaries to check on the meanings and grammatical categories of the words if they are not sure. Explain that some of the base words only have one other related form. Also explain that the verbs in the table are very commonly used in the passive form in signal processing – hence the focus on past participles.

Feed back with the whole class. Check students can pronounce all the words correctly. The word stress in these words does not change between the verb and noun forms.

Answers

Model answers:

Base form	Other related forms	
code (n, C/U, v)	coding (n U)	codification (n U)
convert (v)	conversion (n C/U)	converted
extract (v)	extraction (n C/U)	extracted
filter (n C, v)	filtration (n U)	filtered
hold (v)		held
plot (n C, v)		plotted
process (n C, v)	processing (n U)	processor (n C) processed
sample (n C, v)	sampling (n U)	sampled
smooth out (v)		smoothed out
soundproof (v)	soundproofing (n U)	soundproofed

Language note

With a good class, you can spend plenty of time on the issue of whether each noun is used as countable or uncountable or both, i.e., can the word be made plural, and if so, does that change the meaning?

Closure

It is important that students are familiar with the terminology of signal processing from this lesson. On the board, write some terms from the lesson and ask students to give a definition; choose items from Exercises A and D. Or read out a definition and ask students to tell you the appropriate word or phrase. Check the pronunciation. This exercise can also be done as a dictation.

Alternatively, write the words and definitions on different cards and give a card to each student. The student then reads out the word or the definition and the rest of the class must produce the correct answer.

9.2 Listening

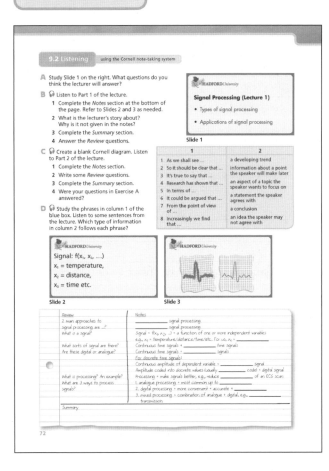

General note

Read the *Skills bank – Using the Cornell note-taking system* at the end of the Course Book unit. Decide when, if at all, to refer students to it. The best time is probably at the very end of the lesson or the beginning of the next lesson, as a summary/revision.

Lesson aims

● use the Cornell note-taking system

Further practice in:

● listening for an established purpose
● understanding fractured text
● recognition of fixed phrases and what type of information comes next
● using abbreviations and symbols in note-taking

Introduction

1 Review some of the compound nouns from Lesson 9.1 by writing a selection of the compounds on the board and asking students to put them in groups, e.g., *signals*, *noise*, giving reasons for their decisions.

2 Revise note-taking symbols and abbreviations by using extra activity 3 at the end of this unit.

3 Introduce the elements of the Cornell note-taking system. Try to elicit some of the R words. Ask students to try to think of five words beginning with *re~* with six or seven letters that are good strategies to use when studying and taking notes. Write the words as follows on the board:

RE _ _ _ _ = *record*
RE _ _ _ _ = *reduce*
RE _ _ _ _ = *recite*
RE _ _ _ _ _ = *reflect*
RE _ _ _ _ = *review*

Discuss with the class what each word might mean when taking notes. Try to elicit the following, helping where needed.

record   Take notes during the lecture.

reduce   After the lecture, turn the notes into one- or two-word questions or 'cues' which help you remember the key information.

recite   Say the questions and answers aloud.

reflect   Decide on the best way to summarize the key information in the lecture.

review   Look again at the key words and the summary (and do this regularly).

Tell students that in this lesson they will be introduced to this system of note-taking – which can be used for lectures, and also for reading and for revision for exams later. Do not say much more at this point; they will see how the system works as the lesson progresses.

Subject note

The Cornell system was developed by Walter Pauk at Cornell University, USA (Pauk, W. and Owens, R. (2010). *How to Study in College* (10th edition). Boston: Houghton Mifflin). Pauk advised students to use a large, loose-leaf notebook, with holes punched for filing. This is better than a bound notebook, because you can organize the notes in a file binder. You can also take out notes and rewrite them. Pauk's method, which is now called the Cornell system, is based on a specific page layout.

Pauk told students to divide up the page into three areas. The first area is a column 5 cm wide on the left side of the page. This is the cue area. The main part of the page is the note-taking area. At the bottom of the page is a row 8 cm high, which is the summary area. The basic grid with information on what each section should contain is reproduced in the additional resources section (Resource 9B).

The note-taking and learning process involves the *Five Rs* in the order listed in the introduction to this lesson (and in the *Skills bank*). There are many references on the Internet for this system. Two useful ones at the time of writing are:

http://lss.info.yorku.ca/resources/note-taking-at-university/#cornell

http://lsc.cornell.edu/LSC_Resources/cornellsystem.pdf

Exercise A

Set for pairwork discussion. Refer students to the lecture slide. Tell them to look at the title and bullet points, and for each bullet point to make questions which they expect the lecturer to answer. Do not explain any words from the slide, or allow students to check in their dictionaries at this point, as the meanings of these words will be dealt with in the lecture.

Feed back with the whole class, asking several students to read out their questions. Write some of the questions on the board if you wish.

🎧 Exercise B

1/2/3 Refer students to the notes at the bottom of the page, and to Slides 2 and 3 on the same page. Tell them that this student has used the Cornell system to take notes but has not managed to complete everything and so has left some gaps. (Note that this is quite a normal occurrence in note-taking – details may need to be filled in later, for example, by checking with other people.)

Allow students time to read the gapped notes. Also make sure they read question 2 and are ready to listen out for a story.

Play Part 1, pausing after each major point if you wish.

Tell students to work in pairs to compare their answers to questions 1 and 2, and to complete the summary in 3. Feed back with the whole class, using an OHT or other visual display of the answers if you wish. The completed notes are reproduced in Resource 9C, in the additional resources section, to facilitate this.

4 Now focus on the *recite* element of the Cornell system. Point out that here the student has completed the *Review* section. Tell students to cover up the *Notes* section of the answer and ask them if they can say anything about the first and second questions in the *Review* section. Then put students in pairs to test each other on the remaining notes.

Answers

Model answers:

1/3/4 See below and Resource 9C.

Review	Notes
2 main approaches to signal processing are …?	1) *Analogue* signal processing 2) *Digital* signal processing
What is a signal?	Signal = f(x_1, x_2, …) = a function of one or more independent variables e.g., x_1 = temperature, x_2 = distance, etc. For us, x_1 = *time*
What sorts of signal are there?	Continuous time signals + *discrete* time signals Continuous time signals = *analogue* signals
Are these digital or analogue?	For discrete time signals: Continuous amplitude of dependent variable = *analogue* signal Amplitude coded into discrete values (usually *binary* code) = digital signal
What is processing? An example?	Processing = make signals better, e.g., reduce *noise* of an ECG scan
What are 3 ways to process signals?	1) analogue processing = most common up to *70s* 2) digital processing = more convenient + accurate + *cheap* 3) mixed processing = combination of analogue + digital, e.g., *telephony* transmission

Summary
There are two main approaches to signal processing: digital and analogue. Digital processing has many advantages and has recently become very important, but is often used in combination with analogue signals.

2 The lecturer talks about an incident from his everyday life that shows how important signals and messages are in the real world. It is not in the notes because it is a digression – that is, as a personal observation it isn't part of the lecture contents.

Part 1

Good morning, everyone. I'm going to talk to you this morning about signal processing, and in particular, the two main approaches: analogue signal processing and digital signal processing. I'm going to look at some of the key advantages of each of them, and also mention the idea of using a mixed approach. As we shall see, a mixed approach is perhaps the best for several reasons, and I want to look at how this works in practice.

First of all, however, let me define some important terms. We talk about signal processing, but what do we mean by the term 'signal'? A formal definition of a signal is as follows. It is a function of – or we could say a variable that depends on – one or more other variables, called independent variables. This is written as shown on Slide 1. Examples of independent variables are temperature, distance, time, et cetera.

As electrical engineers, we are mainly interested in an electrical signal carried by a wire, or perhaps a radio wave. This signal is a function of just one independent variable, which is – time. We can plot this function against the time variable, and we get a graph of a waveform. This waveform is the signal, or rather the form that the signal takes.

Now, there are two main types of signal. There are continuous time signals and discrete time signals. In digital signal processing, time can only take discrete values – for example, 1 second, 5 milliseconds etcetera – and to show this we use a small n as a symbol. In this course, we will mainly be looking at signals involving discrete time. But just because the time variable consists of discrete numbers, this does not automatically make the signal digital. If the amplitude of the signal does not consist of just discrete values, then it is still an analogue signal, not a digital one. It is only when the amplitude is coded in some form – usually in a binary form – that it becomes a digital signal. So it should be clear that analogue and continuous time signals are not two ways of saying the same thing. It all depends on whether or not the value of the amplitude is coded into discrete values. This is an important point, and one which can sometimes cause confusion.

It's very important to study signals, because they may carry information. It's true to say that sending and receiving information, and then reacting to the information we have received, is fundamental to human life.

I have a little story to tell you. This morning, as I was driving here on my way to this lecture, I received a phone message on my hands-free set from my wife. She told me that she couldn't get to work because the car wouldn't start. So I had to go back home, take her to work and then come on here to the university. That's why I was a little bit late for this lecture! But the point of this story is that it illustrates, in a very small way, how important messages and signals are in our everyday life. We really couldn't do without them – they're an integral part of living together in groups or as a society.

So … to get back to the main part of my lecture: what about 'processing'? What does processing involve and why is it so important? Well, we process signals in order to change them into a better form. 'Better' means more useful or convenient. For example, consider the electrocardiogram – or ECG – waveform. The first picture on Slide 3 shows what this waveform usually looks like. It's very important that the signal is clear, so doctors can analyze the trace for any problems or malfunctions. But research has shown that the signal can easily be corrupted by 'noise'. For example, the trace can be corrupted by 50Hz power line pickup from the normal electricity supply. To eliminate this noise, we can use a band-elimination filter when the signal is processed. In this way, we can see how signal processing can give a clearer ECG trace. It has changed the signal into a 'better' and more useful form, as seen in the second picture on Slide 3.

There are three basic ways of processing signals. The first way is analogue processing. Here, the signal is received and processed in analogue form. This was the most common form of processing up until the 1970s. The second way is digital processing. In terms of convenience and accuracy, digital processing is a much better option thanks to the invention and use of microprocessors. It is usually much cheaper too.

The third type of processing is what we call 'mixed', and this means a combination of analogue and digital processing. It could be argued that analogue processing is out of date and no longer needed. After all, we have seen that digital processing is much more effective and economical. But it's not that simple. From the point of view of the real world, most of the signals we meet are analogue in form, and most of the output that we need is analogue. For example, think about telephony: we speak into the phone and generate an analogue signal. This can then be converted into a digital signal and processed in various ways. It can then be transmitted and received by another phone in digital form. But we can't listen to a series of zeros and ones – this is the big problem with digital forms! So we need to convert the digital signal back into an analogue one – in other words back into speech. So increasingly we find that engineers use mixed processing for the best, most useful results. And that's what I want to look at in the next part of the lecture …

🎧 Exercise C

1 Tell students to divide up a page of their notebooks into the three sections of the Cornell system. They should try to take notes in the *Notes* section as they listen. Warn them that they may not be able to complete their notes while writing, so they should leave spaces which they can fill in later.

Play Part 2 straight through. Then put students in pairs to complete any gaps in their notes. Feed back with the whole class. Build up a set of notes on the board.

2/3 Set students to work in pairs to complete the *Review* questions and the *Summary*. Feed back with the whole class.

4 Discuss with the class the extent to which their pre-questions in Exercise A have been answered.

Answers

Possible answers:

See table below.

Transcript 🎧 2.10

Part 2

Let's turn now to filters and have a look at them in a little more detail. We have already mentioned one type of filter – the band-elimination filter, which reduces the level of noise in the ECG graph. From this example, we can see that filters can do two different jobs. First, they can remove the unwanted components of a signal, such as random noise; and second, they can extract and keep the useful parts of a signal, such as the components lying within a particular frequency range.

Just like signals, filters can be analogue or digital. Let's first look at analogue filters. In this type of filter, the signal is an electronic voltage or current which is a representation of the physical quantity that is being processed. It could be, for example, a video signal representing moving images. Analogue filters are made up of electronic circuits and consist of components such as resistors and capacitors. There are clear procedures for designing these sorts of circuit, and exact instructions for arranging the components in such a way that they achieve the desired filtering effect.

Digital filters, on the other hand, are processors that process a digital signal by performing numerical calculations on the discrete values of the signal. The signal in a digital filter is represented by a sequence of numbers, usually in binary code, instead of a voltage or current.

But before the digital filter can begin its work, the analogue input signal must be converted into a digital signal. How is this done? Well, an ADC, or analogue to digital converter, contains a device that analyzes the analogue input in two ways. The device first samples the input signal and then holds the signal constant until it takes the next sample. In this way the analogue input is converted to a digital output using binary code. Once we have a binary digital signal, this can then be processed using numerical calculations.

After it has been processed in some way, the digital output needs to be converted back into an analogue signal. In other words, we need to convert the discrete values in the digital signal to the continuous variation of an analogue signal.

Review	Notes
What do filters do?	• remove unwanted parts of signal, e.g., noise • extract useful parts of signal, e.g., particular frequencies
What types of filter are there? What do they consist of? What signals do they work with?	• analogue = electronic circuit with components, e.g., resistors/capacitors. Signal = electronic voltage or current • digital = computer which performs numerical calculations. Signal = series of numbers (in binary code)
How are analogue signals converted to digital signals and then back to analogue?	<u>Conversion A➔D➔A</u> analogue input ➔ device (switch): samples input and holds it constant until next sampling ➔ digital output (binary signal) processing discrete values converted back to continuous analogue signal ➔ low-pass filter eliminates sudden steps in signal ➔ analogue output
What are 3 advantages of digital filters?	<u>Digital filters:</u> 1. programmable & easily changed 2. very stable – no drift or problems with temperature 3. effective in a very wide range of frequencies
Summary	
Filters can be analogue or digital, and each works with different types of signal. Digital filters need to use ADCs, but they are better than analogue filters.	

However, when the amplitude value changes rapidly, the conversion can result in a series of rapid steps, which can be a problem.

<u>That reminds me</u> of an experiment I did some time ago, when computers had very little processing capability and were very slow. Using a record of a song by Elvis Presley, we used an ADC and then converted the digital signal back to analogue again – just to see what would happen. Well, the sampling was very slow, because the computer simply couldn't hold very much information, and the resulting output was very, very strange. It certainly didn't sound anything like Elvis Presley – more like a robot singing! A very funny experiment – although modern equipment would be able to do this extremely easily and quickly of course …

Now where was I? Oh yes, right, I was talking about the problems of converting from digital to analogue. Well, to smooth out these steps, or sudden changes in value, we can use a low-pass filter. This conditions the signal by reducing the amplitude of signals with high frequencies. At this point, we now have a useful analogue output signal.

There are many advantages of digital filters. First of all, they are programmable and can be easily changed without touching the circuitry or hardware. This is not true for analogue filters, which can only be changed by redesigning the circuits.

Secondly, analogue filters tend to be subject to something called 'drift'. This is the phenomenon that occurs when the circuit is switched on – there is an uncontrolled slow change in the way it operates. Analogue filters are also sensitive to temperature. So we can see that they tend to be rather unstable. Digital filters, on the other hand, are extremely stable.

A third advantage of digital filters is that they work very effectively with low-frequency signals – we'll look at this in a future lecture. This is an area where analogue filters have great difficulty in operating. In the past, digital filters had trouble with high-frequency signals in the radio frequency domain, but this is changing thanks to new technology. This means that digital filters are now able to operate in a very wide range of frequencies.

🎧 **Exercise D**

Allow students time to read the phrases and the types of information, making sure that they understand any difficult words. Note that they are being asked not for the words that the speaker uses but what *type* of information the words represent. Note also that the information types may be needed more than once. Play the sentences one at a time, allowing time for students to identify the type of information which follows. Check answers after each sentence, making sure that students understand the actual information that follows.

Answers

Model answers:

	Fixed phrase	Type of information that follows	Actual words/information
1	As we shall see, …	information about a point the speaker will make later	a mixed approach is perhaps the best for several reasons
2	So it should be clear that …	a conclusion	analogue and continuous time signals are not necessarily the same
3	It's true to say that …	a statement the speaker agrees with	sending and receiving information, and then reacting to the information we have received, is fundamental to human life
4	Research has shown that …	a statement the speaker agrees with	the [ECG] signal can easily be corrupted by 'noise'
5	In terms of …	an aspect of a topic the speaker wants to focus on	convenience and accuracy, digital processing is a much better option thanks to the invention and use of microprocessors
6	It could be argued that …	an idea the speaker may not agree with	analogue processing is out of date and no longer needed
7	From the point of view of …	an aspect of a topic the speaker wants to focus on	the real world, most of the signals we meet are analogue in form, and most of the output that we need is analogue
8	So, increasingly we find that …	a developing trend	engineers use mixed processing

Transcript 🎧 2.11

1 As we shall see, a mixed approach is perhaps the best for several reasons.

2 So it should be clear that analogue and continuous time signals are not necessarily the same.

3 It's true to say that sending and receiving information, and then reacting to the information we have received, is fundamental to human life.

4 But research has shown that the signal can easily be corrupted by 'noise'.

5 In terms of convenience and accuracy, digital processing is a much better option thanks to the invention and use of microprocessors.

6 It could be argued that analogue processing is out of date and no longer needed.

7 From the point of view of the real world, most of the signals we meet are analogue in form, and most of the output that we need is analogue.

8 So increasingly we find that engineers use mixed processing.

Closure

Predicting information: play short sections from the lecture again. Stop the recording just before a word or phrase that you want students to produce and ask them what comes next in the lecture. For example:

> Now, there are two main types of signal. There are [STOP] … *continuous time signals and discrete time signals.*
> So it should be clear that analogue and continuous time signals are not two ways of saying the same thing! It all depends on whether or not [STOP] … *the value of the amplitude is coded into discrete values.*

Alternatively, do this exercise by reading out parts of the transcript.

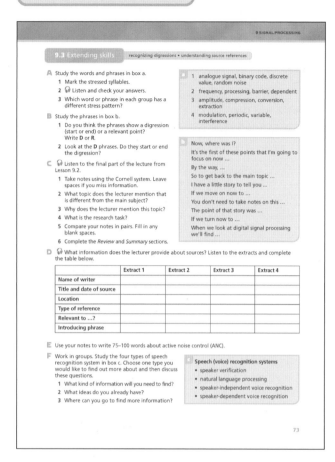

Feed back with the whole class, checking students' pronunciation, and eliciting the odd ones out.

Answers

Model answers:

1/3 (odd one out in italics)

1 'analogue 'signal, 'binary 'code, *disc'rete 'value* (stress is on second syllable of first word), 'random 'noise

2 'frequency, 'processing, 'barrier, *de'pendent* (stress is on second syllable)

3 *'amplitude* (stress is on first syllable), com'pression, con'version, ex'traction

4 modu'lation, peri'odic, *'variable* (stress is on first syllable), inter'ference

Transcript 🎧 2.12

1 'analogue 'signal, 'binary 'code, disc'rete 'value, 'random 'noise

2 'frequency, 'processing, 'barrier, de'pendent

3 'amplitude, com'pression, con'version, ex'traction

4 modu'lation, peri'odic, 'variable, inter'ference

Exercise B

Point out that the phrases in the box are likely to introduce either a digression or a relevant point. The students' task is to identify which is more probable. Set for individual work and pairwork checking. Feed back with the whole class. Note that most of these phrases occurred in the lecture in Lesson 9.2. Some have occurred in previous units and one or two are new. Note also that the end of a digression is actually a transition back to the main point.

Answers

Model answers:

Now, where was I? D (end)

It's the first of these points that I'm going to focus on now ... R

By the way, ... D (start)

So to get back to the main topic ... D (end)

I have a little story to tell you ... D (start)

If we move on now to ... R

You don't need to take notes on this ... D (start)

The point of that story was ... D (end)

If we turn now to ... R

When we look at digital signal processing, we'll find ... R

Lesson aims

- recognize digressions: start and end
- understand reference to other people's ideas: source, quotes, relevance

Further practice in:
- stress within words and phrases
- leaving space in notes for missing information

Introduction

Revise the lecture in Lesson 9.2 by asking students to use their Cornell notes. They should cover up the *Notes* section and use the *Review* and *Summary* sections to help recall the contents of the lecture. They could work in pairs to do this.

🎧 Exercise A

1 Set for individual work and pairwork checking. Students can underline the stressed syllables.

2 Play the recording and get students to check their answers.

3 Set for individual work and pairwork checking. Tell students they need to identify the odd one out in terms of stress (not the meanings of the words).

🎧 Exercise C

Refer students to the lecture slide in Lesson 9.2. Ask them what they know already about signal processing. What would they like to know?

Tell them to prepare a page to take notes using the Cornell system. Remind them that they may not get all the information. If they miss something, they should leave a space. They can fill it in after the lecture.

Let them read the questions through and tell them to listen out for the answers to questions 2, 3 and 4.

1 Play Part 3 straight through. Students should complete the *Notes* section.

2–4 Set for pairwork. Feed back with the whole class. Ask for suggestions for phrases to use to find out about the importance of digressions, e.g., *Why did the lecturer start talking about …? I didn't understand the bit about … Is it important?* and so on (see *Skills bank*). Set question 3 for pairwork.

5/6 Set for pairwork. Students compare their notes, complete any blank spaces and then write the *Review* and *Summary* sections.

Feed back with the whole class, building a set of notes on the board.

Answers

Possible answers:

1 See notes below.

2 The Cornell note-taking system.

3 It's important to know how to take good notes.

4 The research task is to find out about one type of speech (or voice) recognition technology.

5/6 See notes.

Review	Notes
ANC stands for …? Passive NC means …?	<u>A</u>ctive <u>N</u>oise <u>C</u>ontrol passive NC → no added power, e.g., earplugs/soundproofing
What does ANC do? How does it work?	ANC eliminates unwanted audio signal <u>Method</u>: incoming sound analyzed → identical wave with inverted phase generated emitted via a speaker → interference of two waves → phase cancellation → zero/small output signal
Speaker location? Advantages/disadvantages?	<u>3 models</u>: 1. near source: ANC needs same power level as source 2. near ear: lower power level required, but only for 1 listener 3. in another location: only for stationary listeners
ANC best for what type of sounds?	<u>ANC works best with</u>: • low frequencies • periodic audio signals
How do noise-cancelling headphones work?	• passive NC: headphones form physical barrier • ANC: microphone in headphone → picks up external sounds → device analyzes sound signal → generates new wave in antiphase → speaker in headphone emits wave → interference greatly reduces noise
Features of noise-cancelling headphones	• battery powered • can be used with normal audio output, e.g., radio • 20 db noise reduction

Summary
ANC cancels unwanted sound by generating and emitting a similar wave in antiphase to the original sound, e.g., noise-cancelling headphones.

Transcript 🎧 **2.13**

Part 3

OK, so let's move on to look at some of the applications of signal processing and filters. There are so many applications that it's actually been quite difficult to choose just one of them, but I have chosen what I consider to be one of the most important. In fact, as Ansari and Valbonesi point out in *The Electrical Engineering Handbook*, which is one of your core texts – the 1st edition was published in 2004 – signal processing is everywhere in everyday life, although this may not be evident to most people.

Anyway, today I'm going to focus on active noise control, or ANC. This is an extremely important application of signal processing – both analogue and digital – and has resulted in some very useful devices, as we shall see. We use the term *active* because there are also passive methods of controlling or reducing noise, which you may be familiar with – ear plugs, for instance, or soundproofing using sound-absorbing ceiling tiles. We call these *passive* because there is no added power to the noise control system.

One definition of active noise control, given by thefreedictionary.com on the Web, is: 'A method of reducing unwanted sound.' So ANC is basically a way of taking an unwanted audio signal and eliminating it – or at least greatly reducing it. Let's first look at what sound is exactly. Well, as you probably already know, sound is a pressure wave. It consists of two phases: a compression phase and a rarefaction phase. Please note that while rarefaction begins with the spelling R-A-R-E, the *e* is pronounced as a separate syllable, so we say rar-e-fac-tion – I'll just write that on the board for you. In ANC, a computer analyzes the waveform of the incoming unwanted sound and then generates, and emits via a speaker, a sound wave which is identical – or directly proportional – to the original audio signal in terms of amplitude. However, the wave has an inverted phase compared to the original wave. This means that it is 180 degrees out of phase with the wave associated with the noise. We also call this *antiphase*. This means that the two waves combine and form a new wave – we call this process *interference*. The waves basically cancel each other out. This destructive interference is known as *phase cancellation* and results in an output signal which has such a small amplitude that it may not be audible.

There are three basic models of ANC, and in each one the speaker or sound / wave transmitter is placed in a different location. In one model, the speaker is located next to the source of the unwanted sound. It follows from this that the speaker must emit its cancellation signal at the same power level as the source – probably quite a high level. In another model, the speaker is located where the sound reduction is required – and that means near the listener's ear. Of course, in this case, we can use a much lower power level. However, it does mean that each listener needs his or her own speaker – so the situation becomes a little more complicated in that sense. Sometimes the speaker is put in a third position – neither at the source nor at the ear. However, this can work only with a stationary listener, because as soon as he or she moves, the sound and cancellation signals will no longer match, and the interference will no longer be effective.

By the way, I see that some of you are using the Cornell note-taking system. That's very good. Do you all know about this? No? Right, well, if you want to know more about it, I suggest you look at *How to Study in College* by Walter Pauk, the 10th edition, published in 2010. It's very good, and it should be in the university library. I'm sure that you all know the importance of taking good notes – and this system is particularly useful.

So to get back to the main topic … as you can imagine, active noise control works much better than passive methods. And this is particularly true at low frequencies, for which passive soundproofing is less successful. ANC also works best when the sound is periodic. Don't forget that when we use *periodic* in electrical engineering we mean *repetitive* – this is different from the general English meaning of *periodic*, to mean something that happens not very often. And the fact that ANC works well with periodic signals holds true even if the signal is quite complex. It also follows from this that random sounds – by which I mean non-periodic sounds – create more of a problem in terms of cancellation.

Let's now look at a specific application of ANC: noise-cancelling headphones. These consist of a pair of headphones which completely cover the ears and form a physical barrier that can help block high-frequency sound waves. They therefore use classic passive noise cancellation methods. But they combine these with active methods too, and it's this concept that interests us today. A microphone inside the headphone cup picks up the external sounds that cannot be blocked passively. An electronic device located next to the microphone analyzes the amplitude and frequency of the external sound signal to generate a new wave in antiphase to the original. Circuitry feeds this new wave into a speaker located in the headphones and destructive interference erases the noise. All this is powered by a rechargeable battery. The great thing about these headphones is that ANC can be used in parallel with a normal audio signal coming through the speaker, such as when we are listening to the radio or watching a video. The speaker simply emits the *anti-sound* wave created by the ANC device, together with the normal audio. And the result can be surprisingly effective – providing a reduction of up to 20 decibels in addition to the passive noise control that the headphones provide.

Now, I think that's all I'm going to say for the moment on ANC. Are there any questions so far? No? OK. Now, when I see you in tutorials we'll look at how digital signal processing developed in the 1960s and 1970s, and the inventions that helped this development take place. In the meantime, I'm going to set you a research task.

Now, as I said before, it's easy to forget just how many applications of signal processing there are. To quote Ansari and Valbonesi, 'Users may be familiar with JPEG, MPEG and MP3 without recognizing that these tools are rooted in signal processing.' Right, now listen carefully … your research task is to find out about one important application of signal processing in more detail: speech recognition, otherwise known as *voice recognition*. Now, there are several different systems included under the general term of *speech recognition*. I'd like you to work in groups of four. I want each group to find out about *one* speech recognition system and report back on their findings.

Exercise D

Tell students that lecturers will often give references while they talk and it is important to note these down. The kinds of information may differ – they may just be names of books or articles, they may be an exact quotation (a 'direct quote') or they may be a paraphrase (sometimes called an 'indirect quotation'). Refer students to the table and check that they know what each row represents.

Play each extract and allow students time to complete the sections of the table. Check with the whole class.

Answers

Model answers (see below):

Transcript 🎧 2.14

Extract 1

There are so many applications that it's actually been quite difficult to choose just one of them. In fact, as Ansari and Valbonesi point out in *The Electrical Engineering Handbook* (one of your core texts – the 1st edition was published in 2004), signal processing is everywhere in everyday life, although this may not be evident to most people.

Extract 2

One definition of active noise control, given by thefreedictionary.com on the web, is: 'A method of reducing unwanted sound.'

Extract 3

By the way, I see that some of you are using the Cornell note-taking system. That's very good. Do you all know about this? No? Right, well, if you want to know more about it, I suggest you look at *How to Study in College* by Walter Pauk, the 10th edition, published in 2010. It's very good, and it should be in the university library.

Extract 4

Now, as I said before, it's easy to forget just how many applications of signal processing there are. To quote Ansari and Valbonesi, 'Users may be familiar with JPEG, MPEG and MP3 without recognizing that these tools are rooted in signal processing.'

Language note

A 'core text' is the main text for the course. Students are usually told they should buy a copy of the core text for their course.

	Extract 1	Extract 2	Extract 3	Extract 4
Name of writer	Ansari and Valbonesi		Walter Pauk	Ansari and Valbonesi
Title and date of source	*The Electrical Engineering Handbook* 1st edition 2004	thefreedictionary.com	*How to Study in College* 10th edition 2010	as in 1
Location	core text	web	university library	as in 1
Type of reference	indirect quotation/paraphrase	direct quotation	name of book	direct quotation
Relevant to …?	prevalence of signal processing in everyday life	ANC	Cornell note-taking	many unrealized applications of signal processing
Introducing phase	as Ansari and Valbonesi point out in …	One definition of … given by …	I suggest you look at …	To quote Ansari and Valbonesi …

Exercise E

Set for individual work – possibly homework – or else a pair/small group writing task. If the latter, tell students to put their writing on an OHT or other visual medium so that the whole class can see and comment on what has been written. You can correct language errors on the OHT.

Exercise F

Tell students to work in groups of three or four. Either give each group one voice recognition system or allow them to choose. Make sure that each system is covered by at least one group, and preferably two.

Feed back on questions 1–3 with the whole class. Tell them that each student should now carry out research into the group's topic. They should each look at a different source and so will need to decide who is going to look at which one. You will also need to arrange the date for the feedback and discussion of the information – this is the focus of Exercise D in Lesson 9.4. Tell students that in Lesson 9.4 they will take part in a seminar on this topic.

Answers

Possible answers:

1 Information to find: What is this system? How does it work? What applications does it have? What are its advantages/disadvantages?

3 Use subject course books, the library and the Internet to find out the necessary information. Some example websites at the time of writing are:

www.howstuffworks.com

www.thefreedictionary.com

Alternatively (or in addition) – depending on your teaching situation and access to the sources of information – you can refer students to the information in the back of the Course Book.

Closure

Ask students if they have come across voice recognition in their everyday life, e.g., selecting menu options when phoning a company, or giving instructions to their mobile phone. Ask them what they think of the experience, and if the recognition system worked or not. Don't go into too much detail here, though, since this topic is discussed in Lesson 9.4. Focus mainly on personal experiences and stories.

9.4 Extending skills

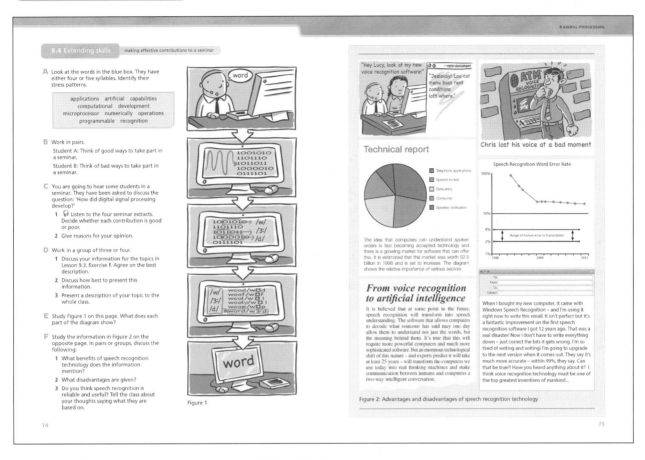

General note

Students will need the information they researched for Lesson 9.3, Exercise F.

Decide how you want students to present their information, e.g.,

- short talk with/without PowerPoint, OHT or other visual medium
- to the whole class or to another group

Make sure that students understand the options for the presentation types.

Lesson aims

- make effective contributions to a seminar

Further practice in:

- stress within words

Introduction

Use a few of the review cues from the Cornell notes in Lesson 9.3 for students to try to recall the ideas on active noise control in the lecture. If students appear to be having difficulty remembering, ask them to look again at their own notes from Exercise C in Lesson 9.3. Check that students are clear about the difference between active and passive noise control. Ask them to define active noise control and to describe how noise-cancelling headphones work.

Exercise A

Set for individual work and pairwork checking.

Answers

Model answers:

oOoo	development, numerically, programmable
ooOo	applications, artificial, operations, recognition
ooOoo	capabilities, computational, microprocessor

Exercise B

This is revision from Unit 5. Set for individual work and pairwork checking. Feed back with the whole class. Give a time limit and see which pair can think of the most Dos and Don'ts in the time. Refer to Unit 5 Lesson 4 for suggestions if you need to.

Answers

Possible answers:

See table on next page.

Do	Don't
prepare the topic beforehand	
ask politely for information	demand information from other students
try to use correct language	
speak clearly	mumble, whisper or shout
say when you agree with someone	get angry if someone disagrees with you
link correctly with previous speakers	
build on points made by other speakers	
make a contribution, even if you are not sure if it is new or relevant	stay silent, waiting for 'the perfect moment'
be constructive	be negative
give specific examples to help explain a point	be vague
listen carefully to what others say	start a side conversation
allow others to speak	dominate the discussion
paraphrase to check understanding	
use clear visuals	

🎧 Exercise C

Check that students understand the topic for the seminar discussion. Ask them what they might expect to hear. Work through these extracts one at a time. Complete questions 1 and 2 for each extract before moving on to the next.

1 Set for individual work.
2 First check that students have understood the extract as well as possible. Then ask for opinions from the whole class on the contribution.

Answers

Model answers:

	✓	✗	Reasons
Extract 1	✓		speaks clearly explains the point clearly answers correctly uses good fixed phrases
Extract 2		✗	doesn't speak clearly doesn't answer the question talks about applications of signal processing, not its development doesn't use visuals well
Extract 3		✗	speaks clearly, but doesn't answer the question makes points that are not relevant to the question talks about benefits of analogue signal processing
Extract 4	✓		speaks clearly explains the point clearly answers correctly uses good fixed phrases has prepared well has a good visual

Transcript 🎧 2.15

Extract 1

Digital signal processing started in the 1960s with the development of digital computers. These computers were able to run the number-crunching applications which were necessary to analyze the frequency spectrum of the input signal, and to do this in real time. Before the 1960s, these techniques were simply impossible due to the lack of suitable technology.

Extract 2

... erm, I think signal processing is very important. It's possible ... er ... we can see how this is very important. So let's look at the chart and ... oh, sorry, that's the wrong chart, just a minute ... right, so this shows some of the main applications of signal processing ... er you can see I think, these applications ... do you have any questions about this chart?

Extract 3

Digital signal processing is usually considered to be superior to analogue signal processing – it's much more powerful and also much cheaper. However, we should not forget that analogue signal processing has capabilities that make it more suitable in certain situations. For example, if the input signal is in analogue form, it can be expensive and complicated to use an ADC. More importantly, it can result in a delay – and this may make it unusable for systems that need to operate in a real-time environment.

Extract 4

In the late 1970s, the invention of the microprocessor meant that digital signal processing became used in an extremely wide range of situations. General-purpose microprocessors led to the development of *digital signal processor* chips – or DSP chips. These are specialized programmable microprocessors which were designed specifically for the numerically intensive operations that digital signal processing requires. If we look at the chart I've prepared here, we can see some of the operations that DSPs are able to carry out. Over the last few years, faster and more powerful versions of these DSPs are appearing on the market, and their sales make up an ever-increasing share of the world market for electronic devices.

Exercise D

Students should work in the same groups as their research groups from Lesson 9.3, Exercise F. They will need to have with them the research they have done individually on the group's chosen topic.

1 Tell each group to discuss the information that they have found and agree on the best description of the type of voice recognition system they have researched.

2 In discussing this question, students will need to decide who is going to speak when and say what. Encourage them to practise presenting to each other before talking to the whole class.

3 Allow each group a maximum of five minutes for the presentation. Then allow some time for questions. If more than one group have done the same topic, encourage disagreement and critical analysis. Remind the groups when discussing to use all the *good* techniques and phrases they have learnt.

Exercise E

The diagram shows stages in the process of a voice recognition system. With the whole class, elicit the words needed to discuss the different stages of the process shown.

- Words are spoken into a microphone, and the analogue waves are converted into a digital signal.
- The processor analyzes the signal and splits it up into separate sounds (phonemes).
- These are compared with words the computer has in its dictionary.
- The software finds the best match and shows it on the screen.

What aspects does the class think a developer will need to focus on in order to improve the accuracy of such a system?

Exercise F

Put students in pairs (or threes). For question 3, each pair can join another pair and agree a decision.

1/2 In their pairs, students can divide the information between them and then summarize the information for their partner. If there are words that they do not understand, they will need to check meanings in dictionaries or online.

3 In coming to a conclusion on this, students should use the information presented in Figure 2, as well as any information or experience they already have of voice recognition technology that they feel is relevant.

Closure

Use the *Vocabulary bank* at the end of the Course Book unit to check that the group can remember the meaning, spelling and pronunciation of the vocabulary of this unit.

This unit contains a lot of technical and semi-technical vocabulary. Students will need lots of practice with this.

1 Work through the *Vocabulary bank* and *Skills bank* if you have not already done so, or as revision of previous study.

2 Use the *Activity bank* (Teacher's Book additional resources section, Resource 9A).

   A Set the crossword for individual work including homework) or pairwork.

   Answers:

   B Ask students to look at the nouns in the table: are plural forms of the nouns possible? Tell students to use an English–English dictionary or online definitions to help them find out the answers to the following questions.

   1 Which forms are countable and which uncountable?

   2 Do the countable and uncountable forms have different meanings?

Answers

Noun	Countable or uncountable?	Notes
amplitude	C	
barrier	C	
cancellation	C/U	usually U in engineering, e.g., *cancellation of noise*
digitization	C/U	
echo	C/U	
editing	U	
domain	C	
image	C	
interference	U	
noise	C/U	active noise control passive noise control
pick-up	C/U	U = the reception of a signal by a processing device C = the device or apparatus which receives the signal
pressure	C/U	
radar	U	
recognition	U	speech recognition voice recognition
variable	C	
verification	U	

3 Revise note-taking symbols – see the list at the back of the Course Book. Check back to Unit 5 if necessary. Give the meanings and ask students to write down the symbol (or do it the other way round). Then ask students to think about and discuss which ones they actually use. Are there any other ones that they have come across that they think are useful?

Alternatively, write the meanings on a set of cards. Put students in groups of about six with two teams in each group. Give each group a pile of cards. A student from each team picks a card and, without showing the members of his/her team, draws the appropriate symbol. The members of his/her team must say what the symbol stands for. If the student writes the correct symbol and the team gets the meaning right, the team gets a point. If the student writes the wrong symbol and/or the team gets it wrong, the team loses a point. The teams take it in turns to pick a card.

4 Identify electrical engineering abbreviations which will be useful for your students. Use the same procedure as in Activity 3. The following are some examples from recent units:

Abbreviation	Meaning
AC	alternating current
ADC	analogue to digital converter
AM	amplitude modulation
ANC	active noise control
ANR	active noise reduction
BW	bandwidth
CAD	computer-aided design
CCM	cruise control module
CPU	central processing unit
CRT	cathode ray tube
DAC	digital to analogue converter
DSP	digital signal processor
DVD	digital versatile disk
FM	frequency modulation
LCD	liquid crystal display
LED	light-emitting diode
PDP	plasma display panel
PID controller	proportional integral derivative controller
VSS	vehicle speed sensor

Some useful glossaries are at:

www.all-acronyms.com/tag/electrical_engineering

www.interfacebus.com/Engineering_Acronyms.html

10 ELECTRIC CARS

This unit looks at electric cars, the reasons why they have become popular, and some of their advantages and disadvantages compared to traditional internal combustion engine cars. It considers the problems that electric cars pose for electrical engineers, such as the need to balance issues of efficiency, weight, environmental concerns etc.

Skills focus

Reading

- recognizing the writer's stance and level of confidence or tentativeness
- inferring implicit ideas

Writing

- writing situation–problem–solution–evaluation essays
- using direct quotations
- compiling a bibliography/reference list

Vocabulary focus

- 'neutral' and 'marked' words
- fixed phrases related to cars, both petrol-driven and electric, and to the topic of pollution
- fixed phrases from academic English

Key vocabulary

brilliant	insignificant	recharge
carbon emissions	last (v)	rocket (v)
charge (n and v)	lead-acid	run (v)
claim (v)	lifespan	side-effect
collapse (n and v)	lithium	significant
contribute	manufacture (n and v)	slump (n and v)
damage (v)	massive	soar
discharge (v)	minimal	store (v)
enormous	outstanding	superb
exhaust pipe	plummet	support (v)
fossil fuel	plunge (v)	tremendous
hidden	pollution	
huge	powerful	

10.1 Vocabulary

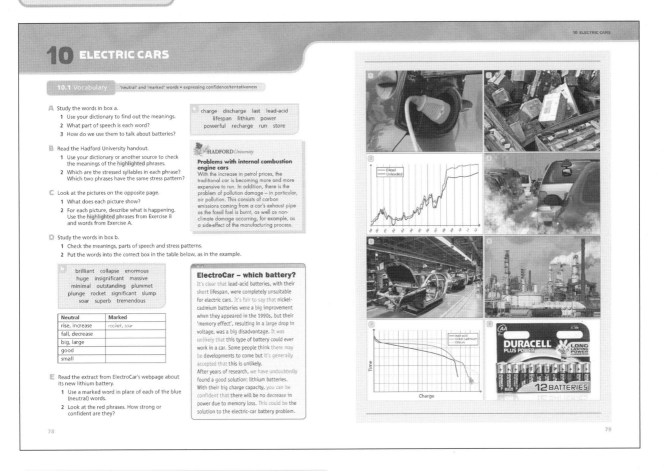

10 ELECTRIC CARS

General note

Read the *Vocabulary bank* at the end of the Course Book unit. Decide when, if at all, to refer your students to it. The best time is probably at the very end of the lesson or the beginning of the next lesson, as a summary/revision.

Lesson aims

- understand when words are 'neutral' and when they are 'marked' (see *Vocabulary bank*)
- understand and use phrases expressing confidence/tentativeness (see *Vocabulary bank*)

Further practice in:

- fixed phrases/compound nouns from the discipline
- fixed phrases from academic English
- stress within words and phrases
- synonyms

Introduction

1 Ask the students to write down all the parts of a car that they know. For example:

wheels
engine
seats
windows
seatbelts
air-conditioning system
roof
battery

2 Revise the following phrases used in academic writing. Ask students what sort of information will follow these phrases.

On the other hand, ...
In conclusion, ...
To put it another way, ...
As Smith (2011) pointed out, ...
Research has shown that ...
Part of the difficulty is ...
To start with, ...
This can be defined as ...
As a result, ...
Finally, ...
Given what has been shown above, ...

Exercise A

Set for individual work and pairwork checking. Feed back with the whole class.

Answers

Model answers:

Word	Part of speech	Meaning and use connected to batteries (definition)
charge	n (C), v (T)	*the battery's charge / to charge a battery* • the battery's charge is the amount of electricity it contains (unit of measurement: coulomb or ampere-hour) • to charge a battery means to pass an electric current through it so it is more powerful, or lasts longer to restore its power
discharge	v (T)	*to discharge the battery* to release the stored energy of the battery
last	v (I/T)	*the battery lasts two days / the battery will last you until tomorrow* can be used for that amount of time because there will still be enough charge available
lead-acid	n (U) + n (C/U)	*a lead-acid battery** a traditional type of battery containing lead and sulphuric acid
lifespan	n (C)	*the battery's lifespan* the length of time a battery can be used, after which it must be replaced
lithium	n (U)	*a lithium battery** a battery made up of lithium-ion (Li-ion) cells
power	n (U), v (T)	*the battery's power, to power a battery / the battery is powered by ...* the rate at which a battery transfers its energy (unit of measurement: watt)
powerful	adj	*a powerful battery* a battery of high power
recharge	v (T)	*to recharge a battery* to put electrical charge back into a battery
run	v (T)	*the battery runs a device* the device uses a battery as its source of energy
store	v (T)	*the battery stores energy* the battery contains and keeps energy until it is needed

* noun–noun compound

Exercise B

1 Set for individual work and pairwork checking. Other sources besides dictionaries could be textbooks, other reference books, or the Internet.

2 Show students how they can draw the stress pattern for the whole word as well as just locating the stressed syllable. If they use the system of big and small circles shown in the Answers section, they can see the pattern for the whole phrase quite easily.

Answers

Model answers:

1

petrol prices	the prices at which petrol is sold to the public
traditional car	a car with a traditional internal combustion engine that runs on petrol
pollution damage	the physical harm that dirty and poisonous substances do when they are put into the water, air or land
air pollution	dirty and poisonous substances put into the air
carbon emissions	carbon dioxide and other carbon compounds that are released into the atmosphere from burning fossil fuels
exhaust pipe	a piece of tubing that carries waste gases away from a car's engine and discharges them into the air
fossil fuel	an energy source formed of hydrocarbon deposits, e.g., coal, petroleum and natural gas
non-climate damage	the physical harm that dirty and poisonous substances (but not carbon emissions) do when they are put into the water, air or land
side-effect	an unplanned and usually negative effect that occurs together with the main result of a process
manufacturing process	the production of goods on a large scale by machinery

2

petrol prices Oo Oo

traditional car oOoo O

pollution damage oOo Oo

air pollution O oOo

carbon emissions Oo oOo

exhaust pipe oO O

fossil fuel Oo O

non-climate damage oOo Oo

side-effect Ooo

manufacturing process ooOoo Oo

Pollution damage and *non-climate damage* have the same stress pattern.

Exercise C

Set for pairwork or class discussion. Encourage students to speculate about what might be happening. Students should use the highlighted phrases and other words that are useful from the text in Exercise B; they can also use words from Exercise A.

Feed back with the whole class. Accept anything reasonable.

Answers

Possible answers:

1 Someone is **recharging** an electric-car battery in the city centre.

2 There are a lot of dumped **lead-acid** car batteries. Here there is a possible **side-effect** in the form of **non-climate pollution damage** due to lead and chemicals in the battery leaking into the environment. The batteries are used in traditional cars.

3 This is a graph of rising **petrol prices** and the price of diesel, which is another example of a **fossil fuel**.

4 A car's **exhaust pipe** is emitting fumes, contributing to the formation of smog. This is an example of **air pollution** and **carbon emission** in particular, due to the burning of **fossil fuels**.

5 This shows the **manufacturing process** for electric cars in a modern factory.

6 Smoke is coming out of a factory chimney. This is an example of possible **air pollution**, and this can be a **side-effect** of the **manufacturing process.**

7 The graph shows the **lifespan** of different types of battery: **lead-acid** vs. nickel-cadmium vs. **lithium.** It shows the different levels of **charge** in each type of battery over time.

8 The photo shows a pack of Duracell batteries. Duracell famously use a toy rabbit in their advertising campaigns to show how long toys which **run** on their batteries **last.**

Exercise D

Introduce the idea of 'neutral' and 'marked' vocabulary (see *Language note* below and *Vocabulary bank*). Set for individual work and pairwork checking.

Feed back, discussing any differences of opinion about whether the words are marked, and in what sense they are marked. (Some students may argue that *minimal, significant* and *insignificant* are not marked, for example. Others may argue that they are marked, because they suggest not just that something is big/small, but that it is important/unimportant. Compare *There is a small problem with the program* and *There is an insignificant problem with the program.*)

Answers

Model answers:

Neutral	Marked
rise, increase	'rocket, soar (v)
fall, decrease	co'llapse (v and n), 'plummet (v), plunge (v and n), slump (v and n)
big, large	e'normous, huge, 'massive, sig'nificant, tre'mendous* (adj)
good	'brilliant, out'standing, su'perb, tre'mendous* (adj)
small	insig'nificant, 'minimal (adj)

* *tremendous* can mean both very large and very good, so students may place this word in either category

Language note

One way of looking at vocabulary is to think about 'neutral' and 'marked' items. Many words in English are neutral, i.e., they are very common and do not imply any particular view on the part of the writer or speaker. However, there are often apparent synonyms which are 'marked' for stance or opinion. Neutral words are usually thought of as basic vocabulary (the adjectives often have opposites, e.g., *big/small*; *light/dark*). Marked words tend to be less frequent and are therefore learnt later.

The marked words in Exercise D are not totally synonymous. Their appropriate use and interpretation will be dependent on the context and also on collocation constraints. For example, one can say that a building is 'massive' but not (in the same sense) 'significant'.

Exercise E

1 Set for individual work and pairwork checking. Make sure that students understand any words they are not sure of. Feed back with the whole class by asking individual students to read out a sentence. Make sure that the pronunciation and stress patterns of the marked words are correct.

2 Put the table from the Answers section on the board. Make sure that students understand *confident* and *tentative*. Elicit answers from the whole class and complete the table. Point out that these phrases are usually found in conversation or in informal writing such as this. Academic writing also requires writers to show degrees of confidence and tentativeness. The mechanisms for this will be covered in the next lesson.

Answers

Model answers:

1 **ElectroCar – which battery?**

It's clear that lead-acid batteries, with their (*short*) minimal/insignificant lifespan, were completely unsuitable for electric cars. It's fair to say that nickel-cadmium batteries were a (*big*) huge/massive/enormous/tremendous improvement when they appeared in the 1990s, but their 'memory effect', resulting in a (*large*) significant/massive/huge drop in voltage, was a (*big*) massive/significant/huge disadvantage. It was unlikely that this type of battery could ever work in a car. Some people think there may be developments to come but it's generally accepted that this is unlikely.

After years of research, we have undoubtedly found a (*good*) brilliant/outstanding/superb solution: lithium batteries. With their (*big*) enormous/huge/massive/superb charge capacity, you can be confident that there will be no (*decrease*) slump/plummet in power due to memory loss. This could be the solution to the electric-car battery problem.

2

	Very confident	Fairly confident	Tentative (= not confident)
It's clear that	✓		
It's fair to say that		✓	
It was unlikely that		✓	
there may be			✓
it's generally accepted that		✓	
we have undoubtedly	✓		
you can be confident that	✓		
This could be			✓

Closure

1 For further practice of neutral and marked vocabulary, ask students to write down some basic words, e.g., four verbs, four nouns and four adjectives. Put a list of these on the board and ask students if they are neutral or marked. See if you can find any opposites. Ask students to find some synonyms for neutral words – they can use a dictionary. A synonyms dictionary or Microsoft Word thesaurus can be useful here as well.

2 Ask pairs or groups to define as accurately as they can three of the fixed electric car-related phrases from the *Vocabulary bank*. Give them a few minutes to think of their definitions, then feed back and discuss as a class.

10.2 Reading

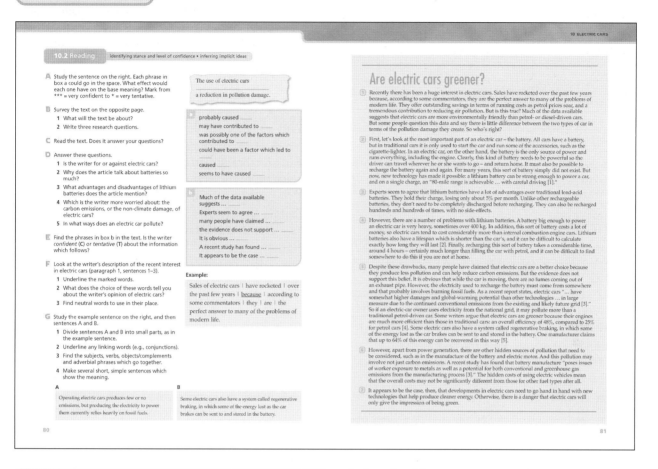

General note

Read the *Skills bank – Identifying the parts of a long sentence* at the end of the Course Book unit. Decide when, if at all, to refer students to it. The best time is probably at the very end of the lesson or the beginning of the next lesson, as a summary/revision.

Lesson aims

- identify the writer's stance on information from the use of marked words
- identify the writer's level of confidence in the research or information
- infer implicit ideas

Further practice in:

- finding the main information in a sentence

Introduction

Introduce the idea of degree of confidence in information, which is usually shown in academic writing. More often than not, writers will avoid very categorical statements such as 'X was the cause of Y' and will demonstrate the extent to which they are sure about something through various different linguistic devices such as modals and hedging words and phrases.

Put this table on the board to help explain the idea:

100% *** definitely true. The writer is very confident	X caused Y
75% ** probably true. The writer is a little tentative	X probably/is likely to have caused Y
50% * possibly true. The writer is very tentative	X may/might/could have/possibly caused Y

Exercise A

Set the exercise for pairwork. Students should refer to the table on the board to explain the rating system. Feed back with the whole class, pointing out the aspects of the language that contribute to the degree of confidence.

Answers

Model answers:

Word/phrase	Rating	Words which show less than 100% confidence
probably caused	**	probably
may have contributed to	*	may have contributed (i.e., there are other reasons)
was possibly one of the factors which contributed to	*	possibly a factor not the factor (i.e., there are other factors)
could have been a factor which led to	*	could
results in	***	–
seems to have caused	**	seems

Exercise B

Remind students that surveying the text means scanning and skim-reading to get an approximate idea of the text contents. They should:

- look at the title
- look at the first few lines and the final few lines of the text
- look at the first sentence of each paragraph

Note that this is in order to get a very approximate idea of the contents of the text. This will enable students to formulate questions about the text for which they might try to find answers. Students should be discouraged from reading deeply at this point, as they will be able to do this later.

Set for individual work and pairwork discussion. Each pair should agree three questions. Feed back with the whole class. Write some research questions on the board.

Exercise C

Set for individual work followed by pairwork discussion. Feed back with the whole class. Ask whether the questions you have put on the board have been answered in the text.

Exercise D

These questions require students to 'infer' information – that is, understand what is not directly stated.

Set for individual work and pairwork checking. Feed back with the whole class, making sure that students understand the answers.

Answers

Model answers:

1 The writer is neither for nor against electric cars. He/she believes that electric cars have advantages and disadvantages, and that more research is needed before we can decide if they are greener than petrol cars.

2 The battery is the key device which is holding back the development of electric cars, due to problems with weight, cost, lifespan and recharging time. The writer seems to suggest that if technology could find an efficient battery, electric cars would be much more successful.

3 Three advantages of lithium batteries: hold their charge, no need for complete discharge, no memory loss. Five disadvantages: weight, cost, limited lifespan, unknown lifespan, recharging time.

4 The writer appears to be more worried about non-climate damage. He/she seems to agree with the evidence that carbon emissions are lower with electric cars, due to engine efficiency and regenerative braking. He/she is concerned that there may be hidden pollution damage in the manufacturing process of the car and its battery.

5 An electric car pollutes by using electricity from the grid, which may come from fossil-fuel power stations. The manufacturing process of the cars and batteries may also result in pollution.

Exercise E

Set for individual work and pairwork checking. Feed back with the whole class. Point out that these phrases are very important in academic writing and will help to determine whether something is a fact or an opinion – an important aspect of reading comprehension. They are also used by writers in developing their arguments for or against a particular point of view.

Answers

Model answers:

Much of the data available suggests that electric cars are more environmentally friendly than petrol or diesel-driven cars.	T
Experts seem to agree that lithium batteries have a lot of advantages over traditional lead-acid batteries.	T
… many people have claimed that electric cars are a better choice …	T
… the evidence does not support this belief.	C
It is obvious that while the car is moving there are no fumes …	C
A recent study has found that battery manufacture "poses issues of worker exposure to metals as well as a potential for both conventional and greenhouse gas emissions from the manufacturing process."	C
It appears to be the case, then, that developments in electric cars need to go hand in hand with new technologies …	T

Exercise F

Set for pairwork. Feed back with whole class. Discuss any differences in students' answers, and whether neutral equivalents are hard to find for some of the words.

Answers

Possible answers:

1 Recently there has been a <u>huge</u> interest in electric cars. Sales have <u>rocketed</u> over the past few years because, according to some commentators, they are the <u>perfect</u> answer to many of the problems of modern life. They offer <u>outstanding</u> savings in terms of running costs as petrol prices <u>soar</u>, and a <u>tremendous</u> contribution to reducing air pollution.

2 The writer uses marked words to highlight the enthusiasm that some people have had for electric cars, and to emphasize the strong claims they have made for them. It does not mean that the writer believes in these claims – as the rest of the piece makes clear.

3

Marked word	Neutral alternative
huge	big, (a) lot of, (a) significant amount of
rocketed	increased, grown
(the) perfect	(a) possible
outstanding	good
soar	increase, go up
tremendous	big, large

Exercise G

Draw the table from the Answers section on the board. Ask students to look at the example sentence and say which box each part of the sentence should go in. Complete the table for the example sentence as shown. Point out how each of the noun phrases is made up of several words. In each case, elicit which words are the core of the noun phrases (shown in bold in the table in the Answers section). Do the same with the verb phrases. Ask students to suggest how the sentence can be rewritten in several short, very simple sentences in which noun phrases and verb phrases are reduced to the core meaning as far as possible. Demonstrate with these examples if necessary:

Sales have rocketed.

Electric cars are the answer to many problems.

Point out how in the actual sentences the noun phrases have been expanded so that there is:

sales + of electric cars

the + perfect + answer to + many + of the + problems + of modern life

Set questions 1–4 (relating to sentences A and B) for individual work and pairwork checking. Feed back with the whole class.

Answers

Model answers:

1/2 A Operating electric cars | produces | few <u>or</u> no emissions, | <u>but</u> | producing the electricity to power them | currently | relies | heavily | on | fossil fuels.

 B Some electric cars | also | have | a system called regenerative braking, | in which | some of the energy lost | as | the car | brakes | can be sent to and stored | in the battery

3 See table on next page.

	Subject noun phrases	Verb phrases	Object/complement noun phrases	Adverbial phrases	Notes
Example	**Sales** of electric cars	**have rocketed**		over the past few years	*because* is a linking word or conjunction. It joins two clauses
	they (electric cars – not 'sales')	**are**	the perfect **answer** to many of the problems of modern life.	according to some commentators	
A	**Operating** electric cars	**produces**	few or no **emissions**		*but* is a linking word or conjunction. Here it joins two clauses
	producing the electricity to power them	**relies** (on)	fossil **fuels**	currently heavily	
B	Some electric **cars**	**have**	a system (that is) called **regenerative breaking**	also	the object noun phrase contains a reduced relative clause, using the past participle 'called'
	some of the **energy** (which is) lost	**can be sent** (to)	the **battery**		*in which* is a relative pronoun introducing the relative clause of the second part of the sentence. The subject noun phrase of the relative clause contains a reduced relative clause, using the past participle 'lost'
	the **car**	**brakes**			*as* is a linking word or conjunction. The clause 'as the car brakes' is an adverbial clause of time
	some of the **energy** (which is) lost	**can be stored** (in)	the **battery**		*and* is a linking word or conjunction. Here it joins two verb phrases: 'can be sent to' and '(can be) stored in'

4 Possible sentences:

A Operating electric cars produces few emissions.

Operating electric cars produces no emissions.

Electricity powers electric cars.

Producing electricity relies on fossil fuels.

B Electric cars have an energy system.

This is called regenerative braking.

The car brakes.

Energy is lost.

The energy can be sent to the battery.

The energy can be stored in the battery.

Language note

1 Subjects and objects will always be nouns, with or without modifying adjectives.

Complements can be

● nouns: *He is a doctor.*

● adjectives: *He is French.*

● adverbs: *He arrived late.*

2 There are several types of conjunction in English.

Coordinating conjunctions such as *and, or, but* link elements of equal grammatical status.

Correlative conjunctions have two items: *either … or … ; both … and … .*

Subordinating conjunctions relate clauses to each other using single words (e.g., *that* with verbs of saying, thinking, etc., *after, as, before, if, although, while*) or phrases (e.g., *as soon as, in order to, provided that …*).

See a good grammar reference book for full explanations.

3 Adverbial phrases add information about the actions or processes described by the verb phrase.

Closure

Put these sentences from an advertising campaign for an electric car (The Bean) on the board. Get students to identify the marked words and phrases that show the company's stance and level of confidence in their product. Get more neutral alternatives.

'The Bean' – our new electric car

Everyone knows that carbon emissions are destroying the planet.

Research shows that this is a result of petrol cars.

Why not do your bit to help save the planet? Make your next car electric!

University studies have shown The Bean is the cleanest car available.

Experts agree: The Bean will make the difference.

Answer:

Many people believe (Everyone knows) that carbon emissions are damaging (destroying) the planet.

Research suggests that one cause might be (this is a result of) petrol cars.

University studies claim (have shown) the Bean is one of the cleanest cars available.

Experts seem to agree: The Bean may (will) make a (the) difference.

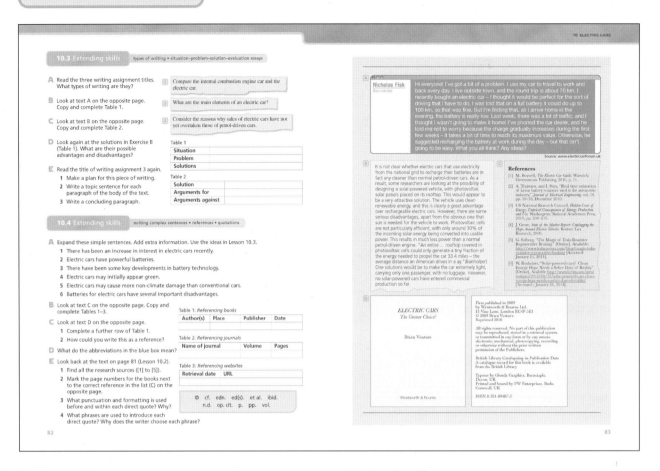

10.3 Extending skills

Lesson aims

- understand situation–problem–solution–evaluation structure in pieces of writing such as reports
- understand the use of information in this type of structure to:

    describe

    give cause and effect

    compare

    evaluate

Further practice in:

- identifying required types of writing
- producing an outline
- writing key sentences – which can be expanded in the next lesson into longer sentences

Introduction

Revise the different types of writing that were examined in Unit 8. Say or write on the board some key words or phrases from written assignment titles, such as the following:

State …

Outline …

Describe how a … works.

Compare …

Contrast …

What are the stages of …?

Why …?

How …?

Ask students to say

- what type of writing is required
- what type of organizational structure should be used

If students find this difficult, refer them to the *Skills bank* for Unit 8.

Exercise A

Set for individual work and pairwork checking.

Feed back with the whole class. Point out that in real life, written assignments given by lecturers often involve several types of writing in one piece of work. This is the case with writing example 3. Tell students that in fact a possible structure for piece 3 would be the following, which is commonly found in many types of writing (including newspapers and academic writing).

Situation: description of a situation/object, often giving some reasons and background information	description
Problem(s): the problems which are caused by the situation; plus the effects of these problems	description (cause and effect)
Solution(s): ways of dealing with the problems (i) which may have been tried in the past or are being tried now; (ii) which will, may or could be tried in the future	description (+ possibly suggestion)
Evaluation of solution(s): comparison of solutions; opinion on how successful the solutions are or could be + justification; an opinion on which is the best option + justification	comparison and argument

Tell students they will plan (and possibly write) this piece of text.

Answers

Model answers:

1 Comparison.

2 Outline/research report.

3 Description, then comparison and evaluation/argument/opinion, plus support (see table above).

Exercise B

Set for individual work and pairwork checking. Feed back with the whole class.

Answers

Model answers:

Situation	the person has recently bought an electric car to commute to and from work every day – a 70 km round trip
Problem	the car is only just managing to cover the daily distance; the person is worried that one day soon the car's battery might run out of power
Solutions	• wait a few weeks, since the power of the battery might continue to increase with use • try to recharge the battery at work during the day

Exercise C

Set for individual work and pairwork checking. Feed back with the whole class.

Answers

Model answers:

Solution	a solar-powered vehicle would be much greener than present electric cars
Argument for	the vehicle would use sunlight, which is a clean, renewable source of energy
Argument against	direct sunlight is needed for the vehicle to work; also, the vehicle needs to be very light and can carry only one passenger

Exercise D

Set for pairwork discussion. Feed back with the whole class. Accept any reasonable suggestions. Common-sense answers are also suitable here.

	Advantages	Disadvantages
Wait a few weeks	• no need to do anything	• may not work and the person will find him/herself in the same situation • battery may no longer be under warranty
Try to recharge the battery at work	• no worries about reaching home after a working day (8 hours) • the battery can be completely recharged • recharging may be free, depending on the employer	• suitable charging point necessary, near a parking area, available for the whole of the working day • charging point with appropriate voltage and socket-type required

Exercise E

1 Set for pairwork discussion. Remind students to refer back to the text in Lesson 10.2 for ideas and information, as well as the texts they have discussed in this lesson. Remind students about the basic structure of this type of writing (introduction – main body – conclusion).

If you wish, you can give students the first two columns of the table in the Answers section, with the third column empty for them to complete. The table is reproduced in the additional resources section (Resource 10B) for this purpose.

Feed back with the whole class. Build the plan on the board, using the ideas in the Answers section to help.

2 Ask students to write some topic sentences for the four body paragraphs, using the information in the plan. Remind students that topic sentences need to be very general. Set for individual work.

Feed back with the whole class, writing some examples on the board.

3 Set for pairwork, then discussion with the whole class. Or if you prefer, set for individual homework. The ideas should be those of the students. Remind them to introduce their ideas with suitable phrases.

Note: Students will need their plans again in Lesson 10.4.

Answers

1 Possible plan:

Introduction	Examples of ideas	
introduce the topic area give the outline of the report	electric cars → still not very popular *In this writing assignment, I will discuss the problems …*	
Body	**Para 1:** situation/problems (general)	interest in electric cars has increased recently ∵ 1. ↑ petrol prices 2. worries: fossil fuels → high carbon emissions
	Para 2: solutions	• electric cars: powerful batteries → travel reasonable distances • battery technology: new lithium batteries → advantages
	Para 3: evaluations of solutions – arguments for	• electric cars: produce no pollution while driving, engines more efficient → greener, regenerative braking → saves energy • lithium batteries: longer life, lighter
	Para 4: evaluations of solutions – arguments against	• electric cars: electricity needed for recharging → cars initially appear green (may not be true ∵ how electricity produced: e.g., using fossil fuel) • electric cars: may cause more non-climate damage than conventional cars: manufacture of cars+batteries (evidence: a recent study) • batteries: limited range, limited lifespan, expensive, recharging time
Conclusion	*In my view/As I see it, the main reason why … is because …* *Firstly …* *Secondly …* *Thirdly …*	

2 Possible topic sentences:

Para 1	Recently, there has been a lot of criticism of our reliance on vehicles powered by fossil fuels.
Para 2	As a result of the problems of petrol cars, a lot of research and new technology has been dedicated to the invention of an electric car.
Para 3	Electric cars appear to have some important advantages over traditional petrol cars.
Para 4	However, there are also some disadvantages associated with electric cars.

3 Students' own concluding paragraphs.

Language note

Although 'situation–problem–solution–evaluation
of solution' is often said to be an organizing
principle in writing, in practice it is sometimes
difficult to distinguish between the situation and
the problem: they may sometimes seem to be the
same thing. The important thing is to be clear
about the main *focus* of the piece of writing – that
is, the answer to the question *What am I writing
about?* – and to structure the piece of writing
around this.

Closure

Set up a discussion activity: 'The next car we buy
should be an electric one.' Divide the class into two
groups. Tell one group that they agree with the
statement, and the other group that they disagree with
it. Give them 5–10 minutes to brainstorm ideas in their
group to support their view.

Then create pairs, with one student from each group,
and tell them to argue their case to their partner. In
feedback, get some responses from the whole group on
whether they managed to convince their partner to
change their mind. Ask which were the most
convincing arguments, and, finally, ask what they *really*
think about the issue, i.e., not necessarily the opinion
you told them to argue for.

10.3 Extending skills — types of writing • situation–problem–solution–evaluation essays

A Read the three writing assignment titles. What types of writing are they?

B Look at text A on the opposite page. Copy and complete Table 1.

C Look at text B on the opposite page. Copy and complete Table 2.

D Look again at the solutions in Exercise B (Table 1). What are their possible advantages and disadvantages?

E Read the title of writing assignment 3 again.
1 Make a plan for this piece of writing.
2 Write a topic sentence for each paragraph of the body of the text.
3 Write a concluding paragraph.

1 Compare the internal combustion engine car and the electric car.

2 What are the main elements of an electric car?

3 Consider the reasons why sales of electric cars have not yet overtaken those of petrol-driven cars.

Table 1
Situation	
Problem	
Solutions	

Table 2
Solution	
Arguments for	
Arguments against	

10.4 Extending skills — writing complex sentences • references • quotations

A Expand these simple sentences. Add extra information. Use the ideas in Lesson 10.3.
1 There has been an increase in interest in electric cars recently.
2 Electric cars have powerful batteries.
3 There have been some key developments in battery technology.
4 Electric cars may initially appear green.
5 Electric cars may cause more non-climate damage than conventional cars.
6 Batteries for electric cars have several important disadvantages.

B Look at text C on the opposite page. Copy and complete Tables 1–3.

C Look at text D on the opposite page.
1 Complete a further row of Table 1.
2 How could you write this as a reference?

D What do the abbreviations in the blue box mean?

E Look back at the text on page 81 (Lesson 10.2).
1 Find all the research sources ([1] to [5]).
2 Mark the page numbers for the books next to the correct reference in the list (C) on the opposite page.
3 What punctuation and formatting is used before and within each direct quote? Why?
4 What phrases are used to introduce each direct quote? Why does the writer choose each phrase?

Table 1: Referencing books
Author(s)	Place	Publisher	Date

Table 2: Referencing journals
Name of journal	Volume	Pages

Table 3: Referencing websites
Retrieval date	URL

cf. edn. ed(s). et al. ibid.
n.d. op. cit. p. pp. vol.

General note

This lesson focuses on writing references for a bibliography according to the IEEE (Institute of Electrical and Electronic Engineers) system. Before the lesson, it would be useful to familiarize yourself with this system. For more detailed information, see websites such as http://libguides.murdoch.edu.au/content.php?pid=144623&sid=1229929 or http://owl.english.purdue.edu/owl/section/2/

Lesson aims

• use quotations with appropriate punctuation and abbreviations such as *ed.* (edition)
• write a reference list (IEEE system)

Further practice in:

• the reverse activity to Lesson 10.2, i.e., putting extra information into simple sentences in an appropriate way

Introduction

Introduce the idea of using sources in writing. Look back at the text in Lesson 10.2 and ask students to find all the places where a reference to a source is mentioned. Ask them to find a quotation and a paraphrase. What are the main differences?

Exercise A

Remind students of the writing plan in Lesson 10.3. If you wish, you can reproduce the following table for them. They should try to get all the information in each numbered point into one sentence.

Para 1	1. interest in electric cars has increased recently ∴ (i) ↑ petrol prices, (ii) worries: fossil fuels → high carbon emissions
Para 2	2. electric cars: powerful batteries → travel reasonable distances 3. battery technology: new lithium batteries → advantages
Paras 3 & 4	4. electric cars: electricity needed for recharging → cars initially appear green (may not be true ∴ how electricity produced? e.g., using fossil fuels) 5. electric cars: may cause more non-climate damage than conventional cars: manufacture of cars+batteries (evidence: a recent study) 6. batteries: limited range, limited lifespan, expensive, recharging time

Do the first sentence with the whole class as an example on the board. Students should feel free to add words as appropriate to make a coherent sentence.

Set the remaining sentences for individual work.

Answers

Possible answers:

1 There has been an increase in interest in electric cars recently due to rising petrol prices and worries that fossil fuels produce high carbon emissions.

2 Electric cars have powerful batteries, which allow them to travel reasonable distances.

3 Recently, there have been some key developments in battery technology, resulting in lithium batteries, which have some interesting advantages over older models.

4 Electric cars may initially appear green, since they do not use fossil fuels; however, the electricity they need for recharging needs to be produced somehow, for example, by a fossil-fuel power station.

5 A recent study suggests that electric cars may cause more non-climate damage than conventional cars as a result of side-effects of the manufacturing process when building the car and its battery.

6 Batteries for electric cars have several important disadvantages, such as having a limited range and lifespan, being expensive, as well as requiring considerable recharging time.

Exercise B

Tell students that this is a list of references from the text in Lesson 10.2. Note that it is called 'References' because it lists all the references actually given (it is not a list of all the references the author might have consulted but not referred to – that is a bibliography).

Set for individual work and pairwork checking. Note that these tables are intended to help students identify some key information. For a full set of categories to include in a reference list, see the *Skills bank*. Tell students that when writing a reference list, they will need to pay close attention to the detail of the layout which is in the IEEE style (the Institute of Electrical and Electronics Engineers). See the *Skills bank* for a website which (at the time of writing) gives further details. In particular, students should note and will need to practise:

- putting the references in order of their appearance in the text, numbering from [1]
- using the right spacing and punctuation for names of writers and multiple writers
- writing all numbers correctly, including dates and page references
- using punctuation, including the role and placing of full stops, commas and colons
- laying out the references in the correct style with the correct positions (e.g., of indents and tabs)

- using standard IEEE style features such as italic, quotation marks and square brackets

Answers

Table 1:

Author(s)	Place of publication	Publisher	Date of publication
M. Boxwell	Warwick	Greenstream Publishing	2010
J. Grose	Boston	Lux Research	2009
US National Research Council	Washington	National Academies Press	2010

Table 2:

Name of journal	Volume	Pages
Journal of Electrical Engineering	10	p. 10–16

Table 3:

Retrieval date	URL
January 24, 2014	http://www.teslamotors.com/blog/magic-tesla-roadster-regenerative-braking
January 24, 2014	http://www.forbes.com/sites/realspin/2012/08/15/solar-powered-cars-clean-energy-hype-needs-a-sober-dose-of-reality/

Language and subject note

In the case of journals, there is an increasing tendency to refer to the volume number only in reference lists, omitting the issue number. Thus, for example, *English for Specific Purposes, vol. 16, no. 1, pp. 47–60* might become *English for Specific Purposes, vol. 16, pp. 47–60*. Furthermore, journals are now most frequently referred to by their Digital Object Identifier, or 'DOI'.

Exercise C

Set for individual work and pairwork checking.

Answers

1

Author(s)	Place of publication	Publisher	Date of publication
B. Venture	London	Wentworth & Bourne Ltd.	2010

2 B. Venture, *Electric Cars: The Greener Choice?* London: Wentworth & Bourne, 2010.

Exercise D

Many of these were covered in Unit 5, so ask students to check back if they are not sure, or they can refer to the list at the back of their books; they can also check online at the IEEE referencing system sites given at the beginning of this unit and in the *Skills bank*.

Set for individual work and pairwork checking.

Answers

Model answers:

©	copyright
cf.	compare
edn.	edition
ed(s).	editor(s)
et al.	and other authors
ibid.	same work (or place in a work) as cited in immediately preceding reference
n.d.	no date (used in a reference list if there is no date – as is often the case with web articles)
op. cit.	the work already referred to
p.	page
pp.	pages
vol. (journal); Vol. (book)	volume

Exercise E

Remind students (if you have not done so already) of the two main ways in which they can use sources (i.e., references to other writers' work) in their writing:

- by giving the exact words used by another writer
- by paraphrasing another writer's ideas, i.e., rewriting the ideas using their own, different words but retaining the meaning

The first method is referred to as quotation or direct quotation. Short direct quotations should be in double quotation marks, and incorporated into the paragraph. Quotations of more than one sentence should be 'display quote' style, i.e., on a new line, and indented.

The second method is referred to as paraphrase, summary or indirect quotation. Note that around 90% of the paraphrase should be new words.

1/2 Set for individual work. Tell students to look for all the direct quotations. These are numbered [1] and [3] in the reading text. (References [2], [4] and [5] do not contain direct quotations.) They should then locate the source in the reference list on page 83 of the Course Book. Writing the page numbers on the reference list may seem a mechanical exercise, but it is useful for students to get into the habit of doing this. It will enable them to find an original source book, refer to the relevant part of the book, and read more about the subject.

3/4 Students should identify the punctuation and introducing phrases used. Emphasize that unlike other referencing systems, such as APA, the IEEE systems includes reference numbers in square brackets before the closing quotation mark.

Feed back with the whole class.

Answers

Model answers:

See table on next page.

Quote	Source	Punctuation/formatting before/within each direct quote	Introducing phrase + reason for choice
"80-mile range is achievable … with careful driving [1]."	page 11 of Boxwell, M. (2010). *The Electric Car Guide*. Warwick: Greenstream Publishing	"xxx[ref. no.]."	… on a single charge, an reason: the quote gives an example of what a single charge can achieve, so there is no need for an introducing phrase
"… have somewhat higher damages and global-warming potential than other technologies … in large measure due to the continued conventional emissions from the existing and likely future grid [3]."	pages 200–219 of US National Research Council (2010). *Hidden Costs of Energy: Unpriced consequences of energy production and use*. Washington: National Academies Press	"Xxx[ref. no.]."	As a recent report states, electric cars reason: the quote backs up the assertion in the previous statement, as shown by the use of use of 'as'. 'a recent report' gives authority to the view.
"poses issues of worker exposure to metals as well as a potential for both conventional and greenhouse gas emissions from the manufacturing process [3]".	page 200 of US National Research Council (2010). *Hidden Costs of Energy: Unpriced consequences of energy production and use*. Washington: National Academies Press	"xxx[ref. no.]."	A recent study has found that battery manufacture reason: the introducing phrase tells the reader the quote gives evidence to support the point made in the previous sentence and gives authority to this assertion.
"An entire … rooftop covered in photovoltaic cells could only generate a tiny fraction of the energy needed to propel the car 33.4 miles – the average distance an American drives in a day."	W. Banholzer, "Solar-powered cars? Clean Energy Hype Needs a Sober Dose of Reality." [Online]. Available: http://www.forbes.com/sites/ realspin/2012/08/15/solar- powered-cars-clean-energy- hype-needs-a-sober-dose-of- reality/ [Accessed: January 24, 2014].	"xxx." (author's surname)	No introducing phrase. The quote gives an example to illustrate what was said in the previous sentence. The relationship is clear, so no introducing phrase is needed.

Language and subject note

Use *and* (preceded by a comma) rather than an ampersand (&) for two or more authors. For three or more authors, the authors should be separated by commas, with the final author preceded by a comma, then *and*. For more than six authors, et al. should be used after the first author's name.

A full stop is inserted at the end of a URL, followed by [Accessed: date, year].

Dates are (for example) April 7 not April 7th.

Closure

Refer students to the *Skills bank* for a summary of writing references. Study how the following are used:

order of references

- punctuation (capital letters, full stops, commas, colons)
- layout (indentation, spacing)
- style features (italics, brackets)

For further practice, use Resource 10C from the additional resources section. Ask students to check the references in a library database or on the Internet (discuss which sources are likely to be the most accurate and give them all the information they need – often the best way to check bibliographical details is to use a university library catalogue, as information found on the Internet is frequently inaccurate or incomplete). They should also make any necessary changes to ensure the references fit the IEEE model used in this unit. If possible, they should use the online website references (see *Skills bank*) to help them. Remind students that they will also need to put the references in the order in which they are cited in the text.

Correct versions are:

[1] P. L. Carrell, and J. G. Carson, "Extensive and intensive reading in an EAP setting," *English for Specific Purposes*, vol. 16, 1997, pp. 47–60.

[2] A. El Shahat, and H. El Shewy, "PM synchronous motor drive system for automotive applications." *Journal of Electrical Systems*, vol. 6, no. 2, 2010, pp. 10–20.

[3] D. A. Kirsch, *The Electric Car and the Burden of History.* Rutgers: Rutgers University Press, 2000.

[4] G. B. Kliman, and H. A. Toliyat, *Handbook of Electric Motors*, 2nd ed. Boca Raton: CRC Press, 2004.

[5] F. Romero, (2009). "A Brief History of the Electric Car." [Online]. Available: http://www.time.com/time/business/article/0,8599, 1871282,00.html [Accessed: December 11, 2013].

Extra activities

1 Work through the *Skills bank* and *Vocabulary bank* if you have not already done so, or as revision of previous study.

2 Use the *Activity bank* (Teacher's Book additional resources section, Resource 10A).

    A Set the wordsearch for individual work (including homework) or pairwork.

Answers

    B Set for individual work (including homework) or pairwork. Accept all reasonable answers. Students should be able to explain the meaning.

3 Ask students to choose one of the other writing types in Lesson 10.3 and make a plan. They can also write topic sentences for each paragraph in the piece of writing.

Answers

Possible answers:

rechargeable, lithium, lead-acid, dead, flat, car	battery
regenerative	braking
electric, petrol-driven	car
carbon, exhaust	emissions
internal combustion, two-stroke, turbine	engine
electricity	generation
electric, petrol, diesel	motor
air, water, land, non-climate, industrial, lead, vehicle, nuclear	pollution
exhaust	pipe
air-conditioning, computer, electronic, audio, stereo, sound, satellite, alarm, heating	system

11 MICROELECTROMECHANICAL SYSTEMS

This unit looks in more detail at MEMS and NEMS (micro- and nanoelectromechanical systems), and covers how they are manufactured and some of their applications. Examples of devices using MEMS and NEMS are given, along with potential future developments.

Skills focus

 Listening

- recognizing the speaker's stance
- writing up notes in full

Speaking

- building an argument in a seminar
- agreeing/disagreeing

Vocabulary focus

- words/phrases used to link ideas (*moreover*, *as a result*, etc.)
- stress patterns in noun phrases and compounds
- fixed phrases from academic English

Key vocabulary

See also the list of fixed phrases from academic English in the *Vocabulary bank* (Course Book page 92).

accelerometer	electromechanical	MEMS	sensor
acid	etching	microscopic	shade (n)
actuator	fraction	mirror	shut
airbag	glue	nano	spread (v)
attach	hearing aid	NEMS	spring (n)
base	hinge	pattern	surface (n)
beam (n)	huge	photosensitive	tiny
blood	instantly	place (v)	transduction
building block	lab-on-a-chip	projector	tray
cantilever (n)	layer	radiation	tyre
carbon nanotube	main	reflection	urine
deposition	mask	saliva	X-rays
dissolve	mass	screen (n)	
drawback	massive	secure (v)	

11.1 Vocabulary

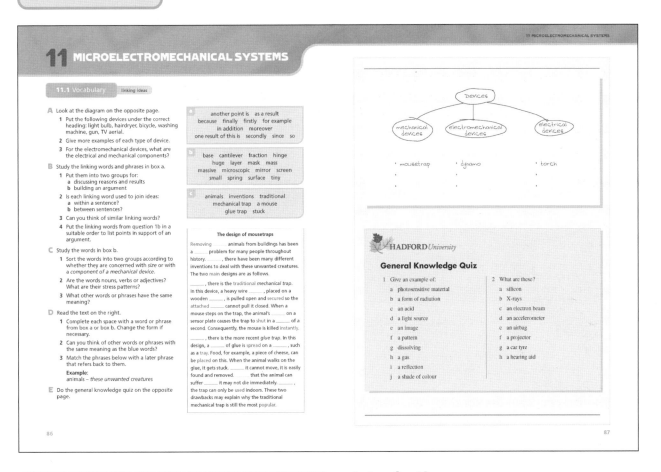

General note

Read the *Vocabulary bank* at the end of the Course Book unit. Decide when, if at all, to refer your students to it. The best time is probably at the very end of the lesson or the beginning of the next lesson, as a summary/revision.

Lesson aims

- use rhetorical markers: to add points in an argument; to signal cause and effect (between- and within-sentence linking)
- further understand lexical cohesion: the use of superordinates/synonyms to refer back to something already mentioned; building lexical chains

Further practice in:

- synonyms, antonyms and word sets from the discipline
- abbreviations and acronyms

Introduction

1 Revise some vocabulary from previous units. Give students some key words from the previous unit (in italic below) and ask them to think of terms connected with these words:

petrol prices/cars, electric *cars*, air *pollution*, *carbon* emissions, *exhaust* pipe, fossil *fuel*, side-*effects*, *manufacturing* process, *lead-acid* battery, lithium *battery*, pollution/non-climate *damage*

2 Introduce the topic: before asking students to open their books, ask them what they remember from Unit 2 about the development of the microprocessors.

Exercise A

Ask students to open their books and look at the diagram on page 87.

1 Set for pairwork. Feed back with the class.

2/3 Set for pairwork. Ask a few pairs to feed back to the class. Accept any reasonable suggestions.

Answers

Possible answers:

1 See diagram.

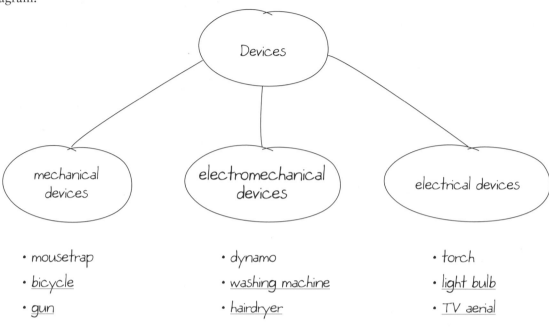

2 Some more examples of devices are:

Mechanical: a bicycle pump/a gear lever/a car bumper

Electromechanical: a car starter motor/a door bell/ a switch

Electrical: battery/a fuse/a spark plug

3 For the electromechanical devices, the electrical and mechanical components are:

	electrical components	mechanical components
Dynamo:	coil of wire magnet	brushes wheel
Washing machine:	motor cable	gearbox steel tub damping system concrete block (counter weight)
Hairdryer:	motor cable heating element	fan

For other examples, accept all reasonable answers and correct where necessary.

Add some of these to the diagram, as appropriate and as students suggest them. It would be a good idea to make a large poster-sized copy of the diagram or put it on an OHT or other visual medium, to which you can add more examples as the unit progresses.

Exercise B

1 Set for individual work and pairwork checking. Feed back with the whole class, building the table in the Answers section.

2 Explain what is meant by 'within' a sentence and 'between' sentences: 'within-sentence' linking words or phrases join clauses in a sentence; 'between-sentence' linking words or phrases connect two sentences. Demonstrate with the following:

Within-sentence linking words:

A TV aerial isn't a mechanical device, <u>because</u> there are no moving parts.

Make sure students can see that within-sentence linking words precede dependent clauses.

Between-sentence linking words:

A hairdryer is powered by electricity, but has some moving parts. <u>As a result</u>, it is an electromechanical device.

Point out that with between-sentence linking words there is usually a comma before the rest of the sentence.

Ask students to say which of the other words in box a are 'between' and which are 'within'.

3 Ask for suggestions for synonyms and add to the table.

4 First, make sure that students understand the basic principle of an argument, which is:

```
┌─────────────────────┐
│      Statement      │
└─────────────────────┘
           +
┌─────────────────────────────────┐
│  one or more support(s) for statement │
│  (= more facts, reasons, results,      │
│      examples, evidence, etc.)         │
└─────────────────────────────────┘
```

Constructing a complex argument will usually entail a statement plus several supports.

With the whole class, elicit suggestions for how to use the linking words/phrases when constructing an argument. Build the table in the Answers section on the board.

Answers

Possible answers:

1/2/3

Linking words/phrases	Use for	Within or between sentence	Other similar words/phrases
another point is	building an argument	between	and another thing
as a result	reasons and results	between	consequently
because	reasons and results	within	as
finally	building an argument	between	lastly
firstly	building an argument	between	to begin with/to start with for one thing
for example	building an argument	between	for instance
in addition	building an argument	between	also
moreover	building an argument	between	furthermore
one result of this is	reasons and results	between	one consequence of this is because of this
secondly	building an argument	between	next then
since	reasons and results	within	as
so	reasons and results	between	therefore thus hence

4 A typical argument is constructed like this:

firstly	making the first major support point
for example	supporting the point with a specific example
in addition	adding another related point in support
secondly	making the second major support point
another point is	adding another related point in support
moreover	adding more information to the point above
finally	making the last point

Language note

1 Note that within-sentence linking words may be placed at the beginning of the sentence with a comma after the first clause, as in:

Because there are no moving parts, a TV aerial isn't a mechanical device.

2 Although the between-sentence linking words are described above as joining two sentences, they can of course link two independent clauses joined by coordinating linking words *and* or *but*, as in:

*A hairdryer is powered by electricity, but has some moving parts, and, **as a result**, it is an electromechanical device.*

Exercise C

1 Set for individual work. Note that students should try to put each word into one of the two categories, even if it is not immediately clear how it could be relevant.

2/3 Set for pairwork. Feed back with the whole class if you wish.

Answers

Model answers (see next page):

Word	Suggested categories	Part of speech	Other words/phrases
base	component	n (C)	support
'cantilever	component	n (C)	
'fraction	size	n (C)	a small percentage
hinge	component	n (C)	
huge	size	adj	massive, enormous, gigantic
layer	component	n (C)	covering, coating
mask	component	n (C)	cover, screen
mass	component	n (C)	weight
'massive	size	adj	huge, enormous, gigantic
micro'scopic	size	adj	minuscule, minute, tiny
'mirror	component	n (C)	
screen	component	n (C)	
small	size	adj	little
spring	component	n (C)	
'surface	component	n (C)	top
tiny	size	adj	very small, microscopic

Exercise D

Note: Students may need to use dictionaries in question 2.

Students should first read through the text to get an idea of the topic.

1/2 Set for individual work and pairwork checking. Feed back with the whole class.

Point out that, having answered these questions, students should now be able to say whether the words in box b can be put into a 'size' or a 'component of a mechanical device' group. The point here is that the context will make clear what the meaning of a word should be. This is important when it comes to making a guess at the meaning of a word you are not sure of initially.

3 It is also common to use synonymous or superordinate words and phrases to refer back to something already mentioned. Ideally, use an OHT, or other visual medium, of the text (see Resource 11B in the additional resources section), and with a coloured pen draw a line to show how *animals* is referred to later in the text by *these unwanted creatures*. Set for individual work and pairwork checking. Feed back with the class (linking the phrases with coloured pens if using Resource 11B).

Answers

Model answers:

1 Removing <u>small</u> animals from buildings has been a <u>huge</u> problem for many people throughout history. <u>As a result</u>, there have been many different inventions to deal with these unwanted creatures. The two main designs are as follows.

<u>Firstly</u>, there is the traditional *mechanical trap*. In this device, a heavy wire <u>hinge</u>, placed on a wooden <u>base</u>, is pulled open and secured so the attached <u>spring</u> cannot pull it closed. When a mouse steps on the trap, the animal's <u>mass</u> on a sensor plate causes the trap to shut in a <u>fraction</u> of a second. Consequently, the mouse is killed instantly.

<u>Secondly</u>, there is the more recent *glue trap*. In this design, a <u>layer</u> of glue is spread on a <u>surface</u>, such as a tray. Food, for example, a piece of cheese, can be placed on this. When the animal walks on the glue, it gets stuck. <u>Since</u> it cannot move, it is easily found and removed. <u>One result of this is</u> that the animal can suffer <u>because</u> it may not die immediately. <u>In addition</u>, the trap can only be used indoors. These two drawbacks may explain why the traditional design is still the most popular.

2

Word	Synonym
removing	eliminating, getting rid of
main	principal, key, primary
traditional	classic, conventional
secured	fixed, fastened
attached	connected, joined
shut	close
instantly	immediately, right away
spread	distributed
tray	board
placed	put
used	employed, utilized, operated
popular	common, widespread

3

First phrase	Second phrase
animals	these unwanted creatures
inventions	designs
traditional mechanical trap	this device
a mouse	the animal
glue trap	this design
stuck	cannot move

Exercise E

Time this general knowledge quiz if you wish. Alternatively, set it for homework for students to research the answers. Make sure that students understand they need to give an example of the items in the first column, and a definition or explanation of the items in the second column.

In order to be able to follow the lecture in Lesson 11.2, students will need to be familiar with these words.

Answers

Model answers:

1 a photosensitive material – photographic film
   b radiation – light
   c an acid – citric acid
   d a light source – a light bulb
   e an image – a photo taken by a digital camera
   f a pattern – stripes on a shirt
   g dissolving – stirring sugar in tea
   h a gas – oxygen
   i a reflection – an image in a mirror
   j a shade of colour – pink

2 a silicon – a brittle metalloid element used in electronic components
   b X-rays – a type of electromagnetic radiation between UV and gamma rays
   c an electron beam – streams of electrons in vacuum tubes, also known as cathode rays
   d an accelerometer – a device for measuring the acceleration of a moving body to which it is attached.
   e an airbag – a vehicle safety device consisting of a flexible, expandable envelope that inflates rapidly during a crash to prevent passengers hitting the interior of the vehicle
   f a projector – an optical device that creates an image on a surface or screen
   g a car tyre – the rubber ring on a car wheel
   h a hearing aid – an amplifying device to improve the hearing of people who are deaf or hard of hearing

Closure

Play the guessing game: 'Electrical, mechanical or electromechanical'. Give an example first with the whole class. Think of an object, e.g., a light bulb. Students have to ask questions to try to guess what the object is. The first question is always: 'Is it electrical, mechanical or electromechanical?' So the answer for a light bulb is 'electrical' since there are no moving parts. After this question, students can ask ten further questions, which can be answered by only *yes* or *no*. If, after these ten questions, they have not guessed what the object is, tell them. Then divide the class into small groups to play the game amongst themselves.

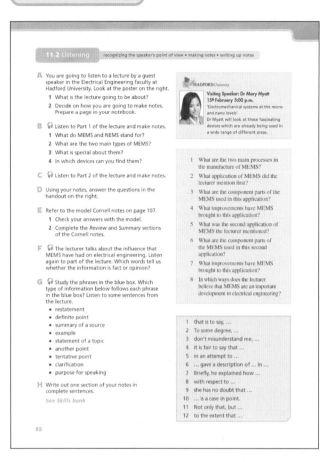

General note

Read the *Skills bank – Writing out notes in full* at the end of the Course Book unit. Decide when, if at all, to refer students to it. The best time, as before, is probably at the very end of the lesson or the beginning of the next lesson, as a summary/revision.

Lesson aims

- recognize and understand phrases that identify the speaker's point of view
- use background knowledge in listening comprehension
- convert notes into full sentences and paragraphs

Further practice in:

- making notes (use of heading systems and abbreviations)
- referring to sources
- general academic words and phrases

Introduction

1 Review phrases indicating a speaker's view of the truth value of a statement. Write a sentence such as the following on the board (i.e., a 'fact' about which there may be differences of opinion): *Electronic engineering is the most exciting branch of engineering.*

Ask students to say whether they think this is true or not. Elicit phrases they can use before the sentence to show how certain they are about their opinion.

Dictate or write on the board the following phrases. Ask students to say what the effect of each phrase is when put before the sentence on the board. In each case, does it make the writer sound confident or tentative?

The research shows that …

A survey found that …

The evidence does not support the idea that …

It appears to be the case that …

The evidence suggests that …

The evidence shows that …

It is clear that …

It is possible that …

2 Revise the Cornell note-taking system. Elicit the R words. Ask students to describe how to divide up the page (refer to Unit 9). Revise the other ways to take notes (see Units 1 and 3).

3 Revise note-taking symbols and abbreviations (see Units 5 and 9, and Unit 9 extra activity 4).

Exercise A

Refer students to the Hadford University lecture announcement. Tell them to look at the title and the summary of the talk. Check that they know the meaning of 'micro' and 'nano': micro = prefix denoting 10^{-6} (ten to the power minus six, i.e., one millionth); nano = prefix denoting 10^{-9} (i.e., one billionth).

Set the exercises for pairwork discussion. Feed back with the whole class.

Answers

1 Accept any reasonable suggestions.

2 The lecturer is clearly going to talk about two types of electromechanical device: micro and nano. This suggests that possibly a table or two columns might be a suitable form of notes (as in Unit 1), as well as the Cornell system (which is used here) or the more conventional numbered points system.

🎧 Exercise B

Play Part 1 once through *without* allowing students time to focus on the questions.

Put students in pairs to answer the questions by referring to their notes. Feed back with the whole class, building a set of notes on the board if you wish.

Ask students which method they are going to use to make notes, now that they have listened to the introduction. They should make any adjustments necessary to the page they have prepared in their notebooks.

Answers

Model answers:

1 MEMS = microelectromechanical systems; NEMS = nanoelectromechanical systems.

2 (a) Sensors, which collect data, and (b) actuators, which follow commands.

3 They are very small: between one and a hundred micrometres (1–100 μm).

4 Inkjet printers, car tyre pressure sensors, video projectors, hearing aids.

Transcript 🎧 2.16

Part 1

Good morning. My name is Dr Mary Myatt and I'm an electrical engineer and researcher working in the field of microsystems technology, or MST. It's a pleasure to be here today. I'm going to explain some of the main developments that are happening in the field of microelectromechanical systems, that is to say, I shall be looking at very small mechanical devices built onto semiconductor chips. To some degree, I believe that the area of microelectromechanical systems – or MEMS for short – is perhaps the most interesting sector of electrical engineering at the present time. Now, don't misunderstand me, I'm not implying that other areas of electrical engineering are boring! But it is fair to say that there is something particularly exciting about the developments in MEMS and, recently, at a nano level – NEMS.

So, in an attempt to give you an overall picture of this field, let's start with the question: What are MEMS? Well, although they are very modern, they were first predicted in 1959 by Richard Feynman. Feynman gave a description of smaller and smaller machines in his famous talk: 'There's plenty of room at the bottom.' Briefly, he explained how building and controlling devices at smaller scales would have a wide range of potential applications. And this is exactly what has happened with respect to a number of common electrical products.

MEMS consist of an electrical element and a mechanical element. The electrical element is a central microprocessor, which processes data. The mechanical element acts in response to this data. Now, there are two main types of MEMS: sensors and actuators. *Sensor* devices collect data, whereas *actuators* follow commands with highly controlled movements. The thing to remember about MEMS is their size: between one and a hundred micrometres – about the thickness of a human hair. Yes, tiny! MEMS can be found in inkjet printers, car tyre pressure sensors, video projectors, hearing aids and many, many other products. Today, I want to look at how MEMS are manufactured, and explore two uses of MEMS in more detail: in car crash sensors and in the latest video projectors.

🎧 Exercise C

Play the whole of the rest of lecture through *once* without stopping. Students should make notes as they listen.

Answers

See *Notes* section of the table in the Answers section for Exercise E.

Transcript 🎧 2.17

Part 2

Let's first look at how MEMS are made. The manufacturing process is similar to that of typical microelectronic products, and uses the same materials – silicon, for example. Extremely thin layers of various materials are deposited onto a base. This is the *deposition* stage. After this, a pattern, or design, is transferred onto the layers. This is usually done using a photosensitive material – a material which changes its physical properties when exposed to a radiation source, such as an electron beam or X-rays. The important point here is that the material is not uniformly exposed to the radiation. Some of it is masked, and, so … we've got two parts. The properties of the two parts become different. I mean, the parts of the material which were exposed develop different properties from the parts which were hidden. These differences can then be exploited, and exposed parts removed by dissolving them in a chemical solution, such as an acid, or by allowing them to react to a gas or a combination of gases. This process of removing parts of a layer is known as *etching*. Etching leaves a microscopic three-dimensional surface. In this way, both electrical and mechanical components are constructed.

Now let's look at some applications of MEMS. First, I want to talk about car crash sensors. The MEMS that are used here are a form of accelerometer – they measure changes in the car's speed. Inside the tiny device, there is a weight attached to a spring or hinge, and this mass moves as the car slows down or speeds up. The MEMS contain electrical sensors that can send data about the movement of the mass to a microprocessor, which monitors this information. In a crash, there is a sudden negative acceleration – a deceleration – and when this reaches a certain critical level, the airbags open. All this happens in a fraction of a second. Now, airbags in cars have been around for some time, so you might wonder what's so special about using a MEMS for this. Well, I have a colleague who's been directly involved in the development of these new sensors, and she has no doubt that the use of MEMS has meant a huge improvement on earlier versions, making the sensors more reliable – and this means safer – as well as cheaper.

Another product that has been greatly improved by the use of MEMS is the video projector. Do you remember I talked about some MEMS being actuators? Well, this is a case in point. These actuators use micro-mirror devices to improve image quality. Micro-mirror devices consist of extremely small mirrors attached to hinges. The mirror can move on the hinge in two directions: towards the light source, which means the mirror will reflect the light, or away from the light source, which means the light will be blocked. Each mirror corresponds to one pixel of the projected image, so if the mirror reflects the light source there will be a tiny point of light on the screen. Not only that, but the amount of time the mirror reflects light will also give the perception of brightness: the longer it reflects, the brighter the point. In this way, up to sixteen million different shades of colour can be achieved. Now this is a massive improvement on previous technology, to the extent that it is now being used in cinemas, and replacing old film projectors.

Some people say that MEMS don't bring anything new to electrical engineering – it's simply a case of making existing devices smaller. But the evidence shows that this is not really the whole story. In my view, both the examples I have presented today show how MEMS can *improve* existing products, making them more reliable and more accurate, and sometimes doing the task more cheaply. If we don't recognize the benefits that MEMS can bring, and act on them, we could get left behind and that would be a disaster. As Feynman said in his excellent talk, the whole of technology benefits as a result of developing smaller-scale devices. Actually,

MEMS are destined to become more and more important in the future, in all sorts of different ways. Now, I'm going to stop at this point and …

Note

Source references for lecture:

R. Feynman, "There's plenty of room at the bottom". This was a famous lecture given by physicist Richard Feynman at an American Physical Society meeting at Caltech on December 29, 1959. It was printed in *Engineering and Science,* 23:5, pp. 22–36, February 1960.

Exercise D

Put students in pairs to answer the questions by referring to their notes. Feed back with the class to see how much they have been able to get from the lecture. If they can't answer something, do not supply the answer at this stage.

Answers

Model answers:

1 deposition and etching

2 a form of accelerometer in car crash sensors

3 a central mass, a spring or hinge, electrical sensors, a microprocessor

4 sensors with MEMS are more reliable, safer and cheaper

5 an actuator in a video projector

6 micro mirrors, hinges

7 more detail: each mirror = one pixel and more shades of colour. More shades of colour can be achieved, which improves image quality.

8 She believes that MEMS make existing products more reliable, accurate and cheaper. She is also in agreement with Feynman that at a more fundamental level, small-scale devices such as MEMS benefit the whole of technology.

Exercise E

1 Set for individual work.

2 Set for individual work and pairwork checking. Feed back with the whole class.

Answers

Possible answer: See next page.

Review	Notes
How are MEMS manufactured?	1 Manufacture of MEMS:
What materials are used?	Materials: similar to other microelectronic products, e.g., silicon
What are 2 main stages and what happens in each?	(a) Deposition stage: thin layers of material deposited on base (b) Etching: pattern transferred onto layers. Photosensitive layer → masked → exposed to radiation → properties of exposed parts change → dissolved in acid/gas/gases: 3-dimensional surface
What are 2 applications of MEMS?	2 Applications of MEMS:
What do the MEMS do in 1ˢᵗ app.?	(a) Car crash sensors MEMS = accelerometer (measures changes in car's speed)
What are the component parts? How does it work?	Mechanism: central inertial mass attached to spring/hinge. Car slows down/speeds up → mass moves. Electrical sensors send data about movement of mass → microprocessor. Microprocessor monitors information: rapid ↓ in acceleration (= crash) → critical level reached = airbags open very rapidly.
What are the advantages of using MEMS in this device?	Advantages of MEMS = sensors more reliable = safer/cheaper.
What do the MEMS do in 2ⁿᵈ app.?	(b) Video projectors MEMS = actuator
What are the component parts? How does it work?	Mechanism: small mirrors attached to hinges. Mirror moves towards light source (= light reflected) or away (= blocked). 1 mirror = 1 pixel of image. Time mirror reflects light = brightness of pixel → many different shades of colour possible.
What are the advantages of using MEMS in this device?	Advantage of MEMS = ↑ image quality

Summary

MEMS are manufactured in two main stages, deposition and etching, using materials similar to other microelectronic products. This creates a 3-dimensional surface. Two applications of MEMS are car crash sensors and video projectors. MEMS improve these devices by making them more accurate. Small-scale devices such as MEMS can benefit the whole of technology.

🎧 Exercise F

Discuss the question with the whole class. Ask them if they can remember any phrases which signal whether comments are fact or just opinion.

Play the extract. Ask students to tell you to stop the recording when they hear key phrases. Write the phrases on the board.

Remind students that it is important to recognize when someone is giving only their opinion, which others might well disagree with.

Answers

Model answers:

Some people say that (MEMS don't bring anything new to electrical engineering …)	This phrase can be used to give a speaker's own opinion as well as an opposing view.
But the evidence shows that this is not really the whole story.	Sometimes, to put their case strongly, people will present opinions as facts, very strongly stated, with no tentativeness.
In my view, both the examples I have presented today show how MEMS can improve existing products …	This is clearly the lecturer's opinion.
If we don't recognize the benefits that MEMS can bring, and act on them, we could get left behind and that would be *a disaster*.	Getting left behind would be a problem, but whether it is a disaster is a matter of opinion.
As Feynman said in his *excellent talk*, the whole of technology benefits as a result of developing smaller-scale devices.	Whether something is 'excellent' or 'interesting' is always a matter of opinion.
Actually, MEMS are destined to become more and more important in the future, in all sorts of different ways.	The lecturer means 'contrary to what most people think'. Again the lecturer is stating the case very strongly to persuade the listener.

Transcript 🎧 2.18

Some people say that MEMS don't bring anything new to electrical engineering – it's simply a case of making existing devices smaller. But the evidence shows that this is not really the whole story. In my view, both the examples I have presented today show how MEMS can *improve* existing products, making them more reliable and more accurate, and doing the task more cheaply. If we don't recognize the benefits that MEMS can bring, and act on them, we could get left behind and that would be a disaster. As Feynman said in his excellent talk, the whole of technology benefits as a result of

developing smaller-scale devices. Actually, MEMS are destined to become more and more important in the future, in all sorts of different ways.

🎧 Exercise G

Allow students time to read the phrases and the types of information, making sure that they understand any difficult words. Remind students that 'type' of information tells you what the speaker *intends to do* with the words. The words themselves are something different.

Ask students to try to match the phrases and types of information as far as they can. Note that it is not always possible to say what the function of a phrase is outside its context, so they may not be able to match all the phrases and information types before hearing the extracts. Note that some types of information are needed more than once.

When they have done as much as they can, play the extracts one at a time, allowing time for students to identify the type of information which follows. Check answers after each extract, making sure that students understand the information that actually follows the phrase. If possible, students should also give the actual words.

Fixed phrase	Type of information which follows the phrase
1 that is to say, …	restatement
2 To some degree, …	tentative point
3 don't misunderstand me, …	clarification
4 it is fair to say that …	tentative point
5 in an attempt to …	purpose for speaking
6 … gave a description of … in …	summary of a source
7 Briefly, (he) explained how …	summary of a source
8 with respect to …	statement of a topic
9 (she) has no doubt that …	definite point
10 … is a case in point.	an example
11 Not only that, but …	another point
12 to the extent that …	clarification

Transcript 🎧 2.19

Extract 1

I'm going to explain some of the main developments that are happening in the field of microelectromechanical systems, that is to say, I shall be looking at very small mechanical devices built onto semiconductor chips.

Extract 2

To some degree, I believe that the area of microelectromechanical systems – or MEMS for short – is perhaps the most interesting sector of electrical engineering at the present time.

Extract 3

Now, don't misunderstand me, I'm not implying that other areas of electrical engineering are boring!

Extract 4

But it is fair to say that there is something particularly exciting about the developments in MEMS and, recently, at a nano level – NEMS.

Extract 5

So, in an attempt to give you an overall picture of this field, let's start with the question: What are MEMS?

Extract 6

Feynman gave a description of smaller and smaller machines in his famous talk: 'There's plenty of room at the bottom.'

Extract 7

Briefly, he explained how building and controlling devices at smaller scales would have a wide range of potential applications.

Extract 8

And this is exactly what has happened with respect to a number of common electrical products.

Extract 9

Well, I have a colleague who's been directly involved in the development of these new sensors, and she has no doubt that the use of MEMS has meant a huge improvement on earlier versions …

Extract 10

Do you remember I talked about some MEMS being actuators? Well, this is a case in point.

Extract 11

Not only that, but the amount of time the mirror reflects light will also give the perception of brightness …

Extract 12

Now this is a massive improvement on previous technology, to the extent that it is now being used in cinemas, and replacing old film projectors.

Exercise H

Use this section from the Cornell notes to demonstrate what to do:

Notes
1 Manufacture of MEMS:
Materials: similar to other microelectronic products, e.g., silicon
(a) Deposition stage: thin layers of material deposited on base
(b) Etching: pattern transferred onto layers. Photosensitive layer ➜ masked ➜ exposed to radiation ➜ properties of exposed parts change ➜ dissolved in acid/gas/gases: 3-dimensional surface

Elicit from students suggestions on how to write up the notes in complete sentences. Write the suggestions on the board.

Ask students to say what they need to add in to the notes to make a good piece of writing, e.g.,

> *Grammar*: relative pronouns, articles and determiners, prepositions, auxiliary verbs, linking words, 'there was/were' clauses.

> *Vocabulary*: some vocabulary may need to be added, particularly where symbols are used in the notes, or where extra words are required to make sense of the information or give a good sense of flow in the writing.

Note that this of course works the other way: when making notes, these elements can be excluded from the notes.

Set another section for individual writing in class or for homework. Ask students to refer either to their own notes, or to the Cornell notes on page 107 of the Course Book.

Closure

1 Tell students to review and make a list of the main topics and arguments presented in this lesson. Then ask them to try to summarize the viewpoints, using some of the language they have practised.

2 They could also give a two- or three-sentence summary of anything that they themselves have read, e.g., *I read a useful article on X by Y. It said that …*

3 Ask students to do some research and to make a list of useful or interesting books/articles/websites on the topics in this lesson. They should draw up a list, including correct referencing, and share their sources with other students.

11.3 Extending skills

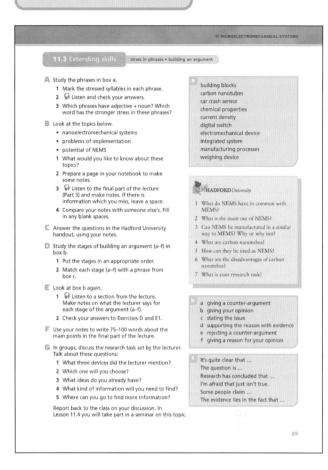

Lesson aims

- recognize stress patterns in noun phrases
- understand how to develop an argument:
  stating the issue
  giving a counter-argument
  rejecting a counter-argument
  giving opinions
  supporting opinions
- understand more general academic words and
  phrases mainly used in speaking

Further practice in:

- expressing degrees of confidence/tentativeness
- reporting back

Introduction

1 Revise the lecture in Lesson 11.2. Ask students to
use the model Cornell notes on page 107. They
should cover up the *Notes* section and use the
Review and *Summary* sections (which they
completed in Lesson 11.2) to help recall the
contents of the lecture. They could work in pairs to
do this.

2 Revise phrases which express degrees of confidence
in 'facts'. Dictate these phrases. Do they show that
the speaker is certain or tentative?

There is no question that (= certain)

We have to accept the evidence (= certain)

Some people claim that (= tentative)

What seems obvious is that (= certain)

As everyone is aware (= certain)

To some degree (= tentative)

This means ultimately that (= certain)

It's quite clear that (= certain)

We could argue that (= tentative)

🎧 Exercise A

1/2 Set for individual work and pairwork checking.
This is an exercise in perceiving rhythm. At this
point, there is no need to distinguish between
different levels of stress. Students can underline all
the stressed syllables. They will also need to count
all the syllables.

Feed back with the whole class, checking
pronunciation of the phrases and meanings.

3 Discuss this with the class first. Demonstrate with
digital 'switch, showing how if you say *'digital
switch*, it appears that a contrast is being made
with another type of switch. Tell students that the
usual pattern for the adjective + noun phrase is for
a heavier stress to go on the noun. *Building blocks*
is, however, different: it is a compound made from
a noun + noun, and the stress is: *'building blocks* –
i.e., the heavier stress normally goes on the first
noun. *Carbon 'nanotubes* is an exception – it is also
a noun + noun compound, but the heavier stress is
on the second noun. Set students to pick out the
other adjective + noun patterns, writing each one
on the board. Elicit the stress patterns and give
students time to practise the phrases.

Answers

Model answers:

1/2 'building blocks

  'carbon nanotubes

  'car crash sensor

  chemical 'properties

  'current density

  digital 'switch

  electromechanical de'vice

  integrated 'system

  manu'facturing processes

  'weighing device

3 Adjective + noun (second word has stronger stress): chemical properties, digital switch, electromechanical device, integrated system.

Transcript 🎧 2.20

'building blocks
'carbon nanotubes
'car crash sensor
chemical 'properties
'current density
digital 'switch
electromechanical de'vice
integrated 'system
manu'facturing processes
'weighing device

🎧 Exercise B

1 Look at the three topics. Discuss with the class what they know already these topics and find out what opinions they may have. Put students in pairs and ask each pair to write down one question to which they would like an answer in the lecture.

2 Set for individual work.

3 Play Part 3 straight through; students make notes.

4 Put students in pairs to compare their notes and fill in any gaps they may have.

Transcript 🎧 2.21

Part 3

So, now we've seen what MEMS are, let's look at something even smaller! We will move from the microscale to the nanoscale. And, just as we had *microelectromechanical* systems, we can have *nanoelectromechanical* systems, or, in other words, NEMS. The principle is the same: a combination of electrical and mechanical devices working together, but this time measuring from one to a hundred nanometres. To give you an idea of this size, a human hair is around 100,000 nanometres wide!

If you recall, earlier today I spoke about the two main uses of MEMS for sensors and actuators. Well, NEMS seem to have a lot of potential as sensors. Research has shown that they are highly sensitive detectors of various quantities such as mass, charge, energy and displacement. To give an example, do you remember the MEMS used as a car crash sensor? Well, imagine that sort of device consisting of a mass attached to a hinge, but now imagine it much, much smaller. At this scale, the electrical circuit measuring the deflection of the hinge is capable of sensing the weight of an individual atom or molecule which is resting on it.

It becomes a tiny weighing device!

This sort of device would need to be built in a very similar way to how MEMS are built. The question is: How small can we go? Some people claim that there is no limit in terms of size, and that the same manufacturing processes used in MEMS can be used to produce NEMS: deposition and etching. I'm afraid that just isn't true. It's quite clear that the main problem in the development of NEMS is with the transduction element of the system. A transducer converts mechanical energy – for example, a vibration – into electrical energy. Research has concluded that making transducers at a nanoscale level is not at all easy. The evidence lies in the fact that as electromechanical devices are made smaller and smaller, it becomes very difficult to create an efficient and finely controlled integrated system.

However, there is another approach available for creating NEMS, using the chemical properties of single molecules. Perhaps the most exciting materials are *carbon nanotubes*. These are molecules of carbon allotropes – allotropes are different forms which a chemical element can take. Carbon nanotubes look like very long thin cylinders. Their diameter is only a few nanometres, but they can be up to several centimetres in length. They are extremely strong and have interesting electrical characteristics, acting as semiconductors in some circumstances. This means that they can be used to create nanotube-based transistors – one of the key building blocks in any electronic device. For example, a carbon nanotube can be employed as a digital switch, using a single electron. Some carbon nanotubes can also conduct high current densities, so can be seen as a type of *wire* – another fundamental component of any electrical system.

We need to remember, however, that there are problems regarding the use of carbon nanotubes. First of all, when they are exposed to oxygen, their electrical properties change significantly. As a result, new environments will need to be developed for these electronic devices. Their conductivity also seems to be extremely variable, depending on various factors in the production process that have not been completely understood and which are not easy to control. Finally, carbon nanotubes may be extremely toxic, causing lung cancer when inhaled.

But let's finish by looking at some of the potential of NEMS. Since NEMS are built so very small, their potential is huge. It is expected that they will make a significant impact on many areas of technology. And, since they will be even more efficient, smaller and cheaper to run and manufacture, they will one day perhaps even take

199

the place of MEMS. So, all in all, I hope you agree with me when I say that MEMS and NEMS are very exciting fields of electrical engineering!

Now, I'm going to set you a task which will involve investigating some of the points I've raised. I want you to do some research into some of the most common applications of MEMS. I've chosen three of these. The first one is a very common device and I'm sure many of you have one at home: an *inkjet printer*. The second is a *gyroscope*. And the last application I want you to investigate is a *portable blood pressure sensor*.

Exercise C

Set for individual work and pairwork checking. Feed back with the class on question 7 to make sure that it is clear.

Answers

Model answers:

1 They both involve a combination of electrical and mechanical devices.

2 As sensors.

3 To some extent, yes. But there is a limit to how small manufacturing processes used for MEMS can go. It's difficult to make a transducer at a nano level.

4 Single molecules of carbon allotropes that form long, thin cylinders.

5 They act like semiconductors, so they can be used as switches and wires.

6 They cannot be exposed to air, their conductivity is very variable, and they may be toxic to humans.

7 Do some research on three applications using MEMS technology: an inkjet printer, a gyroscope and a portable blood pressure monitor.

Exercise D

1 Set for pairwork discussion. Point out that there is no one 'correct' order; students should try to identify the most logical sequence for the argument. Explain that a 'counter-argument' means an opinion which you do not agree with or think is wrong. 'Issue' means a question about which there is some debate.

2 Set for individual work and pairwork checking.

Do not feed back with the class at this point but move on to Exercise E, where the answers will be given.

🎧 Exercise E

1 Play the extract. Tell students to stop you when they hear each item. Make sure students can say exactly what the words are in each case. Ask them also to paraphrase the words so that it is clear that they understand the meanings.

2 If necessary play the extract again for students to check that they have the phrases and types of statement correct. Ask how many students had the stages of an argument (Exercise D, question 1) in the same order as the recording/model answers below. Discuss any alternative possibilities (see *Language note* below).

Answers

Model answers for Exercises D and E: see table below.

Type of statement	Phrase	Lecturer's words
c stating the issue	The question is …	The question is: How small can we go?
a giving a counter-argument	Some people claim …	Some people claim that there is no limit in terms of size …
e rejecting a counter-argument	I'm afraid that just isn't true.	I'm afraid that just isn't true.
b giving your opinion	It's quite clear that …	It's quite clear that the main problem in the development of NEMS is with the transduction element of the system.
f giving a reason for your opinion	Research has concluded that …	Research has concluded that making transducers at a nanoscale level is not at all easy.
d supporting the reason with evidence	The evidence lies in the fact that …	The evidence lies in the fact that as electromechanical devices are made smaller and smaller, it becomes very difficult to create an efficient and finely controlled integrated system.

Transcript 🎧 2.22

This sort of device would need to be built in a very similar way to how MEMS are built. The question is: How small can we go? Some people claim that there is no limit in terms of size, and that the same manufacturing processes used in MEMS can be used to produce NEMS: deposition and etching. I'm afraid that just isn't true. It's quite clear that the main problem in the development of NEMS is with the transduction element of the system. A transducer converts mechanical energy – for example, a vibration – into electrical energy. Research has concluded that making transducers at a nanoscale level is not at all easy. The evidence lies in the fact that as electromechanical devices are made smaller and smaller, it becomes very difficult to create an efficient and finely controlled integrated system.

Language note

A common way in which an argument can be built is to give a counter-argument, then reject the counter-argument with reasons and evidence. There are, of course, other ways to build an argument. For example, the counter-arguments may be given after the writer/speaker's own opinion. Or all the arguments against may be given followed by all the arguments for an issue (or vice versa), concluding with the speaker/writer's own opinion.

Exercise F

Set for individual work – possibly homework – or else a pair/small group writing task. If the latter, tell students to put their writing on an OHT or other visual medium, so that the whole class can look and comment on what has been written. You can correct language errors on the OHT.

Exercise G

Set students to work in groups of three or four. Make sure they understand that they should choose to focus on one of the three devices: an inkjet printer, a gyroscope or a portable blood pressure sensor. Allow each group to choose their device. Make sure that each device is covered by at least one group, preferably two. Ask one person from each group to present the results of the group's discussion.

Tell the class that they should carry out research into their group's device. You will also need to arrange the date for the feedback and discussion of the information – this is the focus of Exercise F in Lesson 11.4.

Closure

Arguments, counter-arguments and giving opinions

Ask students to think about the methods seen above for building an argument. As they do this, write the statements below on the board or display them on an OHT or other visual medium. Ask them to think about whether they agree with the statements. They should prepare a brief summary of their viewpoints on the topics; they should also try to use some of the phrases featured in this lesson.

1 Electrical engineering is the most important branch of engineering.

2 Nanoelectromechanical systems are going to produce life-changing developments in the next ten years.

3 'Smaller is always better' as far as electrical devices are concerned.

4 Electrical devices are always better than mechanical devices.

5 MEMS don't bring anything new to electrical engineering.

6 We can't live without mechanical devices, but we could live without electrical devices.

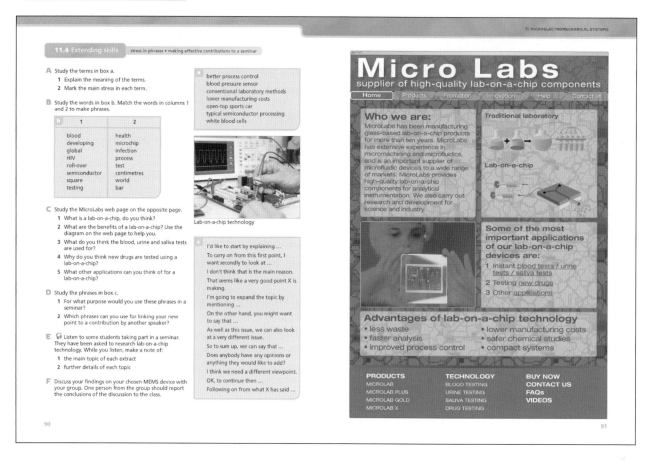

Lesson aims

- recognize stress in compound phrases
- link a contribution to previous contributions when speaking in a seminar
- understand vocabulary in the area of lab-on-a-chip

Further practice in:

- taking part in seminars:

  introducing, maintaining and concluding a contribution

  agreeing/disagreeing with other speakers

Introduction

1 Remind students that they are going to be presenting their research findings later in this lesson. Check that they can remember the main points from Lesson 11.3 lecture extracts using the following questions:

> *What's the difference between MEMS and NEMS?* (mainly a question of size – they do similar things)

> *Which uses of NEMS were mentioned?* (as sensors, e.g., as weighing machines)

Are NEMS made in the same way as MEMS? (no, MEMS are made by deposition and etching, NEMS are single molecules)

2 The following activity is a good way to check that students are familiar with the terminology and vocabulary from Lesson 11.3. Ask students to write down 5–10 words or expressions from the previous lesson relating to nanoelectromechanical systems. Then use two or three students as 'secretaries'. Ask the class to dictate the words so that the secretaries can write the vocabulary on the board. Use this as a brainstorming session.

Exercise A

These are more complex noun phrases than in Lesson 11.3, since they are made up of three words. In some cases, the pattern is noun + noun + noun. In this case, there may be a compound made from the first two nouns, or the last two nouns. In other cases, the pattern is adjective + noun + noun, in which the second and third words make a compound. These patterns should become clear once the meaning is understood.

1 Discuss a *blood pressure sensor* with the class as an example. Elicit that it is a sensor for measuring the pressure of the blood. Set the remaining phrases for

individual work and pairwork discussion. Feed back with the whole class, writing each phrase on the board and underlining the words which make a compound noun.

2 Tell students to try to identify where the main stress should come in each phrase. The key to this is finding the two- or three-word compound which is at the base of the three-word phrase. The stress will normally fall in the same place as if this two-word compound was said without the third word. Demonstrate this with *blood pressure sensor*. The two-word compound here is not *pressure sensor*, but *blood pressure*. This is a noun + noun compound, so the rules say this will normally be stressed on the first noun 'blood pressure. The main stress remains in its original place when the third word is added.

Tell students only to identify the syllable on which the heaviest stress in the phrase falls. (See also *Language note*.)

Answers

Model answers:

The basic compound is underlined in each case.

better 'process control	process control that is better
'blood pressure sensor	a sensor for measuring the pressure of the blood
conventional la'boratory methods	conventional methods that are used in laboratories
lower manu'facturing costs	manufacturing costs that are lower
open-top 'sports car	a sports car with an open top
typical 'semiconductor processing	typical processing by a semiconductor
white 'blood cells	blood cells that are 'white'

Language note

Stress placement, especially in complex compound noun phrases, is notoriously unstable.

Stress may often move, depending on the context: for example, *bad-'tempered* – but *bad-tempered 'teacher*. It's also possible that some native speakers may not agree about some of the phrases above. The main point is to try to notice where the main stresses fall.

Exercise B

Set for individual work and pairwork checking. Tell students that, although in some cases it will be possible to make a phrase with more than one option, they must use each word once, and they must use all the words.

Feed back with the whole class. Check that the meaning of all other phrases is understood. Check pronunciation.

Answers

Model answers:

blood	test
developing	world
global	health
HIV	infection
roll-over	bar
semiconductor	microchip
square	centimetres
testing	process

Language note

Although in most noun–noun compounds the main stress comes on the first element, there are some compounds where this is not true. Definitive pronunciation of compounds can be found in a good pronunciation dictionary.

Exercise C

Refer students to the web page on page 91 of the Course Book. Set for pair or small group discussion. For all questions, students need to try to make informed guesses, using the information they have on the web page. Do not correct or confirm students' responses at this stage as they will hear the answers in the listening activity in Exercise E.

Answers

1 A lab-on-a-chip performs the analysis and diagnosis that a traditional laboratory does, but it is much smaller.

2 A lab-on-a-chip is smaller, quicker and cheaper than a traditional laboratory.

3 The tests can be used to check for bacteria, viruses, cancers and allergies. They can also be used to measure the level of certain chemicals.

4 Testing new medicines on a lab-on-a-chip is safer than testing on animals or humans. The medicines might have dangerous side-effects.

5 Other applications include preparing blood samples, extracting DNA, and monitoring the healing of wounds.

Exercise D

This is mainly revision. Set for individual work or pairwork discussion. Feed back with the whole class.

Answers

Model answers:

I'd like to start by explaining …

= beginning

To carry on from this first point, I want secondly to look at …

= maintaining/continuing a point

I don't think that is the main reason.

= disagreeing

That seems like a very good point X is making.

= confirming

I'm going to expand the topic by mentioning …

= adding a new point to someone else's previous contribution

On the other hand, you might want to say that …

= disagreeing

As well as this issue, we can also look at a very different issue.

= adding a new point to someone else's previous contribution

So to sum up, we can say that …

= summarizing/concluding

Does anybody have any opinions or anything they would like to add?

= concluding

I think we need a different viewpoint.

= disagreeing

OK, to continue then …

= maintaining/continuing a point

Following on from what X has said …

= adding a new point to someone else's previous contribution

🎧 Exercise E

Before students listen, tell them to look at the exercise and questions. Check that students understand the topic for the seminar discussion. Ask them what they might expect to hear.

Play the extracts one at a time and ask students to identify the main topic and some further details. Feed back with the whole class.

Answers

Model answers: see table below.

	Main topic	Further details
Extract 1	definition of a lab-on-a-chip	a semiconductor microchip which can analyze the composition of fluids
Extract 2	example of a lab-on-a-chip	blood tests, which require only a drop of blood – the chip analyzes the blood and sends the results to a computer
Extract 3	advantages of a lab-on-a-chip	requires only a very small quantity of fluid → less waste ● faster → better control ● very small device → cheap to make
Extract 4	applications of a lab-on-a-chip	analyze blood, urine and saliva ● look for bacteria, viruses and cancers ● test for allergies ● test new drugs to see if they are safe and if they work

Transcript 🎧 2.23

Extract 1

MAJED: The lecturer we listened to last week introduced a number of interesting issues. In my part of the seminar, I would like to build on what he said and talk about a subset of MEMS called *lab-on-a-chip*, or LOC. I'd like to start by explaining what a lab-on-a-chip is. In common with other MEMS, a lab-on-a-chip is very small: ranging from a few square millimetres to a few square centimetres. As the name suggests, a lab-on-a-chip is an analytical tool involving a semiconductor microchip, and it combines typical semiconductor processing with the control and manipulation of very small quantities of fluids. The idea is that a lab-on-a-chip is able to analyze the composition of these fluids. Clearly, this will have a wide range of applications. I think this is what Evie wants to talk about.

Extract 2

EVIE: Actually, I'm going to give an example of a lab-on-a-chip and how it works. One of the main applications of LOCs is analyzing, for medical purposes, the fluids that are in a person's body. The example I want to talk about involves one of these fluids: blood. Usually, when we have a routine blood test in a hospital, we have to give quite a lot of blood. A lab-on-a-chip only needs a drop of blood to do the same thing. The process is quite complicated and entails creating a micro-emulsion, which is a drop of fluid – blood in this case – inside a layer of another substance. The emulsion can then be positioned very accurately on the chip, and tests can be carried out, with the results transmitted immediately to a computer. OK then. Does anybody have any opinions or anything they would like to add?

Extract 3

JACK: Yes, well, following on from what Evie has said, I'd like to mention some of the advantages of LOCs. As you can see from Evie's example of a blood test, a lab-on-a-chip requires a much smaller quantity of fluid, so it's much easier and quicker for the patient. The analysis is faster than with conventional fluid testing, and this, of course, is a very important factor, meaning that there is better process control. Finally, a lab-on-a-chip is obviously very small, and this compactness can have clear advantages, not least in terms of lower manufacturing costs.

Extract 4

LEILA: OK, to continue then, I'm going to look at some of the various applications of LOCs. Evie talked about blood tests, and tests of this sort are one really important application of a lab-on-a-chip. Apart from blood, other bodily fluids are saliva and urine. LOCs can be used with these fluids to detect bacteria, viruses and even cancers. For example, a lab-on-a-chip can be used to diagnose and manage HIV infections in a cheap and simple way – a very important requirement, especially in the developing world. LOCs can also be used to test for allergies by exposing a person's white blood cells to potential allergens and recording their reaction. Yet another application is the testing of new drugs to see if they are safe and effective. Obviously, this would be at the start of the testing process, but using LOCs is cheaper and quicker than conventional laboratory methods. So, to sum up, we can say that a lab-on-a-chip has a lot of potential, particularly in terms of improving global health.

Exercise F

In their groups, students should now present their research findings on the three common devices that use MEMS:

- an inkjet printer
- a gyroscope
- portable blood pressure sensor

Encourage students to use the seminar language practised in this unit and earlier. In addition, students can, of course, make use of the information in Lesson 11.4.

They should be looking at, or at least mentioning, some or all of the following:

- an inkjet printer – introduced in 1980s / places tiny drops of ink on paper / drops are positioned very precisely / inkjet printhead formed of hundreds of MEM ink ejection devices / device ejects ink when heated electrically via tiny resistors.

- a gyroscope – a device to measure angular velocity / gyroscope mechanisms include tuning forks (a pair of masses which resonate), vibrating wheels (tilt of rotating wheel measured) / MEMS gyroscopes use etching to construct micro versions of one of these mechanisms

- portable blood pressure sensor – very small monitor on finger or wrist / contain MEMS pressure sensor / disc or doughnut structure of MEM detects pressure changes

As a group, students should consolidate their research findings, which should then be presented to the rest of the class.

Closure

Ask students to imagine that they are 10–15 years in the future. What differences do they think MEMS and lab-on-a-chip technology will have made to everyday life? Ask students, in groups, to come up with five differences, and then share their predictions with the class. Decide which difference will make the biggest impact.

1 Work through the *Vocabulary bank* and *Skills bank* if you have not already done so, or as revision of previous study.

2 Use the Activity bank (Teacher's Book additional resources section, Resource 11A).

A Set the crossword for individual work (including homework) or pairwork.

Answers

B Set for individual work (including homework) or pairwork. Check students understand the meanings.

Possible answers

blood pressure

hearing aid

inkjet printer

manufacturing costs

mechanical device

radiation source

semiconductor microchip

sports car

square centimetres

3 Tell students to add other words to each of the words below to make as many two-word phrases as possible. Elicit one or two examples, then set for individual work or pairwork.

- blood

- car

- electron

Possible phrases:

blood pressure, blood test, blood cells, blood disease, blood flow, blood transfusion

car tyre, car crash, sports car, racing car, electric car, car engine

electron beam, electron cloud, electron microscope, free electron, electron accelerator, electron orbitals

4 Use an extended activity to allow students to practise some of the ideas they have studied in this unit. Tell students to work in groups. Give each group one of these lab-on-a-chip applications:

- detecting cancer at a very early stage

- measuring blood pressure with a disposable sensor

- diagnosing and monitoring the HIV virus in the blood

- determining what someone is allergic to

- matching the DNA from a drop of blood to a database and finding the identity of the person

Each group is going to argue that their application of a lab-on-a-chip is more important than any of the others and will benefit humankind most. Divide the activity into stages as follows:

a The groups should decide why their application is the most important (even if they don't actually believe this to be the case). Give them some time to come up with a list of reasons.

b Create new groups having at least one person representing each application. Each person in turn presents to the rest of the group why they believe their application is the most important and will benefit humankind most. The members of the group can then vote on who made the most convincing presentation.

12 LIGHTING ENGINEERING

This unit provides an opportunity for extending some of the key skills practised in the book and features key topics within the field of lighting engineering. Lessons 12.1 and 12.2 focus on sources of artificial light, looking at the main lighting devices; incandescent light bulbs, fluorescent lamps and LEDs are discussed in terms of how they work, their applications, and their advantages and disadvantages. Technical report writing in the field of simple circuits with LEDs is covered in Lessons 12.3 and 12.4.

Skills focus

Reading

- understanding how ideas in a text are linked
- note-making from texts
- creating and labelling a spidergram

Writing

- writing a comparison summary from notes
- writing a laboratory report section from notes

Vocabulary focus

- definitions
- referring back using pronouns and synonyms
- words/phrases to describe processes in lighting engineering
- common verb + noun phrases used in laboratory reports

Key vocabulary

anode	emit	parallel circuit
artificial	field	photon
assemble	filament	polarity
brake lights	fixture	practitioner
brightness	flow (v)	release (v)
bulb	fluorescent lamp	reliable
camera flash	forward-biased	repeat (v)
cathode	halogen	reverse-biased
collide	hit (v)	scanner
combustion	holes	series circuit
connect	imperfect	set (v)
considerable	incandescent	shape (n)
create	infrared	significant
decrease (v)	installation	steady (adj)
diffuse	latter	torch
dim (adj)	lifespan	ultraviolet
diode	lightning	valid
domestic (adj)	measure (v)	verify
efficient	mercury	visible
electrode	open circuit	wavelength
electroluminescence	optical	

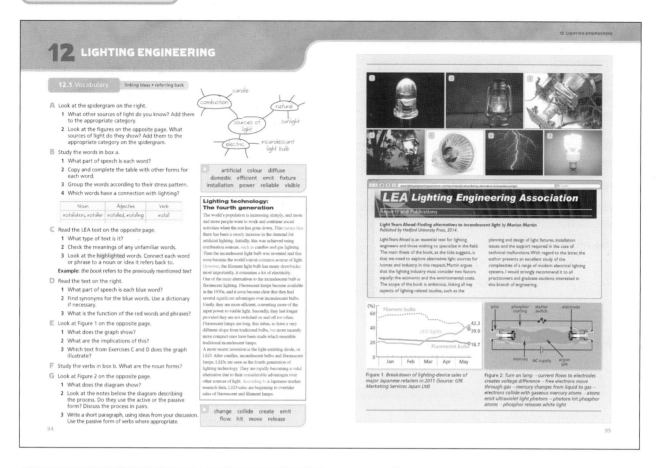

General note

Read the *Vocabulary bank* at the end of the Course Book unit. Decide when, if at all, to refer your students to it. The best time is probably at the very end of the lesson or the beginning of the next lesson, as a summary/revision.

Lesson aims

- further understand lexical cohesion: referring back using synonyms
- interpret charts and diagrams
- explain a process orally and in writing

Further practice in:

- definitions
- word formation
- words and phrases from the discipline

Introduction

1 Revise the following words and phrases from the previous unit. Ask students to say which grammar class the words belong to and to provide definitions of them.

dissolve (v, T/I)

hinge (n, C)

layer (n, C)

main (adj)

mask (n, C; v, T)

massive (adj)

pattern (n, C)

place (v, T)

spread (v, T/I))

spring (n, C)

tiny (adj)

2 Introduce the topic of the unit: write the words *lighting* and *engineering* on the board. Ask students why lighting is a key field in engineering. Elicit the types of engineering connected with lighting (e.g., in domestic and industrial contexts) and what types of process and device are involved. Accept any reasonable suggestions. Do not elaborate, but tell students that this will be the topic of this unit.

Exercise A

Ask students to say briefly what the spidergram shows (*different sources of light*), and make sure they understand the three different categories – natural, combustion and electric – using the examples given.

1 Set for pairwork. Feed back with the whole class. Accept valid suggestions and add them to the spidergram on the board.

2 Set for individual work and pairwork checking. Feed back with the whole class, adding the sources of light to the appropriate category of the spidergram.

Answers

1/2 Model answers (numbers in brackets refer to figure numbers in the Course Book):

See spidergram below.

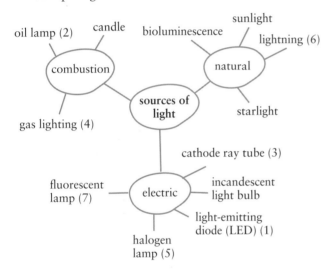

Exercise B

Allow time for students to look at all the questions and copy the table into their notebooks.

1 Set for individual work and pairwork checking. Students should try to identify the part of speech for each word from the suffix. Do not allow the use of a dictionary for this question. Feed back with the class, pointing out that some of the words can be more than one part of speech, e.g., *power, colour, diffuse*. Ask students to think of the common suffixes for nouns (*~tion, ~sion, ~ity,* etc.) and those for adjectives (*~ic, ~able, ~ous, ~ive, ~ed,* etc.)

2 Set for pairwork or individual work and pairwork checking. Allow the use of dictionaries, if necessary. Feed back with the class, building up the table on the board.

3 Set for individual work and pairwork checking. Feed back with the class.

4 Set for pairwork. Tell students that some connections may be obvious, but others may seem to have no connection. Ask them to put a question mark by the words they are not sure about. Feed back with the class to share ideas, making a note of all the words students found difficult to connect. This would be a useful question to return to at the end of Lesson 12.2, when students should be able to explain each word's connection.

Answers

Model answers:

1/2

Noun	Adjective	Verb
artificiality	artificial	—
colour, colouring	coloured, colourful	colour
diffusion	diffused, diffuse*	diffuse
domestication	domestic, domesticated	domesticate
efficiency	efficient	—
emission	emitted, emitting	emit
fixture, fixing	fixed	fix
installation, installer	installed, installing	install
power	powerful, powerless, powered	power
reliability	reliable	rely
visibility	visible	—

* The pronunciation of *diffuse* changes according to whether it is in verb (/z/) or adjective (/s/) form.

3

Oo	colour, fixture, power
oO	diffuse, emit
Ooo	visible
oOo	domestic, efficient
oOoo	reliable
ooOo	artificial, installation

4 Answers depend on students.

Exercise C

1 Set for individual work. For this exercise, tell students to read the text quickly for an overall idea of content and style. This will be sufficient to enable them to answer the question, and is a good skill to develop when close reading is not required. Feed back with the class.

2 Set for pairwork. Tell students to read the text again more closely, and to try to guess the meanings of unfamiliar words from the context, from the part of speech, and from affixes, before using a dictionary. For example, a knowledge of the prefix *mal* would tell students automatically that *malfunction* involves something not working or working badly.

3 Set for individual work and pairwork checking. Remind students of the idea of textual cohesion, created by referring back to previously mentioned words or ideas by the use of words/phrases with a similar meaning, so that the text flows without too much repetition of the same words and phrases. Refer them to Unit 11 *Vocabulary bank*. Feed back with the class.

You can build up the answers to question 3 by copying Resource 12B in the additional resources section onto an OHT or other visual medium.

Answers

Model answers:

1 A book review.

3

Word/phrase	Refers back to	Comments
the field	*lighting engineers* in the same sentence	implied, i.e., field of lighting engineering
the book	*text* in the previous sentence	synonym: avoids using the same word twice in proximity
the title	*Light Years Ahead: Finding alternatives to incandescent light*	refers back to the *meaning* of the full title in the heading (*as the title suggests …*)
(In) this respect	Statement in previous sentence: *… engineers will need to play a key role in developing more effective lighting for homes and industry.*	a phrase used to refer to something previously said as a way of both linking to it and building on it
lighting-related studies	*the field*	another way of referring to lighting engineering
the latter*	*technical malfunctions*	the last of several things just mentioned; has to be used in proximity to the word/phrase it refers back to
the author	*Martin, Marion Martin*	clear reference to Martin in the context
it	*an excellent study, the book, the text*	use of pronoun where the reference should be easily understood in the context (i.e., a book review recommends a book)
practitioners	*lighting engineers*	refers back to beginning of text
graduate students	*those wishing to specialize*	refers back to beginning of text; implies that they are one and the same
this branch	*lighting-related studies, the field* (and generally *lighting engineering*)	use of synonyms throughout the text in a constant referral

* *latter* should only apply to the second or the second mentioned of two items; however, it is frequently used nowadays to mean the last of several items.

Exercise D

The text in this exercise introduces the main theme of Lesson 12.2 by connecting demand for lighting with different sources of electrical light. It features some vocabulary related to the topic without being too technical at this point. Students should first read through the text to get an idea of the topic, and then study all the questions before proceeding.

1/2 Set for individual work and pairwork checking. These two exercises revise and extend work on synonyms without supplying alternative choices within the lesson. The focus on the part of speech in question 1 makes students think about both the function and the meaning of a word in context and helps to reduce reliance on a dictionary. This is an important academic reading skill to develop, and can increase reading speed. Feed back with the class, building up the table on the board.

3 Set for pairwork discussion. Tell students to discuss the general function of the red words and phrases and be able to explain the purpose of each one. Feed back with the class, eliciting alternatives for each word or phrase to check understanding.

Answers

Possible answers:

1/2

Word	Part of speech	Synonym(s)
sharply	adv	rapidly, quickly
steady	adj	constant, regular
common	adj	familiar, standard
drawbacks	n (pl.)	disadvantages
main	adj	principal
significant	adj	considerable
shape	n	appearance, body, model
rapidly	adv	quickly
valid	adj	convincing
considerable	adj	significant

3 The red words and phrases are examples of linking expressions.

Expression	Meaning	Alternatives
means that	to show an implication or a result/consequence	implies that
such as	to introduce examples	including ('for instance' and 'for example' can also be used, but the grammar of the sentence would need adjusting)
However	to present an opposite/contrasting idea/situation	though, nevertheless
but	to show two things or ideas in opposition	though, while, whereas
According to	to introduce supporting evidence for a statement	In the light of research conducted by ...

Exercise E

1 Set for pairwork. Ask pairs to study the graph carefully and compose a precise description of it in one sentence. Feed back with the class, writing some of the suggested sentences on the board. Invite other pairs to judge and, if necessary, improve on the descriptions. Key words that the sentence should contain are underlined in the answers section below.

2/3 Set for individual work and pairwork checking. The purpose of question 2 is to make sure that students link the graph to the text they have just read in Exercise D. For question 3, tell students to be prepared to give any reasons to support their answer. Feed back with the class.

Answers

1 The graph shows the percentage market share of the three main types of lighting devices in Japan over five months in 2011.

2 Sales of traditional incandescent filament light bulbs and fluorescent lamps are declining, but sales of LEDs are increasing and have now overtaken the other two.

3 The graph best illustrates the final sentence of the text in Exercise D.

Exercise F

Set for individual work and pairwork checking. Tell students that these verbs will be needed for the following exercise. Tell them to use their knowledge of suffixes to guess any of the noun forms for verbs they are not familiar with. If you wish to give them a clue, say that four of the verbs have the same noun form, i.e., they do not change. Do not allow the use of dictionaries for this exercise. Feed back with the class, checking pronunciation and the meanings of any unknown verbs.

Answers

Model answers:

Verb	Noun form
change	change
collide	collision
create	creation
emit	emission
flow	flow
hit	hit
move	movement
release	release

Exercise G

1 Set for individual work. Allow enough time for students to study the diagram before feedback, as this will help towards question 2. However, tell them to cover up the notes underneath the diagram for the moment, since only a brief statement is required rather than a full description at this stage. Students will probably realize that the diagram is connected with the subject of the second paragraph of the text in Exercise D.

2 Set for pairwork discussion. Feed back with the class. Invite one pair to share their explanation of the process, with input from others as and when appropriate, so that feedback becomes a collaborative activity. The notes use the active form, but students are likely to use a mix of active and passive expressions. Write some of the suggestions on the board, checking the grammar at the same time.

3 Set for individual work/homework. Before setting the students to write, explain that when writing about a process or procedure, the passive voice is generally used, but not exclusively. Some explanations will only be possible in the active voice. As an example of this, and as a possible prompt for beginning the paragraph, write the following on the board:

When the fluorescent lamp is turned on, current <u>flows</u> to the electrodes and …

Ask students whether it is possible to change this to the passive, and if not, ask how a different verb could be used for a passive sentence, for example:

… current <u>is sent</u> to the electrodes and …

The model paragraph in the answers section below is also available in Resource 12C in the additional resources section. For feedback purposes, you may wish to copy the resource onto an OHT or other visual medium for students to compare with their own paragraph. Alternatively, set students to work in pairs to compare and discuss each other's work. Then ask them to write an improved version, combining their ideas.

Answers

Possible answers:

1 The diagram shows the main parts of a fluorescent lamp.

2 The notes use the active form. Answers depend on students.

3 Model answer:

When the fluorescent lamp is turned on, current flows to the electrodes and a voltage difference is created. This causes free electrons to move through the gas, and, as a result, the mercury present in the tube is changed from liquid into gaseous form. The moving electrons collide with the gaseous mercury atoms and ultraviolet light photons are emitted. These photons hit the phosphor atoms in the casing, and white light is released.

Closure

Put students into small groups. Each student should describe how something works, while trying not to name the item or process or give away too many clues all at once. They should start with just one sentence, adding extra information until the others guess what it is. Encourage them to choose something they can describe in a technical or semi-technical way. Start the activity with the whole class, using the example below if you wish:

This domestic item is driven by an electric motor attached to an inner steel drum.

It has a set of controls for different programmes.

The drum spins and vibrates.

It uses water to perform its function.

The water can be either hot or cold.

The controls determine speed and temperature.

In some models, the drum is accessed from the front, while on others it is accessed from the top.

etc.

Answer: *A washing machine.*

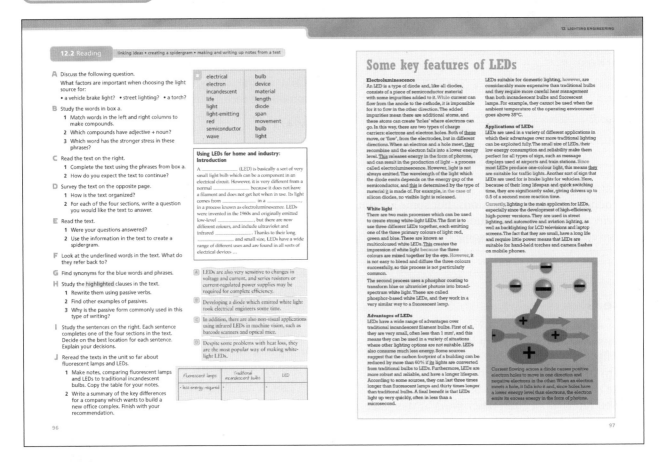

General note

Read the *Vocabulary bank* at the end of the Course Book unit. Decide when, if at all, to refer students to it. The best time is probably at the very end of the lesson or the beginning of the next lesson, as a summary/revision.

Lesson aims

- further understand how ideas in a text are linked: referring back using pronouns and synonyms matching new with given information
- create and label a spidergram from textual information
- understand the use of the passive form in technical writing
- make notes from written sources and write a comparison summary

Further practice in:

- noun + noun and adjective + noun compounds
- predicting content
- words and phrases from the discipline

Introduction

Revise different sources of light from Lesson 12.1. Elicit a definition of each source, or give a simple paraphrased definition and ask students to name the light source.

To prepare students for the lesson's theme, ask them to think about the classroom's lighting and typical sources of lighting in their own country, for example:

What kinds of light source are used in this classroom?

What light sources do you use in your home?

What types of light source do different electrical devices use, e.g., a mobile phone, a camera flash, an airport message board, traffic lights, a television?

Exercise A

Set for small group work. Ask students to brainstorm the question and incorporate their ideas into table. If possible, supply each pair or group with a large sheet of paper or an OHT with pens so that they can display their table during class feedback. Alternatively, copy the table outline in Resource 12D in the additional resources section onto an OHT or other visual medium. During class feedback, elicit students' ideas to complete the table. Accept any reasonable suggestions. However, as the students may only be able to come up with a few ideas at this point, you may wish to return to the activity at the end of Lesson 12.2 and fill in the gaps.

Answers

Possible answers:

	a vehicle brake light	street lighting	a torch
Important factors	• long lifespan • quick switching time • small • excellent visibility from a distance	• low energy consumption • reliability (as difficult to maintain) • long lifespan	• small • not heavy • low power required • cheap

Exercise B

1 Set for individual work and pairwork checking. Allow the use of dictionaries, if necessary. The purpose of this exercise is to prepare students for the texts in Exercises C and D. Most of these compounds are fixed expressions, but some are not (e.g., *electron movement*). Students may come up with several possibilities for some of the words, such as *incandescent/light-emitting/semiconductor material*. However, tell students that each word in each column can be used only once (noting that *bulb* appears in two compounds), so this will narrow down the possibilities. If question 1 proves too difficult at this point, an alternative approach is to move directly on to Exercise C, returning to questions 2 and 3 after students have completed the gaps in the text in Exercise C.

2/3 Set for individual work and pairwork checking. Feed back with the class.

Answers

Model answers:

*<u>electrical</u> device	adj + n
<u>electron</u> movement	n + n
incandescent <u>bulb</u>	adj + n
<u>light</u> bulb	n + n
light-emitting <u>diode</u>	adj + n
red <u>light</u>	adj + n
<u>semiconductor</u> <u>material</u>	n + n
wavelength	n + n (compound)
lifespan	n + n (compound)

* The emphasis will appear on the adjective if a comparison is being made with another type of device.

Exercise C

Students should first read through the text to get an idea of the topic.

1 Set for individual work and pairwork checking. Tell students to look at each gap in the context of the sentence and to pay attention to the words that immediately precede and follow it. If you have moved directly to this exercise from question 1 of Exercise B, remind students that each word from the table can be used only once when making the compound nouns. Once they have completed the gaps, ask them to read the text again to make sure that the phrase they have chosen for each gap makes sense within the context. Feed back with the class.

2 Approach this question with the whole class. Elicit ideas *and* reasons from individuals, i.e., information in the text that lends support to ideas. Accept any reasonable suggestions and write them on the board.

Answers

Model answers:

1 **Using LEDs for home and industry: Introduction**

A <u>light-emitting diode</u> (LED) is basically a sort of very small light bulb which can be a component in an electrical circuit. However, it is very different from a normal <u>incandescent bulb</u> because it does not have a filament and does not get hot when in use. Its light comes from <u>electron movement</u> in a <u>semiconductor material</u>, in a process known as *electroluminescence*. LEDs were invented in the 1960s and originally emitted low-level <u>red light</u>, but now there are different colours, including ultraviolet and infrared <u>wavelengths</u>. Thanks to their long <u>lifespan</u> and small size, LEDs have a wide range of different uses and are found in all sorts of electrical devices. …

2 Answers depend on students. Based on the title of the text (Using LEDs for home and industry), and the topics mentioned in the introduction, the text is likely to continue by providing a detailed description of how LEDs work, including electroluminescence, and discussing various applications of LEDs.

Exercise D

Elicit what surveying a text means, as a reminder (skim-reading to get an approximate idea of the text contents by looking at the title, any headings and diagrams, by looking at the beginning few lines and the final few lines of the text, and by looking at the first sentence of each paragraph).

1 Set for pairwork discussion after giving students one minute to survey the text, to ensure that they skim read rather than close read. Feed back with the class. Ask how the organization of this text helps with skim-reading. Check back on the suggestions students gave about text continuation from the previous exercise and ask who predicted correctly.

2 Set for pairwork. Each pair should agree four questions. Feed back with the class. Write some questions on the board.

Answers

Possible answer:

1 The title states clearly what the text will be about. This is followed by four numbered and labelled sections that describe different aspects of LEDs. Three of the sections are further divided into shorter paragraphs. A text box with a small diagram explains some detail of the text.

The organization helps with reading because of the way the text is divided up into shorter sections. This makes finding and retrieving information easier. The titles of the four sections also give a clear indication of their content.

2 Answers depend on students.

Exercise E

1 Set for individual work followed by pairwork discussion. Feed back with the class. Ask whether the questions you have put on the board have been answered in the text.

2 Set for pairwork. They will need to read the text again, but ask them which type of reading skill they should use to be able to complete the spidergram (scanning for specific information). Feed back with the class. Display the spidergram in Resource 12E in the additional resources section on an OHT or other visual medium so that students can check their answers. The completed spidergram is also provided in the answers section on the next page.

Answers

Model answer:

2

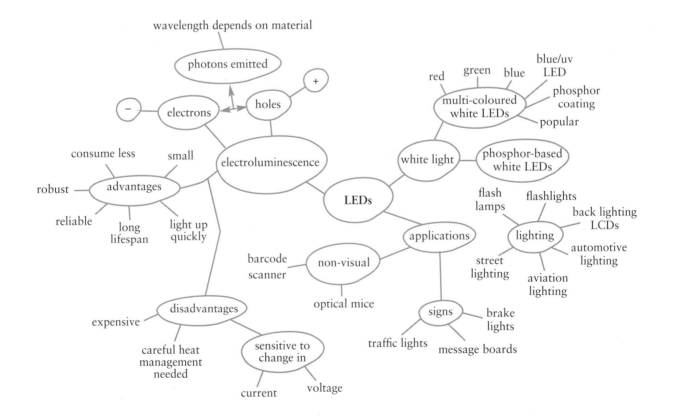

Language and methodology note

When note-making in technical subjects, it is always a good idea to draw quick spidergrams and mind maps where possible and to add notes to any diagrams you are given in handouts, etc. For many people it is easier to learn from a visual aid than from a page full of notes. It is also easier to recall information.

Exercise F

Set for individual work and pairwork checking. Tell students to number the text paragraphs 1–7 to make it easier to provide feedback. Feed back with the class.

Answers

Model answers:

Word	Paragraph	Refers to
these	1	electrons and holes
they	1	an electron and a hole
this	1	the fact that an electron falls into a lower energy level
this	1	the energy gap of the semiconductor
it	1	the semiconductor
this	2	using three LEDs of different colours
its	4	the building's
they	6	LEDs

Exercise G

Refer students to the blue words in the text. Elicit that they are all linking words and phrases either within sentences or between sentences. Remind students that some of these words and expressions were dealt with in Units 7 and 11. Feed back with the class, building up the table below on the board.

Answers

Model answers:

Linking word/phrase	Possible synonym in context
While	Although, Even though
in the case of	in, with regard to, as regards, as far as [silicon diodes] are concerned
because	as, since, due to/owing to the fact that …
However	Nevertheless
however	though
Since	Because, As
Currently	At the present time (warn students about using the word 'presently' as this tends to mean 'soon')

Exercise H

1 Set for individual work and pairwork discussion. Tell students to think about the choice of preposition after the passive verb in each case. Feed back with the class, building up the passive clauses on the board. Ask students whether they think the passive clauses are an improvement on the original active clauses and why/why not. (Some clauses may appear awkward in the passive voice; others may alter the main focus, by making the subject the object of the verb.)

2 Set for individual work and pairwork checking. Tell students to underline examples in the text and to pay particular attention to any examples of passives in reduced clauses. See the *Language note* below the answers section. Tell students to also circle any prepositions following the verbs that indicate an agent or other action, but warn them to be aware of any phrasal verbs. Feed back with the class.

3 Elicit ideas from the whole class. If they find it difficult to explain, use one of the passive examples in the table in the answer key to question 2 below to show why the passive is used. For example:

… its lights <u>are converted</u> from traditional bulbs to LEDs.

If this example was written as an active sentence, there would have to be a subject: something that converts the lights. However, in this case, as in all the other examples, we are not interested in who or what performs the action, but rather what happens to the lights. The use of the passive voice therefore emphasizes the process rather than the agent (which in most cases is either irrelevant, obvious or implied).

Answers

Model answers:

1

Clause from the text	Passive clause
This releases energy in the form of photons …	Energy <u>is released</u> in the form of photons (by this) …
The second process uses a phosphor coating …	In the second process, a phosphor coating <u>is used</u> …
LEDs also consume much less energy.	Much less energy <u>is also consumed</u> (by LEDs).
… they require more careful heat management …	… more careful heat management <u>is required</u> (by them) …
… most LEDs produce one-colour light, …	… one-colour light <u>is produced</u> by most LEDs, …

Paragraph	Examples of passives
1	… a process called *electroluminescence*. (note reduced relative clause)
1	… this <u>is determined</u> by the type of material
1	… it <u>is made</u> of … (note phrasal verb)
1	… no visible light <u>is released</u>.
2	There are two main processes which <u>can be used</u> to create …
2	… the three colours <u>are mixed</u> together by the eye.
2	These <u>are known</u> as multicoloured white LEDs.
3	These <u>are called</u> phosphor-based white LEDs, …
4	… they <u>can be used</u> in a variety of situations …
4	… the carbon footprint of a building <u>can be reduced</u> by more than 60% …
4	… its lights <u>are converted</u> from traditional bulbs to LEDs.
5	… they <u>cannot be used</u> when the ambient temperature of the operating environment goes above 35°C.
6	LEDs <u>are used</u> in a variety of different applications …
6	… their advantages over more traditional lighting <u>can be exploited</u> fully.
6	… such as message displays <u>used</u> at airports and train stations. (note reduced relative clause)
6	Another sort of sign that LEDs <u>are used for</u> is brake lights for vehicles. (note phrasal verb)
7	They <u>are used</u> in street lighting, …

3 In most scientific and technical writing, the passive voice is used to emphasize the process rather than the agent (the person or thing performing the action). See also the explanation in the notes to this question above.

Language note

A *reduced* clause is where the relative pronoun (*who/which/that*) can be omitted, and where the verb is reduced to the past participle. An example sentence from the text, also in the answers section above, would be written the following way if the relative pronoun was included:

… *such as message displays* **which are** *used at airports and train stations.*

Not all relative clauses can be reduced, for example if there is a new subject:

… *such as message boards, which airports sometimes use* … .

See a good grammar reference book for a full explanation.

Exercise I

Set for individual work and pairwork checking. This exercise provides further practice in linking ideas in a text by focusing on the logical flow of information in a paragraph. Ask students to study the four sentences first and try to predict which section the information belongs in before checking with the text. Feed back with the class.

Answers

Model answers:

Sentence	Location in text	Reason
A	at the end of section 3: Advantages of LEDs	it gives a further disadvantage of LEDs, completing the last paragraph of this section
B	at the end of section 1: Electroluminescence	it follows on from the previous sentences in the text, which talk about the wavelength of the light emitted by the diode, and the fact that silicon, a common material used in diodes, does not emit visible light; it also links up with the next section of the text – white light
C	at the end of section 4: Applications of LEDs	it offers a further application of LEDs
D	at the end of section 2: White light	it continues the topic of phosphor-based white LEDs discussed in the second paragraph in this section

Exercise J

Tell students to read both questions carefully. Before they start the exercise, write the following sentences on the board/OHT. Ask them to suggest possibilities for the missing word or words in each sentence and say what type of words they are.

1 *Incandescent light bulbs heat up considerably, _____ fluorescent lamps and LEDs do not change temperature very much.*

(whereas or while = showing contrast)

2 *_____ fluorescent lamps and most white-light LEDs contain a phosphor coating.*

(Both = comparing similar features/things)

3 *Incandescent light bulbs use _____ energy _____ fluorescent lamps.*

(More … than = comparing using the comparative form + *than*)

Ask students to work in pairs to make a list of linking expressions commonly used when comparing or contrasting two or more things. Elicit their ideas, building up the table below on the board.

Compare expression	Contrast expressions
similarly	whereas
similar to	while
compared (with/to)	unlike
also	in contrast (to/with)
the same as	on the other hand
likewise	
like	

Others ways to compare/contrast
both
more than/less than
smaller than/greater than
as … as
not as … as

Language note

Make sure students are aware that the following expressions, commonly found in such compare/contrast lists, are mainly used to show concession (i.e., used to concede/accept a point which simultaneously contrasts with the main point in a sentence or paragraph):

although, though, even though, however, nevertheless, yet, still, at the same time, on the other hand

For example:

Fluorescent lamps use less energy than traditional light bulbs. However, LEDs use even less.

1 Set for individual work (possibly for homework) and pairwork discussion of notes. Before students reread the texts in Lesson 12.1 and earlier in this lesson, refer them to the table containing the given notes. Elicit a logical way to carry on making notes from the texts (they should find points of comparison from the texts and record them side by side in the columns – this makes it easier to write up the notes).

Remind students to use symbols and abbreviations, and to survey the text before closer reading. Tell them that they should also use information from the short text in Exercise C, and from the sentences in Exercise I.

Feed back with the class and ask for some examples of key points from the texts for comparison/contrast. You may wish to display all or part of the model notes in the answers section on the next page (available in Resource 12F).

2 Set for individual work. Alternatively, set for pair or small group work as a collaborative writing activity. Students could write the summary on an OHT or other visual medium, which you can display and give feedback on with the whole class.

To expand on the question to make it more authentic, write the following scenario on the board/OHT, or invent an alternative scenario for your class. Change the wording where appropriate for a collaborative writing activity:

Imagine that a bank you work for is thinking about building a new office complex in a city centre. It wants to make its lighting as efficient and environmentally friendly as possible. As one of the engineers, you have been asked to present your views. Write a summary of around 250 words, comparing fluorescent lamps and LEDs and finishing with your recommendations.

Tell students that they will need to think about which points to select from their notes for the summary, and in what order to present them. This decision will depend on which factors they want to highlight. For example, they might want to focus more on costs than on environmental factors or vice versa, or have a balance of factors. Or they might decide that the most important factor is the technology. Encourage students to think in the role of one of the engineers.

The summary in the answers section below can be used as a model to display and/or as an extra activity in identifying key comparison/contrast and concession words and phrases.

Answers

Model answers:

1

Fluorescent lamps	Traditional incandescent bulbs (IBs)	LEDs
• less energy required than IBs • more efficient than IBs, converting more of the input power to visible light	• world's most common source of light • consume a lot of energy	• consume much less energy than IBs • carbon footprint of a building can be reduced by > 60% if its lights are converted from IBs to LEDs
• lamps are long, thin tubes → very different lamp shape from IBs • more recently more compact fluorescent lamps have been made which resemble traditional IBs	• traditional lightbulb shape	• very small, often < 1 mm² → can be used in a variety of situations where other lighting options not suitable
• reasonably robust, but can be broken	• easy to break	• more robust than IBs → difficult to break
• last longer than IBs, provided they are not switched on and off too often	• don't last very long	• more reliable than IBs → longer lifespan too • LEDs can last 3x longer than fluorescent lamps & 30x longer than IBs
• take time to switch on, although new models are quicker than older ones	• quick light up	• LEDs light up very quickly, often in < 1 µs
		• LEDs very sensitive to changes in voltage and current • series resistors or current-regulated power supplies may be required for complete efficiency
	• filament gets hot	• require more careful heat management than both incandescent bulbs and fluorescent lamps • cannot be used when the operating temperature > 35°C
• less initial capital expenditure – cheaper than IBs and LEDs • common lighting system with low installation costs & cheap replacement parts	• cheap	• initial capital costs high • LEDs suitable for domestic/office lighting cost more than fluorescent lamps
• contain a small amount of mercury		

2 Model summary:

The following summary presents key differences between fluorescent lamps and LEDs that are relevant for the given scenario, focusing mainly on economic considerations and environmental impact.

Both fluorescent lamps and LEDs are suitable for office lighting, and both are relatively cheap compared to traditional incandescent light bulbs. However, there are significant differences between the two technologies that need to be taken into consideration.

Firstly, the initial capital cost of LED lamps is considerably higher than for fluorescent lighting. LED technology is relatively new and LED lamps suitable for this situation are expensive, while fluorescent lamps are an established form of lighting, with significantly lower installation costs. In addition, LEDs are very sensitive to changes in voltage and current, and circuits need to include costly features such as series resistors and current-regulated power supplies. However, the price of LED lamps is undoubtedly going to fall, and this means that replacement parts and eventual future modifications may be more affordable.

The main benefit of using LED lighting is in their efficiency. LEDs consume less energy than fluorescent lamps, making them more environmentally friendly. Lower running costs also mean that the extra initial costs of LEDs will eventually be paid off, although this will take many years.

Another key advantage is that LED lights last up to three times longer than fluorescent lamps. This is especially true if fluorescent lamps are often switched on and off, as may indeed be the case here. LEDs are also very robust, whereas fluorescent lamps can be broken when handled.

Even though fluorescent lamps are a common choice and a more mature technology, my/our view is that LEDs would be the better choice for our company. LEDs have lower energy costs and reflect our company's innovative and environmentally friendly image.

Closure

1 As extra practice in using linking words and expressions to show comparison and concession, copy the gapped sentences below onto an OHT or other visual medium for whole class work.

The sentences are adapted from the information in the texts in the unit. Ask for suggestions to complete the sentences. There may be more than one answer in some cases. You could also ask students to rewrite the sentences using a different expression, paying attention to punctuation and any other changes they would need to make.

a LEDs are cheap to run, _____ they are expensive to install.

b _____ incandescent bulbs, fluorescent lamps do not heat up when in use.

c _____ fluorescent lamps are usually long, thin tubes, more compact shapes are now available and can be used in normal lamps instead of light bulbs.

d LEDs are _____ environmentally friendly _____ incandescent bulbs.

e Fluorescent lamps are _____ energy efficient _____ LEDs.

Answers

Possible answers:

a yet, but (without preceding comma), though, although, nevertheless (preceded by semicolon), at the same time (preceded by semicolon) = concession

b Unlike, In contrast to = showing contrast

c Although, Even though, Though = concession

d more ... than = comparison

e less ... than, not as ... as = comparison

2 Put students into small groups. Ask them to choose one of the following products or a product of their own choice, and say what light source it uses and why they think it was adopted.

mobile phone, car headlamp, solar lamp, lighthouse light, security lighting, floodlighting

Ask them to prepare a short presentation using an OHT or other visual medium to present key points. They should address all the questions below:

What light source does this product use?

Why was it chosen?

What are its advantages?

Are any alternative light sources possible?

Why would they be less successful?

Do you think a different light source will be used in the future for this product?

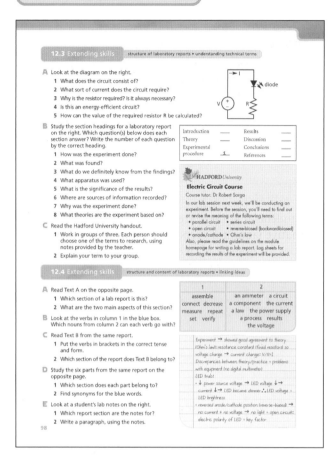

General note

Read the *Vocabulary bank – Understanding technical terms* and the *Skills bank* at the end of the Course Book unit. Decide when, if at all, to refer your students to it. The best time is probably at the very end of the lesson or the beginning of the next lesson, as a summary/revision.

Lesson aims

● understand the structure of a laboratory report

● understand the purpose of each laboratory report section

● understand and explain key terms in lighting engineering

Introduction

In preparation for looking at the structure of a laboratory report, revise the sections for a report: introduction, body, conclusion. Ask students what should go in each section. Elicit ideas for introductions and conclusions. Do not correct at this point.

Language and subject note

The theme of Lessons 12.3 and 12.4 connects with the subject of LEDs by focusing on a typical laboratory experiment involving simple circuits containing LEDs and fixed resistors. The lessons also introduce aspects of writing laboratory reports, but in a simplified way. Laboratory reports are best taught in the context of practical laboratory sessions. However, it is hoped that this short introduction to the genre will be helpful in familiarizing students with an important aspect of engineering practice.

Exercise A

1–5 Set for pairwork discussion. Feed back with the class. Question 4 is designed to prompt students to think about testing, experiments, established mathematical models and calculations, etc., as a lead-in to the topic of laboratory experiments. Feed back with the class.

Tell students that the rest of this lesson and the following lesson will focus on laboratory reports. Tell them that the emphasis will be on the structure and style of lab reports, and that understanding all the details of the experiment is not expected.

Answers

Possible answers:

1 An LED and a resistor, R.

2 An LED circuit requires direct current (DC), and not typical mains electricity, which is alternating current (AC).

3 As mentioned in the text in Lesson 12.2, LEDs are very sensitive to changes in voltage. If the voltage is too low, no current will flow and the LED will not light. If the voltage is too high, the current may cause the LED to heat up and may damage it. Even a small change in voltage can change the current dramatically. It is therefore important that the power source delivers the right voltage. The resistor placed in series with the LED is required to stabilize the current supplied to the LED. However, no resistor is needed if the supply voltage is equal to the LED's voltage drop.

4 This circuit is not particularly efficient, since some energy will be lost in the resistor.

$$\text{resistance } (R) = \frac{\text{power supply voltage } (V_s) - \text{LED voltage drop } (V_f)}{\text{LED current } (I)}$$

5 The resistor value R can be computed using Ohm's law: subtract the forward voltage drop V_f across the LED from the supply voltage V_s, and then divide the result by the desired LED operating current I.

Exercise B

Set for individual work and pairwork checking. Feed back with the class. Explain that there are several variations of lab report structures, but whatever the format, the aim is the same – to record results of an experiment and discuss their significance. (Some of these variations are addressed in Closure activity 2 at the end of the lesson.)

Answers

Model answers:

Introduction	7
Theory	8
Experimental procedure	1, 4
Results	2
Discussion	5, 6
Conclusions	3
References	7

Exercise C

1/2 Set for individual work and small group discussion. Allow time for students to read the handout. Copy and cut up the notes in Resource 12G in the additional resources section, so that there are enough for all the groups.

Allocate a set time for students to study the notes and any diagrams. They should make their own notes from the information provided and then take turns to explain their terms to the group. Encourage those with diagrams in their notes to draw a quick sketch for other group members during their turn, and encourage others to seek clarification where necessary. Monitor the groups to make sure that students are not just reading from the notes provided. Check pronunciation of key terms at the same time.

Feed back with the whole class. Check understanding by asking a few key questions about each term and invite students to ask questions if they need further clarification.

Closure

1 Refer students to the *Skills bank* to consolidate their understanding of the sections of a laboratory report and their contents.

2 Put the following words on the board.

Abstract
Materials
Methods
Findings
Appendix/Appendices

Tell students that these are different headings in alternative laboratory report structures. Ask them to find out for homework what these sections do, and which ones are extra to the model used in this unit.

12.4 Extending skills

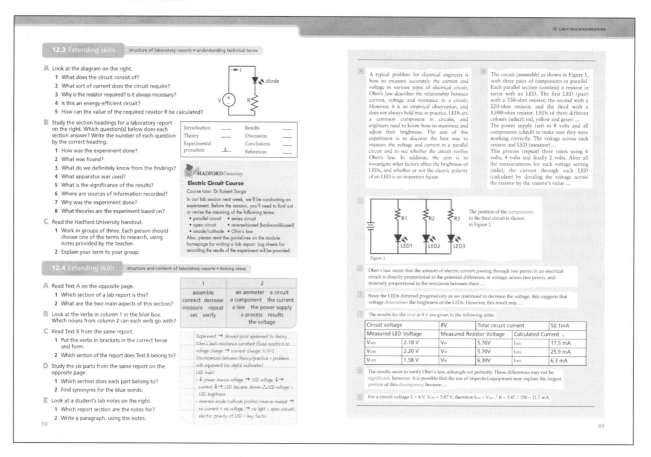

Lesson aims

- identify parts of a laboratory report
- use the correct tense and form (active or passive voice) in laboratory report sections
- write a section of a laboratory report from notes: *Conclusions*

Further practice in:

- synonyms
- passives
- verb and noun collocations from the discipline

Introduction

Write the sections of a laboratory report on the board in an incorrect order. With Course Books closed, ask students to say what the correct order should be. Check stress and pronunciation. Test their understanding of the sections by asking a selection of paraphrased questions from Exercise B in Lesson 12.3:

What <u>equipment</u> was used? (*Experimental Procedure*)

What do the results <u>imply</u>? (*Discussion*)

What was the <u>reason</u> for the experiment? (*Introduction*)

What <u>procedure</u> was followed? (*Experimental*

Procedure)

What was the <u>outcome</u> of the experiment? (*Results*)

What do we <u>know for sure</u> as a result of the experiment? (*Conclusions*)

If you gave students Closure activity 2 from Lesson 12.3, ask them what they found out about the section headings below:

Abstract (= extra to unit model; a clear and concise summary of around 100–200 words at the beginning of the report which summarizes the four key aspects: the aim of the experiment, key results, significance of results and main conclusions. The abstract should help readers to decide whether they need to read the whole report.

Materials (= an alternative report format often has two sections in place of *Experimental Procedure*, namely, *Materials* and *Methods*)

Methods (= see above)

Findings (= another name for *Results*)

Appendix/Appendices (= extra to unit model; would include raw data, calculations, graphs, tables, etc., which are included in *Experimental Procedure* in unit model)

Exercise A

1/2 Set for individual work and pairwork checking. Tell students to focus more on the functional and general academic language than on the actual content. Remind them that it is not necessary for them to fully understand the details of the experiment. Feed back with the whole class.

Bring the class's attention to the tense that is used here (present simple), but explain that the second part of the *Introduction* could also have been written in the past tense: *The aim of this experiment was to discover the best way to measure the voltage and current in a parallel circuit …*

To connect this exercise with the following one on verb and noun collocations, ask the class to say briefly what two specific things will be done in the experiment (*measure the voltage, verify a law*).

Answers

Model answers:

1 *Introduction*
2 The two main aspects are a) background information to the experiment, including known facts, and b) the aim of the experiment (i.e., why the experiment was performed).

Exercise B

Set for individual work and pairwork checking. Explain that these are common verb and noun combinations used when reporting on lab experiments. Make sure students understand that some of the verbs collocate or go with more than one noun. Feed back with the class, building up the table on the board.

Answers

Model answers:

assemble	a circuit
connect	an ammeter, a component
decrease	the current, the power supply, the voltage
measure	a component, the current, the power supply, the voltage
repeat	a process, results
set	the power supply, the voltage (to a value)
verify	a law, results

Exercise C

1/2 Set for individual work and pairwork checking. Tell students to read through the text first for overall understanding. Explain that this text shows only selected extracts from a report section (indicated by the row of three periods or full stops at the end of each paragraph), and remind students that they do not have to fully understand the experiment to be able to do the exercise. Feed back with the class.

If you wish to do question 1 as a whole class activity, copy the text in Resource 12H in the additional resources section onto an OHT or other visual medium.

Answers

Model answers:

1 The circuit (*assemble*) <u>was assembled</u> as shown in Figure 1, with three pairs of components in parallel. Each parallel section (*contain*) <u>contained</u> a resistor in series with an LED. The first LED (*pair*) <u>was paired</u> with a 330-ohm resistor, the second with a 220-ohm resistor, and the third with a 1,000-ohm resistor. LEDs of three different colours (*select*) <u>were selected</u>: red, yellow and green …

The power supply (*set*) <u>was set</u> to 8 volts and all components (*check*) <u>were checked</u> to make sure they were working correctly. The voltage across each resistor and LED (*measure*) <u>was measured</u> …

This process (*repeat*) <u>was repeated</u> three times using 6 volts, 4 volts and finally 2 volts. After all the measurements for each voltage setting (*take*) <u>were taken</u>, the current through each LED (*calculate*) <u>was calculated</u> by dividing the voltage across the resistor by the resistor's value …

2 These are extracts from the *Experimental Procedure* section: an account of how the experiment was carried out.

Language note

The impersonal use of the passive for laboratory reports is not absolutely required. It is often possible to find students' work which contains the use of the first person singular or the third person singular if the report is the result of group work. However, in formal writing – especially for publication in the field – the passive is typically used. In higher education, students should always follow instructions from their subject lecturers with regard to their stylistic preferences.

Exercise D

1 Set for individual work and pairwork discussion. Tell students to read through all six parts first for overall understanding before discussing in pairs. Feed back with the class.

2 Set for individual work and pairwork checking. Remind students that synonyms are not always precise and so they need to be careful that the words they choose are appropriate in the context. The meanings of words such as *significant* and *critical,* for example, are very context-dependent. Feed back with the class.

Answers

Model answers:

1

1	Experimental Procedure
2	Theory
3	Discussion
4	Results
5	Discussion
6	Results

2

Word in context	Possible synonyms
components	devices
determines	regulates (could also be replaced by *is responsible for* in this context)
trial	experiment
significant	important
portion	element (could also be replaced by *reason for* in this context)
discrepancy	difference, problem

Exercise E

1 Set for individual work and pairwork checking. Feed back with the class. Elicit the meanings of the symbols and abbreviations, most of which students have already encountered in previous units.

2 Set for individual work and pairwork checking/review. Alternatively, this task could be done as homework. Tell students to include the section heading when they write the paragraph. As a reminder about things to consider when writing up from notes, elicit aspects of grammar that are commonly omitted in notes, such as prepositions, linking words, articles, punctuation, pronouns and the full forms of verbs. Feed back with the class. Copy the model paragraph in the answers section below, available in Resource 12I, onto an OHT for comparison with students' own work. Underline or highlight salient aspects of the paragraph that show how the notes have been reconstructed into sentences. Invite feedback from students on how the model compares with their own paragraph.

Answers

Model answers:

1 The *Conclusions* section.

2 Possible answer:

Overall, the results obtained in this experiment showed good agreement with Ohm's law and were seen to verify this theory for the circuits used. Because fixed resistors were used, the resistance in the circuits was constant and therefore a change in voltage resulted in a change in current. It was demonstrated that the results follow the formula $V/R = I$. The small differences found between theoretical and practical results are probably due to the equipment used. For instance, the use of a digital multimeter might eliminate these discrepancies in future experiments. The results concerning LEDs showed that, as the power source voltage was decreased, the voltage across the LED decreased and, as a result, the current decreased. The LED became dimmer, indicating that the brightness of an LED depends on its voltage. In addition, when the anode and cathode positions of the LED were reversed, no current flowed through the circuit and there was no voltage. With the LED reverse-biased in this way, there was an open circuit and the LED did not emit any light. It can therefore be concluded that the electric polarity of an LED is a key factor in correct functioning.

Closure

1 Write the following five strings of words on the board or OHT/other visual medium. With books closed, elicit suggestions from students on how to build a complete sentence for each string. Tell them to think about the meaning of the combination of words in the order they are given, and about extra words needed, such as determiners, prepositions, and verbs or correct verb endings. Do the first one with the whole class as an example.

1 *typical problem / electrical engineers / choose / source / light / situation*

2 *results / agreement / theoretical values*

3 *aim / experiment / measure / voltage / resistor*

4 *supply / set / 8 V / components / check / sure / work / properly*

5 *It / demonstrate / brightness / LED / dependent / voltage*

Suggested sentences:

1 A typical problem for electrical engineers is how to choose the best source of light for a given situation.

2 The results showed agreement with theoretical values.

3 The aim of the experiment is/was to measure the voltage across the resistor.

4 The power supply was set to 8V and the components were checked to make sure (that) they were working properly.

5 It was demonstrated that the brightness of an LED is dependent on voltage.

2 Set students to research more about laboratory reports on the Internet. Things to notice in sample reports they find are variations in structure, use of tense in different sections, common verbs for reporting on experiments and standard phrases used in the discipline. The following websites are particularly useful (URLs correct at the time of writing):

http://writing.engr.psu.edu/workbooks/laboratory. html (on the structure of lab reports)

http://writing.engr.psu.edu/workbooks/labreport2. html (a sample authentic report)

www.ncsu.edu/labwrite/index_labwrite.htm (guide to writing lab reports)

1 Work through the *Vocabulary bank* and *Skills bank* if you have not already done so, or as revision of previous study.

2 Use the *Activity bank* (Teacher's Book additional resources section, Resource 12A).

   A Set the wordsearch for individual work (including homework) or pairwork.

   Answers

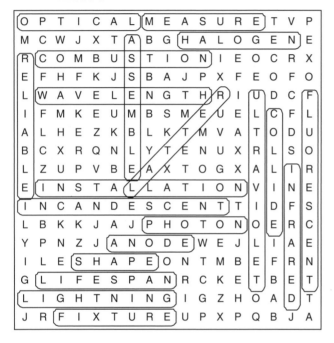

   B Do the quiz as a whole class, or in teams, or set for homework.

   Answers

   1 a multicoloured (white LED)
     b infrared
     c phosphor

   2 a semiconductor
     b electron
     c photon
     d wavelength
     e diode

3 series/parallel/open circuit

   message display

   white-light/ultraviolet/infrared/blue LED

   light/incandescent/filament bulb

   barcode scanner

   phosphor coating

   domestic/artificial/natural/automotive/ aviation/street lighting

   energy gap

   natural/artificial/electric light

   (accept any other words that form acceptable alternative phrases within the discipline)

Activity bank

A Solve the crossword.

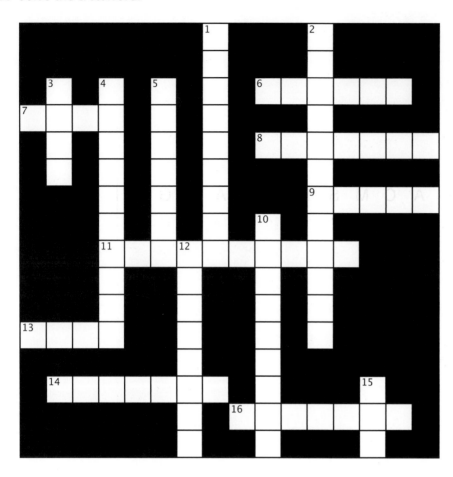

Down

1 An instrument for measuring voltage.

2 Qualified, experienced people in one field of work may belong to a this type of body.

3 A representation of the electric potential energy per unit charge.

4 The opposition to the flow of current through a device or material.

5 The movement of electrons past a reference point.

10 Emission and propagation of energy in the form of rays or waves.

12 The negatively charged particle that revolves around the nucleus of an atom.

15 A statement that is always true, which describes a relationship between two or more things.

Across

6 A stable, positively charged subatomic particle.

7 A connection point or junction in a circuit.

8 Related to heat.

9 A short discharge of electricity between two conductors.

11 An electric generator that produces alternating current.

13 A length of metal rod, usually thin and flexible, used in electrical circuits.

14 One or more cells connected together to produce an electric current.

16 An academic publication consisting of articles on a particular subject or discipline.

B Play noughts and crosses. Use the words in context or explain what they mean.

electromagnetic	kilowatt	ohmmeter	degree	in series	closed circuit
technological	infrared	voltage	electrical charge	satellite dish	inductor coil
leakage	gigabyte	certification	electric field	noise	wave

English for Electrical Engineering – Copyright © Garnet Publishing Ltd 2014

Activity bank

A Find 20 words from this unit in the wordsearch.
- Copy the words into your notebook.
- Check the definition of any words you can't remember.

S	J	O	X	S	I	K	C	O	M	P	O	N	E	N	T	S
E	H	G	N	S	N	P	V	O	L	T	A	G	E	N	E	X
M	T	W	N	Q	S	H	M	W	W	Y	I	J	O	V	W	J
I	E	M	Z	D	U	V	I	I	P	T	M	I	A	C	U	C
C	L	C	S	M	L	A	C	M	S	B	T	W	A	O	G	Q
O	E	I	W	Y	A	C	R	K	J	U	I	E	M	N	E	F
N	C	R	A	X	T	U	O	B	B	L	N	L	P	D	N	T
D	T	C	N	F	E	U	P	I	T	K	D	E	L	U	E	Q
U	R	U	K	Z	D	M	R	E	R	S	U	M	I	C	R	G
C	O	I	E	T	D	T	O	Y	A	W	C	E	F	T	A	O
T	N	T	J	V	S	Y	C	N	N	I	T	N	I	O	T	J
O	I	K	V	I	I	V	E	E	S	T	I	T	E	R	O	M
R	S	V	D	N	G	L	S	T	I	C	O	N	R	L	R	K
M	T	P	X	C	N	C	S	W	S	H	N	O	J	H	Z	S
R	F	N	B	W	A	P	O	O	T	T	R	I	O	D	E	Q
S	N	W	L	B	L	K	R	R	O	O	C	R	P	V	I	V
K	L	D	B	Y	M	I	J	K	R	C	Y	M	O	Z	X	G

B Do the quiz.
1 What is the word for:
   a a three-layer conductor sandwich
   b something that turns electricity on and off
   c a series of transistors arranged in circuits having many degrees of complexity
2 What was discovered/invented in the following years:
   a 1888
   b 1947
3 Name the two types of current.
4 List:
   a three inventions of the second half of the 19th century
   b three inventions made during the Second World War

The history of electrical engineering up to 1950

Electrical phenomena occupied European thinkers as early as the 17th century, but the first notable developments in this field were made in the first half of the 19th century.	Ohm quantified the relationship between electric current and potential difference for a conductor, and constructed an early electrostatic machine in the 1830s. Also around this time, Faraday discovered electromagnetic induction and developed the homopolar generator. The first practical application of electromagnetism was the telegraph, invented by Henry, and exploited commercially by Morse in 1837.
However, many people believe that Electrical Engineering can only be said to have emerged as a discipline in the second half of the 19th century.	This happened when it was associated with the tools of modern research techniques. The Scottish physicist Maxwell summarized the basic laws of electricity in mathematical form in 1864. He predicted that radiation of electromagnetic energy would occur. The radiation later became known as *radio waves*.
As a result of the discoveries in electricity, there was a dramatic increase in work in the area.	Bell invented the telephone in 1876, and Edison invented the incandescent lamp in 1878. Edison provided the world's first large-scale electrical supply network with *direct current* (DC), while Tesla offered a rival form of power distribution known as *alternating current* (AC). AC eventually replaced DC for generation and power distribution, which allowed for the expansion of the electric power industry throughout the world, improving the safety and efficiency of power distribution.
The rivalry between AC and DC systems helped advance electrical engineering.	Tesla's work on induction motors influenced the field for years to come, while Edison's work on telegraphy and the stock ticker helped his company expand. It eventually became General Electric. All these applications meant an increased demand for people trained to work with electricity.
The discovery of the Edison effect and electron theory laid the foundations of radio engineering.	The Edison effect is the name given to the phenomenon of a hot metal cathode emitting electrons and is the principle behind vacuum tubes. Many scientists and inventors were involved in the radio technology that followed as a result of experiments in the Edison effect and electron theory. Hertz transmitted and detected radio waves using electrical equipment in 1888. Tesla, in 1895, was able to detect signals from transmissions at a distance of over 80 km. In 1896, Popov made wireless transmissions over a distance of 60 m, and Marconi, around the same time, made a transmission across 2.4 km. By the end of 1906, Fessenden had sent the first radio broadcast.
In 1930, the term *electronics* was introduced to include radio and the industrial applications of electron tubes.	However, prior to the Second World War, the subject was still commonly known as *radio engineering* and was mainly restricted to aspects of communications, commercial radio and early television. At this time, the study of radio engineering at universities could only be undertaken as part of a physics degree.
The Second World War saw tremendous breakthroughs in the field of electronics.	Key advances were made in radar, as well as in the magnetron developed by Randall and Boot in Birmingham in 1940. Radio location, radio communication and radio guidance of aircraft were all developed in Britain at this time. An early electronic computing device, Colossus, was built by Flowers to decipher German coded messages. Advanced hidden radio transmitters and receivers for use by secret agents were also developed at this time. All these developments ensured that electrical engineering had come of age, and was at the forefront of modern scientific advancement.

The discovery of the electron in 1897 emerged from Edison's work on the electric light bulb and marked the beginning of electronics.

A series of experiments led to the invention of the triode.

Triodes can also work as a switch by using the grid voltage to turn a current on or off.

By the middle of the 20th century, scientists were searching for an alternative to vacuum tubes.

There were pros and cons to the first transistors.

Today, transistors are much cheaper and are often organized in circuits having many degrees of complexity.

The first microprocessor was produced in 1971.

The discovery of the electron in 1897 emerged from Edison's work on the electric light bulb and marked the beginning of electronics.

A series of experiments led to the invention of the triode.

Triodes can also work as a switch by using the grid voltage to turn a current on or off.

By the middle of the 20th century, scientists were searching for an alternative to vacuum tubes.

There were pros and cons to the first transistors.

Today, transistors are much cheaper and are often organized in circuits having many degrees of complexity.

The first microprocessor was produced in 1971.

The history of electronic engineering

The discovery of the electron in 1897 emerged from Edison's work on the electric light bulb and marked the beginning of electronics.	In his experiments, Faraday noticed that a small metal plate placed in front of one of his experimental bulbs picked up an electric current that had crossed the bulb's vacuum from the hot filament. The current passing through the vacuum always travelled in the same direction, from the filament to the plate, even when the filament carried an alternating current. The existence of microscopic particles – electrons – was proposed. The theory was that these particles were moving through the vacuum at high speed.
A series of experiments led to the invention of the triode.	Within the vacuum tube, a grid-like wire was inserted between the filament and the plate. This functioned as an amplifier, meaning that changes in a very small voltage applied to the grid produced parallel changes in the flow of the much larger current between the other two elements. This three-element tube – or triode – had many applications, including long-distance telephony, record players, radio and television.
Triodes can also work as a switch by using the grid voltage to turn a current on or off.	Rapid switching between on and off positions was identified as a way of carrying out complex calculations using the binary numbering system, with different arrangements of switches sufficient to perform any mathematical or logical operation. Vacuum tubes were therefore quickly enlisted for the new computing machines. But, because a very large number of switches are required, the first models of computers were extremely large and expensive to run.
By the middle of the 20th century, scientists were searching for an alternative to vacuum tubes.	Crystalline materials known as *semiconductors*, in which current flows in only one direction, were investigated. It was known that the presence of certain impurities, such as phosphorus, strongly affected the electrical behaviour of semiconductors. The impurities provided a surplus of electrons that were free to contribute to a current. Some investigators were convinced that semiconductors could have the properties of a triode. In 1947, that goal was met in the form of a three-layer semiconductor sandwich, known as a *transistor*. An impurity was added to the outer layers to supply extra electrons, and the middle portion of the sandwich functioned like the grid in a triode, controlling a sizable current flow between the outer layers. This was the beginning of solid-state electronics.
There were pros and cons to the first transistors.	They used much less power than vacuum tubes, did not need to warm up, and were compact. However, their main ingredient was germanium: an expensive, hard-to-handle element, with performance limitations. A turning point came in early 1954, when a transistor was made from silicon, an element of sand. The Silicon Age had arrived. Silicon transistors led to the creation of integrated circuits. An integrated circuit is an assemblage of different components that are wired together and work as a unit. In 1958, it was discovered that a wafer of silicon could be given all the elements necessary to function as a circuit. The design of the wafer was developed and it became better protected and insulated. It also became much easier to connect the circuit elements together. By the mid-1990s, some chips the size of a fingernail contained 20 million components.
Today, transistors are much cheaper and are often organized in circuits that can perform complex functions or tasks..	They can provide electronic memory and carry out particular tasks, such as manipulating audio signals or graphic images. Other uses are in general-purpose devices called *microprocessors*, which are not designed to do one specific job. Instead, they can follow software instructions to perform a range of tasks.
The first microprocessor was produced in 1971. Faster models soon followed, and prices dropped.	Microprocessors are now everywhere, operating in every household appliance and in every mode of communication and transportation. This rate of development shows no sign of slowing. Computing power will continue its incredible expansion and change our future in ways which we cannot imagine at present.

Activity bank

A Solve the crossword.

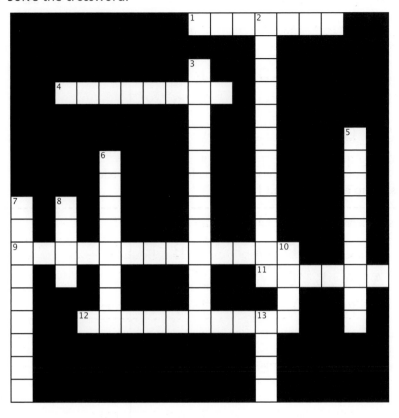

Down

2 Having a constant ratio.
3 Glowing white-hot and emitting light.
5 Contacts on a device through which current enters or leaves.
6 To make or become greater in value.
7 Derived from experiment and observation rather than theory.
8 Having no measurable quantity.
10 Synonym of an *increase*.
13 A spiral form made from a number of turns of a single wire.

Across

1 A device used to find magnetic north.
4 A value that does not change in different working conditions.
9 At an angle of 90 degrees.
11 Consisting of a straight line.
12 The opposition to electric flux.

B Play bingo.

- Think of words for each of the categories and write them on card 1. Each student says one of their words. Cross the squares on card 2 when you hear a word from that category.

1

a unit of measurement	an electronic device	a circuit element
___	___	___
an electromagnetic quantity	an electrical device	a mathematical operation
___	___	___

2

a unit of measurement	an electronic device	a circuit element
an electromagnetic quantity	an electrical device	a mathematical operation

Activity bank

A Find 20 verbs from the first four units in the wordsearch.

- Copy the verbs into your notebook.
- Write the noun for each verb.

P	L	N	B	S	S	Y	D	I	V	I	D	E	U	Y	O
R	D	E	V	E	L	O	P	R	X	W	M	G	Y	O	X
O	D	J	E	H	Y	N	R	G	E	N	E	R	A	T	E
D	S	I	N	S	U	L	A	T	E	D	T	A	M	J	Q
U	A	P	P	L	Y	C	I	T	O	A	U	R	Q	A	N
C	R	E	T	R	A	N	S	M	I	T	O	H	C	M	I
E	O	R	X	W	F	L	V	J	Q	F	W	R	A	P	E
B	M	O	H	P	B	O	A	A	S	L	Y	E	L	L	V
N	E	E	R	C	A	Z	P	N	L	L	U	S	C	I	R
R	A	E	D	D	Y	N	A	L	P	P	L	O	U	F	A
E	S	F	E	Y	I	R	D	I	U	A	E	L	L	Y	D
S	U	C	F	K	T	N	T	N	W	R	X	V	A	J	I
I	R	L	I	M	X	L	A	J	T	C	H	E	T	Z	A
S	E	C	N	A	U	D	U	T	Z	N	I	U	E	A	T
T	B	Z	E	M	K	L	I	P	E	R	F	O	R	M	E
B	D	I	S	T	R	I	B	U	T	E	T	G	I	C	A

B Play noughts and crosses. You must say the abbreviation or acronym and give the original words to place your symbol in a square.

FAQ	CAD	HTTP
MP3	RAM	CAL
ROM	PC	HTML

CAM	LAN	URL
WWW	LCD	ISP
CPU	RTF	PDF

In all fields, the impact of computers has been enormous.

Historically, the development of the computer started relatively recently.

The second-generation computers were more advanced.

The invention of the integrated circuit – or microchip – signalled an important development.

This new technology had important consequences.

In all fields, the impact of computers has been enormous.

Historically, the development of the computer started relatively recently.

The second-generation computers were more advanced.

The invention of the integrated circuit – or microchip – signalled an important development.

This new technology had important consequences.

CAD	CAL
CAM	DVD
HTML	HTTP
ISP	LCD
PIN	ROM
URL	USB
WAN	WWW

Activity bank

A Solve the synonyms crossword. Find words with the same meaning as the clues.

Across

1 appliance
4 wide
6 sharply
10 designed
11 increase
13 called
16 kind
18 concerned
19 thin
20 immovable

Down

2 methods
3 drop
5 quick
7 programme
8 big
9 display
12 place
14 compact
15 aspect
17 image

B Play opposites bingo.

- Choose six words from the box and write one word in each square of your bingo card.
- Your teacher will call out some words. If you have the **opposite** word on your card, cross it out.
- The first person to cross out all the words on their card is the winner.

active cheap easy fall flat heavy
increase large low narrow recent
sharply slightly slow twisted vertical

Describing trends

Verbs	Nouns	Adverbs	Adjectives
rise		gradually	
increase		sharply	
grow		slightly	
improve		markedly	
fall		significantly	
decrease		rapidly	
drop		steeply	
decline		steadily	

Poor contributions	Student A	Student B	Student C	Student D
disagrees rudely				
doesn't explain how the point is relevant				
doesn't understand an idiom				
dominates the discussion				
gets angry when someone disagrees with them				
interrupts				
is negative				
mumbles or whispers				
says something irrelevant				
shouts				
sits quietly and says nothing				
starts a side conversation				
other:				

Good contributions	Student A	Student B	Student C	Student D
allows others to speak				
asks for clarification				
asks politely for information				
brings in another speaker				
builds on points made by other speakers				
contributes to the discussion				
explains the point clearly				
gives specific examples to help explain a point				
is constructive				
links correctly with previous speakers				
listens carefully to what others say				
makes clear how the point is relevant				
paraphrases to check understanding				
says when they agree with someone				
speaks clearly				
tries to use correct language				
other:				

Activity bank

A Find 20 verbs from this unit in the wordsearch.
- Copy the words into your notebook.
- Write the noun for each verb.

```
D  Q  Q  R  Y  R  V  X  T  A  E  B  X  A  U  I
E  T  T  Q  Y  Z  C  A  L  C  U  L  A  T  E  T
D  X  R  S  O  L  V  E  R  L  T  U  X  K  R  E
E  C  I  X  H  I  N  T  E  G  R  A  T  E  S  S
S  X  A  H  G  I  G  Z  M  K  Y  N  Q  F  N  T
T  E  L  K  O  R  U  R  C  E  U  V  P  C  R  S
A  O  M  E  V  A  L  U  A  T  E  S  V  L  S  I
B  F  D  B  G  E  J  I  E  X  L  N  I  C  T  G
I  F  I  E  C  O  N  T  R  I  B  U  T  E  A  N
L  S  R  U  P  J  A  E  X  C  E  E  D  D  B  I
I  E  V  M  X  N  T  U  N  E  A  A  U  G  I  F
Z  T  A  T  I  A  R  R  Q  F  N  S  K  N  L  Y
E  D  C  M  F  L  U  C  T  U  A  T  E  E  I  P
O  S  I  W  B  O  S  C  I  L  L  A  T  E  Z  S
X  L  I  A  S  S  E  S  S  D  J  J  S  H  E  E
E  P  R  E  D  I  C  T  A  W  L  Z  O  I  D  T
```

B Think of a word or words that can go in front of each of the words below to make a phrase from engineering. Explain the meaning.

Example: *conditions = road conditions, ideal conditions, perfect conditions, laboratory conditions, etc.*

_____ conditions	_____ manufacturer	_____ signals
_____ control	_____ mechanism	_____ system
_____ component	_____ operation	_____ temperature
_____ devices	_____ output	_____ time
_____ distance	_____ parameter	_____ tuning
_____ features	_____ pedal	_____ value
_____ heater	_____ sector	_____ wheel

1 Figure 2 shows the oven temperature is _____ at both set values.

2 In Figure 3 the reaction time is _____, but there is a significant overshoot and the _____ oven temperature is below the set temperature value.

3 The final temperature in Figure 3 is unstable because it is _____ .

4 The unstable oscillation has been _____ in Figure 4, but there is still considerable overshoot.

5 The system shown in Figure 5 is damped and stable, with a _____ reaction time.

1 Figure 2 shows the oven temperature is unstable at both set values.

2 In Figure 3 the reaction time is quick, but there is a significant overshoot and the final oven temperature is below the set temperature value.

3 The final temperature in Figure 3 is unstable because it is underdamped.

4 The unstable oscillation has been eliminated in Figure 4, but there is still considerable overshoot.

5 The system shown in Figure 5 is damped and stable, with a quick reaction time.

a This graph shows there is no more ringing, but initially the oven temperature exceeds the set value.

b In this graph, there is tight loop control.

c Temperature stability is never achieved in this graph.

d In this graph the temperature changes quickly, but it initially goes above the set value and there is a significant final offset.

e The system shown in this graph is underdamped and there is oscillation.

Original sentence	Student A	Student B
It must be remembered that every PID control system needs to be tuned.	We must remember that each PID control system must be tuned.	An important feature of PID control systems is tuning.
	not satisfactory: not enough changes: this is patch-writing	*acceptable paraphrase: clause changed to phrase ('It must be remembered' → 'An important feature'); verb phrase changed to noun ('needs to be tuned' → 'tuning'); all words changed except 'control system', which is acceptable*
In the tuning process, the parameters for P, I and D are chosen according to the nature of the system in question.	During this process, the parameters for P, I and D are calculated depending on the type of system in question.	This involves deciding on the values for P, I and D. These will depend on exactly what system is involved.
	not satisfactory: not enough changes: this is patch-writing	*acceptable paraphrase: use of pronoun for anaphoric reference ('this') eliminates need for 'in the tuning process'; use of synonyms ('choose' → 'decide' / 'values' → 'parameters' / 'in question' → 'involved'); passive changed to active ('are chosen' → 'deciding'); prepositional phrase changed to clause ('according to' → 'these depend on'); all words changed except for 'process' and 'system', which is acceptable*
and then tested in practice.	After this they are tested in practice.	After this, the values undergo trials in working conditions.
	not satisfactory: not enough changes: this is patch-writing	*acceptable paraphrase: use of synonyms ('then' → 'after this' / 'in practice' → 'in working conditions' / 'tested' → 'undergo trials'; no words the same as the original*
The use of a PID controller does not necessarily guarantee ideal control	A PID controller does not guarantee ideal control.	This type of system does not automatically provide perfect control.
	not satisfactory: not enough changes: this is patch-writing	*acceptable paraphrase: use of reference ('this type of system') eliminates need to repeat 'PID control systems'; use of synonyms ('necessarily guarantee' → 'automatically provide' / 'perfect' → 'ideal'); all words changed except for 'does not' and 'control', which is acceptable*

Many electrical devices use various types of feedback control.

The simplest type of feedback control is on–off.

The PID controller is a generic control loop feedback mechanism which improves on the on–off system mentioned above.

One possibility is to make the heater output proportional to the difference, or error, in temperature between the oven now and the temperature we have set it at.

The problem with offset or droop can be solved by adding an integral term (I) to the proportional one we have just looked at.

The addition of a third element of control, called the derivative control component (D), can overcome to some extent this problem with overshoot.

It must be remembered that every PID control system needs to be tuned.

Many electrical devices use various types of feedback control.

The simplest type of feedback control is on–off.

The PID controller is a generic control loop feedback mechanism which improves on the on–off system mentioned above.

One possibility is to make the heater output proportional to the difference, or error, in temperature between the oven now and the temperature we have set it at.

The problem with offset or droop can be solved by adding an integral term (I) to the proportional one we have just looked at.

The addition of a third element of control, called the derivative control component (D), can overcome to some extent this problem with overshoot.

It must be remembered that every PID control system needs to be tuned.

English for Electrical Engineering – Copyright © Garnet Publishing Ltd 2014

	Main subject	Main verb	Main object/ complement	Other verbs + their subjects + objects/ complements	Adverbial phrases
A	a derivative control component	was added (to)	the system.	which is based on the rate of change of the error	In the final graph
B	Three different ways	will be described		in which control loop feedback mechanisms can be set up	here.
C	We	can also add	an integrative term	1. … which eliminates droop so successfully 2. … that it is a key component in many common control loop feedback mechanisms 3. … which have been designed	recently.
D	a control mechanism	must react (to)	an input signal.	As well as being stable, …	quickly accurately
E	the control system	performs	its task	Using all three considered parameters, …	effectively.

A accelerator	A electric	A road
A brake	A electrical	A safe
A car	A perfect	A set
A clutch	A feedback	A safety
A cruise	A power	A steering
A domestic	A radar	A warning
A electric	A reaction	B pedal
B conditions	B heater	B sector
B control	B manufacturer	B signals
B control	B output	B time
B detection	B oven	B tuning
B devices	B pedal	B value
B distance	B pedal	B wheel
B features		

Activity bank

A Solve the crossword.

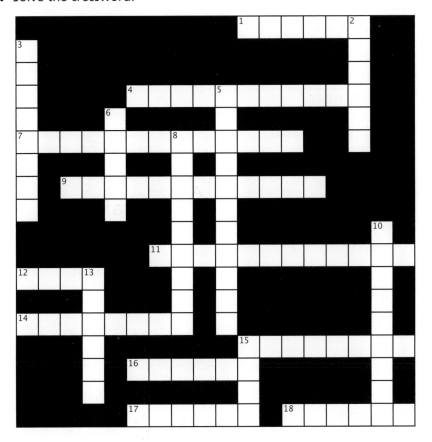

Across

1 A horizontal-axis wind turbine usually has three … .

4 Biofuels can be a good choice for generating power, but only if the system is … .

7 … power is a renewable resource, since the amount of water in the world is constant.

9 … are used to step up or step down the voltage.

11 The … of electricity takes place at a lower voltage than the transmission process.

12 There is always some energy … when electricity is passed through a conductor.

14 A … occurs when there is no electricity distribution for several hours over a large area.

15 Nuclear power stations … electricity with almost no pollution

16 … is commonly used for most electrical conductors.

17 An electrical company needs to balance supply with … .

18 The enormous metal structures that hold up power lines are called … .

Down

2 Most governments consider … and cost the most important factors when considering how to generate electricity

3 Wind turbines are often located …, in the sea.

5 Most electricity is transmitted over long distances in the form of three-phase … current.

6 … power is clean, but can only be used in certain parts of the world where there is an appropriate climate.

8 High voltages are chosen when transmitting electricity because this is more … .

10 Oil-fired power stations produce a lot of … and add to global warming.

13 If you want to use an electrical appliance, you insert the plug into a … .

15 The network of power lines is known as the … .

	Fixed phrase	Followed by ...	Actual information (suggested answers)
1	An important concept (is) ...	an idea or topic that the lecturer wants to discuss	
2	What do I mean by ... ?	an explanation of a word or phrase	
3	As you can see ...	a comment about a diagram or picture	
4	Looking at it another way,	...a different way to think about the topic	
5	In mathematical terms, ...	a general idea put into a mathematical context	
6	Say ...	an imaginary example	
7	The point is ...	a key statement or idea	
8	In this way ...	a concluding comment giving a result of something	

Types of power station: 1 Nuclear
Advantages
- Relatively cheap power
- Low carbon emissions
- One plant can produce large amounts of electricity
- Provide good 'base load' – unvarying over time

Disadvantages
- Lengthy process to design and build
- Expensive to build and run
- Safety issues if there is an accident
- Disposal of waste material
- Locations difficult to find
- Technology related to arms development
- Uranium is not renewable and may only last 60 more years

Types of power station: 3 Hydroelectric
Advantages
- A renewable source of power
- Free/cheap
- No pollution
- No fuel transportation costs
- Often little environmental impact
- Good, if not enormous, level of energy production

Disadvantages
- Depends on rainfall and level of water in rivers
- Damming rivers can have a big environmental impact
- Variable 'base load'

Types of power station: 2 Oil-fired
Advantages
- Fossil fuels are available for the moment
- One plant can produce large amounts of electricity
- Location of plant can be anywhere (as long as oil can be delivered there)
- Quick response time – good for 'topping up' when there is extra demand

Disadvantages
- Very high carbon emissions (carbon dioxide) – polluting the atmosphere and contributing to the greenhouse effect
- Oil transport over long distances is expensive
- Oil is not renewable so one day will run out
- Price of oil is not stable

Types of power station: 4 Solar
Advantages
- Renewable resource of power
- Silent
- No pollution
- Little maintenance required
- Free source of power
- Easy to install
- Technology is improving all the time

Disadvantages
- Expensive to set up
- Cannot provide constant 'base load': no power at night or on cloudy days
- Requires large surface area for energy collection

Activity bank

A Find 15 words from this unit in the wordsearch. All the words are nouns in the texts in this unit.

- Copy the words into your notebook.
- Check the definition of any words you can't remember.

```
Z  J  O  X  C  C  O  C  G  Z  H  P  A  M  W  J
W  V  J  X  W  Y  Q  H  I  P  N  T  A  O  Q  S
S  I  G  N  A  L  O  A  A  M  W  W  O  D  A  Y
U  U  W  R  C  K  J  R  T  S  P  Y  Z  U  T  I
Q  U  K  E  O  I  G  A  E  L  J  A  M  L  R  N
M  D  Q  V  L  E  U  C  F  O  H  S  C  A  A  F
O  E  R  T  L  B  X  T  R  Q  I  V  C  T  N  O
N  V  J  E  R  E  C  E  I  V  E  R  J  I  S  R
D  E  T  E  R  I  O  R  A  T  I  O  N  O  M  M
X  L  Q  A  P  P  L  I  C  A  T  I  O  N  I  A
W  O  B  H  O  U  R  S  J  S  Z  K  U  A  T  T
C  P  B  R  E  A  K  T  H  R  O  U  G  H  T  I
A  M  M  U  U  V  Z  I  R  F  T  Q  D  H  E  O
B  E  A  G  J  T  Y  C  V  F  V  X  I  I  R  N
L  N  P  N  Y  T  E  C  H  N  O  L  O  G  Y  D
E  T  F  H  N  A  M  P  L  I  T  U  D  E  Y  P
```

B Rearrange the letters in the words to form a correctly spelt word from this unit.

Jumbled word	Correct spelling
axocali bleac	
rebif-tocip caleb	
dexif-niel nehop	
ncquerefy ludoonimat	
bolime honep	
lacyhips nechanl	
komes gaslins	
detulipam taludmooni	
rericar veaw	
lexpud	

English for Electrical Engineering – Copyright © Garnet Publishing Ltd 2014

Activity bank

A Solve the crossword.

Down

1 To create a graph showing how a function varies.
2 To use a physical barrier to stop noise getting in.
4 To change, for example, an analogue signal to a digital signal.
5 Relating to information in discrete numerical form.
6 To take small pieces as a representation of the whole.
7 Not continuous – describes a signal having a finite set of values.
8 A device for converting printed images and text into digital information.
12 A line drawn by a recording instrument.
13 Not regular or periodic.

Across

1 To deal with or modify a signal in some way.
3 To keep something in the same position.
9 A sound system with speakers.
10 The amplitude of a digital signal is usually coded in this form.
11 To pass something through a device to remove a part of it.
14 To remove information from a signal.

B Are the nouns countable or uncountable? Use a dictionary to check.

Noun	Countable or uncountable?	Notes
amplitude		
barrier		
cancellation		
digitization		
echo		
editing		
domain		
image		
interference		
noise		
pickup		
pressure		
radar		
recognition		
variable		
verification		

Review reduce + recite + review	Notes record
Here you write only important words and questions; this column is completed *after* the lecture. Later this column becomes your study or revision notes. You can use it by covering the right-hand column and using the cue words and questions here to remember the contents on the right.	This column contains your notes. You should underline headings and indent main ideas. After the lecture or reading you need to identify the key points and write them in the review column as questions or cue words.

Summary
reflect + recite + review
After the class you can use this space to summarize the main points of the notes on the page.

Review	Notes
2 main approaches to signal processing are …?	1) *Analogue* signal processing 2) *Digital* signal processing
What is a signal?	Signal = f(x1, x2, …) = a function of one or more independent variables e.g., x_1 = temperature/distance/time etc. For us, x_1 = *time*
What sorts of signal are there?	Continuous time signals + *discrete* time signals Continuous time signals = *analogue* signals
Are these digital or analogue?	<u>For discrete time signals:</u> Continuous amplitude of dependent variable = *analogue* signal Amplitude coded into discrete values (usually *binary* code) = digital signal
What is processing? An example?	Processing = to make signals better, e.g., reduce *noise* of a ECG scan
What are 3 ways to process signals?	1) analogue processing = most common up to the *70s* 2) digital processing = more convenient + accurate + *cheap* 3) mixed processing = combination of analogue + digital, e.g., *telephony* transmission

Summary (suggested)

There are two main approaches to signal processing: digital and analogue. Digital processing has many advantages and has recently become very important, but is often used in combination with analogue signals.

Activity bank

A Find 20 words from this unit in the wordsearch..

• Copy the words into your notebook.

• Check the definition of any words you can't remember.

```
B E Q A C C E S S O R I E S K Y B W W
N I N J K D A M A G E V S N H P Y D L
P L N G F O L M N T Y B I D M Y A I S
O S F B I H T K K N X S D P S T Q S Q
L U X R Y N N R E K U D E U A X Y C I
L V N A Z U E D G O T G E K L W F H M
U K K K F U D P M J R Y F X S P T A V
T J B E K I M R M A N U F A C T U R E
I R Z B H U O W H P D U E T K H F G N
O G F O I N N C P B D T C H Y W T E M
N Z C H E Z E X G G U V T W X N V I C
L F T B A R V Y C S J L I F E S P A N
B I E W K Y G P O V G S V L E X M U Z
L S C P E T R O L D O W P E M O O C Z
Y I N S I G N I F I C A N T X Y H Z M
P R C H A R G E D F N H A Z S T O R E
E X H A U S T Z M E M I S S I O N S V
```

B Think of a word or words that can go before each of the words or phrases below to make a phrase from electrical engineering relating to electric cars. Explain the meaning.

Example: charge = *electrical charge, positive charge*

battery _____

braking _____

car _____

emissions _____

engine _____

generation _____

motor _____

pipe _____

pollution _____

system _____

Introduction		Examples of ideas
introduce the topic area give the outline of the writing assignment		
Body	**Para 1:** situation/problems (general)	
	Para 2: solutions	
	Para 3: evaluations of solutions – arguments for	
	Para 4: evaluations of solutions – arguments against	
Conclusion		

J.G.Carson & P. L. Carrell (1997). Extensive and intensive reading in an EAP Setting. *English*

for specifiic purposes. Vol. 16: Pages 47–60

Kirsch, David A *The electric car and the Burden of History* (2000) Rutgers University Press (Rutgers)

Hamid A. Toliyat, Gerald B. Kliman, (2004) **Handbook of Electric Motors**. 2nd Edn. published by CRC Press, Boca Raton, USA

A. El Shahat H. El Shewy June 2010 *PM Synchronous Motor Drive System for*

Automotive Applications. "Jour. of Electrical Systems" Volume 6 Issue 2 p. 10–20.

Frances Romero 2009: A BREIF History Of The Electric Car. I accessed website on 24th March 2010: http://www.time.com/time/business/article/0,8599,1871282,00.html

J.G.Carson & P. L. Carrell (1997). Extensive and intensive reading in an EAP Setting. *English*

for specifiic purposes. Vol. 16: Pages 47–60

Kirsch, David A *The electric car and the Burden of History* (2000) Rutgers University Press (Rutgers)

Hamid A. Toliyat, Gerald B. Kliman, (2004) **Handbook of Electric Motors**. 2nd Edn. published by CRC Press, Boca Raton, USA

A. El Shahat H. El Shewy June 2010 *PM Synchronous Motor Drive System for*

Automotive Applications. "Jour. of Electrical Systems" Volume 6 Issue 2 p. 10–20.

Frances Romero 2009: A BREIF History Of The Electric Car. I accessed website on 24th March 2010: http://www.time.com/time/business/article/0,8599,1871282,00.html

Activity bank

A Solve the crossword.

Down

1 A tiny amount or very small proportion of something.

2 A structure joining two things together so that one of them can swing freely.

3 An aspect of something that makes it less acceptable.

6 An instrument used to measure acceleration.

7 An apparatus that causes an enlarged image to appear on a screen or wall.

8 An image that is seen in a mirror.

9 A long piece of material used in a structure, with one end secured and the other end supporting the structure.

11 Molecules of allotropes of carbon which form long cylinders.

12 To apply a thin layer of a substance to a surface.

14 A liquid which can burn or dissolve other substances.

Across

4 The clear aqueous fluid that forms in the mouth.

5 A rubber ring placed round the wheel of a car.

7 A design of lines and shapes on a surface, often repeated.

10 A safety device in a vehicle, which inflates automatically if the car hits something.

13 Responsive to electromagnetic radiation, especially light.

15 Energy, radiation or particles sent out in a particular direction.

16 To mix a substance in a liquid until it disperses.

B Match a word in the first box with a word in the second box to make a two-word phrase. Make sure you know what they mean.

blood hearing inkjet manufacturing mechanical radiation semiconductor sports square

microchip costs device printer aid centimetres car source pressure

The design of mousetraps

Removing small animals from buildings has always been a huge problem for many people throughout history. As a result, there have been many different inventions to deal with these unwanted creatures. The two main designs are as follows.

Firstly, there is the traditional *mechanical trap*. In this device, a heavy wire hinge, placed on a wooden base, is pulled open and secured so the attached spring cannot pull it closed. When a mouse steps on the trap, the animal's weight on a sensor plate causes the trap to shut in a fraction of second. Consequently, the mouse is killed instantly.

Secondly, there is the more recent *glue trap*. In this design, a layer of glue is spread on a surface, such as a tray. Food, for example, a piece of cheese, can be placed on this. When the animal walks on the glue, it gets stuck. Since it cannot move, it is easily found and removed. One result of this is that the animal can suffer because it may not die immediately. In addition, the trap can only be used indoors. These two drawbacks may explain why the traditional design is still the most popular.

Activity bank

A Find 20 words from this unit in the wordsearch.

- Copy the words into your notebook.
- Check the definition of any words you can't remember.

```
O P T I C A L M E A S U R E T V P
M C W J X T A B G H A L O G E N E
R C O M B U S T I O N I E O C R X
E F H F K J S B A J P X F E O F O
L W A V E L E N G T H R I U D C F
I F M K E U M B S M E U E L C F L
A L H E Z K B L K T M V A T O D U
B C X R Q N L Y T E N U X R L S O
L Z U P V B E A X T O G X A L I R
E I N S T A L L A T I O N V I N E
I N C A N D E S C E N T T I D F S
L B K K J A J P H O T O N O E R C
Y P N Z J A N O D E W E J L I A E
I L E S H A P E O N T M B E F R N
G L I F E S P A N R C K E T B E T
L I G H T N I N G I G Z H O A D T
J R F I X T U R E U P X P Q B J A
```

B Do the quiz.

1 What is the word for:
- **a** the white light produced by a red, blue and green LED?
- **b** the radiation produced by a LED in a wireless computer mouse?
- **c** the substance on a fluorescent lamp which produces the light?

2 Rearrange the letters in the words below to form words associated with electroluminescence:
- **a** SMURETONDOCIC
- **b** CRELENOT
- **c** PONHOT
- **d** THEWANGVEL
- **e** ODDIE

3 Think of a word that can go in front of each of the words below to make a phrase from the unit.

_____ circuit	_____ bulb	_____ lighting
_____ display	_____ scanner	_____ gap
_____ LED	_____ coating	_____ light

Light Years Ahead:
Finding alternatives to incandescent light
by Marion Martin

Published by Hadford University Press, 2014

Light Years Ahead is an essential text for lighting engineers and those wishing to specialize in the field. The main thesis of the book, as the title suggests, is that is that we need to explore alternative light sources for homes and industry. In this respect, Martin argues that the lighting industry must consider two factors equally: the economic and the environmental costs. The scope of the book is ambitious, linking all key aspects of lighting-related studies, such as the planning and design of light fixtures, installation issues and the support required in the case of technical malfunctions. With regard to the latter, the author presents an excellent study of the complexities of a range of modern electrical lighting systems. I would strongly recommend it to all practitioners and graduate students interested in this branch of electrical engineering.

When the fluorescent lamp is turned on, current flows to the electrodes and a voltage difference is created. This causes free electrons to move through the gas, and, as a result, the mercury present in the tube is changed from liquid into gaseous form. The moving electrons collide with the gaseous mercury atoms and ultraviolet light photons are emitted. These photons hit the phosphor atoms in the casing, and white light is released.

	a vehicle brake light	street lighting	a torch
Important factors	• • • •	• • • •	• • • •

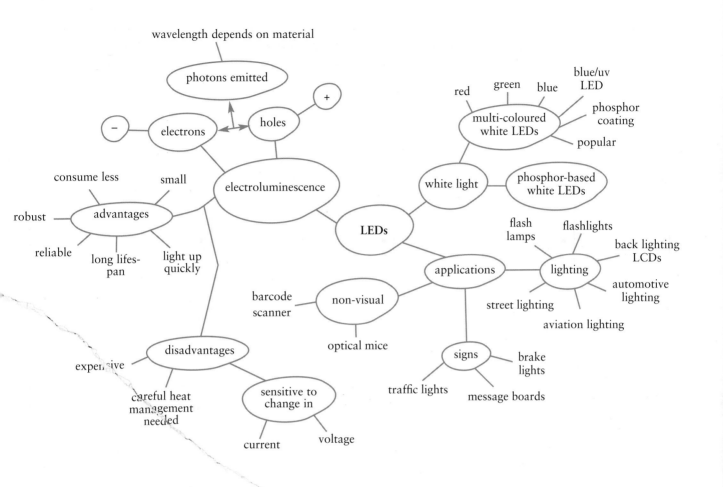

wavelength depends on material

photons emitted

− electrons holes +

electroluminescence

consume less small

robust — advantages

reliable long lifes- light up
pan quickly

red green blue blue/uv
LED

multi-coloured phosphor
white LEDs coating

popular

white light phosphor-based
white LEDs

LEDs

barcode non-visual applications lighting
scanner

optical mice

flash flashlights
lamps

back lighting
LCDs

automotive
lighting

street lighting

aviation lighting

signs brake
lights

traffic lights message boards

disadvantages

expensive

careful heat sensitive to
management change in
needed

current voltage

Fluorescent lamps	Traditional incandescent bulbs (IBs)	LEDs
• less energy required than IBs • more efficient than IBs, converting more of the input power to visible light	• world's most common source of light • consume a lot of energy	• consume much less energy than IBs • carbon footprint of a building ➔ can be reduced by > <u>60%</u> if its lights are converted from IBs to LEDs
• lamps are long, thin tubes ➔ very different lamp shape from IBs • more recently more compact fluorescent lamps have been made which resemble traditional IBs	• traditional lightbulb shape	• very small, often < 1 mm^2 ➔ can be used in a variety of situations where other lighting options not suitable
• reasonably robust, but can be broken	• easy to break	• more robust than IBs ➔ difficult to break
• last longer than IBs, provided they are not switched on and off too often	• don't last very long	• more reliable than IBs ➔ longer lifespan too • LEDs can last 3x longer than fluorescent lamps & 30x longer than IBs
• take time to switch on, although new models are quicker than older ones	• quick light up	• LEDs light up very quickly, often in < 1 µs
		• LEDs very sensitive to changes in voltage and current • series resistors or current-regulated power supplies may be required for complete efficiency
	• filament gets hot	• require more careful heat management than both incandescent bulbs and fluorescent lamps • cannot be used when the operating temperature > 35°C
• less initial capital expenditure – cheaper than IBs and LEDs • common lighting system with low installation costs & cheap replacement parts	• cheap	• initial capital costs high • LEDs suitable for domestic/office lighting cost more than fluorescent lamps
• contain a small amount of mercury		

Parallel circuit

In a parallel circuit, components are connected in such a way that the same voltage is applied to each component. The voltage is the same across each of the components, and the total current is the sum of the currents through each component. If one of the components burns out, the others will still have power. For example:

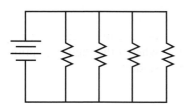

Series circuit

In a series circuit, components are connected along a single path. As a result, the same current flows through each of the components and the voltage across all the components is the sum of the voltages across each component. If one component burns out, the whole circuit stops working, and no current flows. For example:

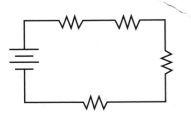

Open circuit

An open circuit exists when a break occurs in the conducting pathway of the circuit, usually in one of the components or in the wire. This happens when a switch is used to turn off a circuit, although it can also be accidental. To restore an open circuit, the cause of the break must be located, and repairs made. This can sometimes be done visually, for example, searching for a burned-out resistor. However, some breaks are not visible to the naked eye. For example:

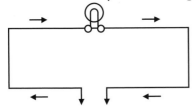

Reverse-biased (backward-biased)

When a diode is placed in a circuit, there are two possibilities. Either the polarity of the battery allows electrons to flow through the diode, in which case the diode is said to be *forward-biased*; or the battery's polarity is reversed, resulting in the diode blocking the current, in which case the diode is said to be *reverse-biased* (or *backward-biased*). In this way, a diode can be seen as a kind of switch: 'closed' when forward-biased and 'open' when reverse-biased.

Anode/cathode

Anodes and cathodes are electrodes through which current passes to complete a circuit. The electrode through which current flows out and where oxidation takes place is called the *anode*, or positive electrode. The electrode through which current flows and reduction takes place is called the *cathode*, or negative electrode. So for a diode we have:

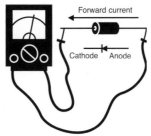

Ohm's law

Ohm's law states that the voltage is equal to the current multiplied by the resistance, or

$$V = I \times R$$

The circuit *(assemble)* as shown in Figure 1, with three pairs of components in parallel. Each parallel section *(contain)* a resistor in series with an LED. The first LED *(pair)* with a 330-ohm resistor, the second with a 220-ohm resistor, and the third with a 1000-ohm resistor. LEDs of three different colours *(select)*: red, yellow and green …

The power supply *(set)* _____ to 8 volts and all components *(check)* _____ to make sure they were working correctly. The voltage across each resistor and LED *(measure)* _____ …

This process *(repeat)* _____ three times using 6 volts, 4 volts and finally 2 volts. After all the measurements for each voltage setting *(take)* _____, the current through each LED *(calculate)* _____ by dividing the voltage across the resistor by the resistor's value …

Conclusions

Overall, the results obtained in this experiment showed good agreement with Ohm's law and were seen to verify this theory for the circuits used. Because fixed resistors were used, the resistance in the circuits was constant and therefore a change in voltage resulted in a change in current. It was demonstrated that the results follow the formula $V/R = I$. The small differences found between theoretical and practical results are probably due to the equipment used. For instance, the use of a digital multimeter might eliminate these discrepancies in future experiments. The results concerning LEDs showed that, as the power source voltage was decreased, the voltage across the LED decreased and, as a result, the current decreased. The LED became dimmer, indicating that the brightness of an LED depends on its voltage. In addition, when the anode and cathode positions of the LED were reversed, no current flowed through the circuit and there was no voltage. With the LED reverse-biased in this way, there was an open circuit and the LED did not emit any light. It can therefore be concluded that the electric polarity of an LED is a key factor in correct functioning.